BLOOM'S

HOW TO WRITE ABOUT

Kurt Vonnegut

JENNIFER BANACH

Introduction by Harold Bloom

BLOOM'S
LITERARY CRITICISM
An imprint of Infobase Publishing

Bloom's How to Write about Kurt Vonnegut

Bloom's Literary Criticism
An imprint of Infobase Learning
132 West 31st Street
New York NY 10001

Library of Congress Cataloging-in-Publication Data
Banach, Jennifer.
    Bloom's how to write about Kurt Vonnegut / by Jennifer Banach ; introduction by Harold Bloom.
        p. cm. — (Bloom's how to write about literature)
    Includes bibliographical references and index.
    ISBN 978-1-60413-856-6 (hardcover)
    1. Vonnegut, Kurt—Criticism and interpretation.   2. Criticism—Authorship.
3. Report writing. I. Bloom, Harold. II. Title. III. Title: How to write about Kurt Vonnegut.
    PS3572.O5Z5354 2011
    813'.54—dc23   2011032298

Bloom's Literary Criticism books are available at special discounts when purchased in bulk quantities for businesses, associations, institutions, or sales promotions. Please call our Special Sales Department in New York at (212)967-8800 or (800)322-8755.

You can find Bloom's Literary Criticism on the World Wide Web at
http://www.infobaselearning.com

Cover design by Ben Peterson
Composition by IBT Global, Troy NY
Cover printed by Yurchak Printing, Landisville PA
Book printed and bound by Yurchak Printing Landisville, PA
Date printed: December 2011
Printed in the United States of America

All links and Web addresses were checked and verified to be correct at the time of publication. Because of the dynamic nature of the Web, some addresses and links may have changed since publication and may no longer be valid.

CONTENTS

Series Introduction   v

Volume Introduction   vi

How to Write a Good Essay   1

How to Write about Kurt Vonnegut   70

    Player Piano   100

    The Sirens of Titan   125

    Mother Night   149

    Cat's Cradle   174

    Slaughterhouse-Five, or The Children's Crusade:
       A Duty-Dance with Death   198

    Breakfast of Champions, or Goodbye Blue Monday   222

Index   246

SERIES INTRODUCTION

Bloom's How to Write about Literature series is designed to inspire students to write fine essays on great writers and their works. Each volume in the series begins with an introduction by Harold Bloom, meditating on the challenges and rewards of writing about the volume's subject author. The first chapter then provides detailed instructions on how to write a good essay, including how to find a thesis; how to develop an outline; how to write a good introduction, body text, and conclusions; how to cite sources; and more. The second chapter provides a brief overview of the issues involved in writing about the subject author and then a number of suggestions for paper topics, with accompanying strategies for addressing each topic. Succeeding chapters cover the author's major works.

The paper topics suggested in this book are open ended, and the brief strategies provided are designed to give students a push forward on the writing process rather than a road map to success. The aim of the book is to pose questions, not answer them. Many different kinds of papers could result from each topic. As always, the success of each paper will depend completely on the writer's skill and imagination.

HOW TO WRITE ABOUT
KURT VONNEGUT:
INTRODUCTION

by Harold Bloom

I

On December 19, 1944, Kurt Vonnegut was captured by the Germans during the Battle of the Bulge; he was twenty-two years old. Sent to Dresden, he survived the firebombing of the city on February 13–14, 1945, in which 135,000 Germans were killed. That is the biographical context (in part) for the novel *Slaughterhouse-Five; or The Children's Crusade* (1969).

Since Vonnegut had begun publishing novels in 1952, it is clear that nearly a quarter century had to go by before the trauma of 1945 could be transmuted into the exorcism of *Slaughterhouse-Five*. I have just reread the novel after thirty years, remembering my shocked admiration for it when it first appeared and not looking forward to encountering it again. As it should, *Slaughterhouse-Five* remains a very disturbed and disturbing book and still moves me to troubled admiration. I prefer *Cat's Cradle*, but *Slaughterhouse-Five* may prove to be an equally permanent achievement.

The shadow of Céline's *Journey to the End of Night* never quite leaves Vonnegut's starker works, including *Slaughterhouse-Five*. I myself read the anti-Semitic Céline with loathing; one sees what is strong in the writing, but a Jewish literary critic is hardly Céline's ideal audience. So it goes.

It is difficult to comment on *Slaughterhouse-Five* without being contaminated by its styles and procedures, which is necessarily a tribute to the book. In "structure" (an absurd term to apply to almost any novel by Vonnegut), *Slaughterhouse-Five* is a whirling medley, and yet it all coheres. Billy Pilgrim, as a character, does not cohere, but that is appropriate, since his schizophrenia (to call it that) is central to the book.

The planet Tralfamadore, where Billy enjoys pneumatic bliss with Montana Wildhack, is certainly more preferable to a world of Nazi death camps and Dresden firebombings. The small miracle of *Slaughterhouse-Five* is that it could be composed at all. Vonnegut always writes from the survivor's stance, where all laughter has to be a step away from madness or fury. So indeed it goes.

Somewhere in the book, the Tralfamadorians tell Billy Pilgrim that their flying saucer crews had verified the presence of seven sexes on Earth, all of them necessary if babies are to go on being born. I think that is one of the useful moral observations I will keep in mind whenever I recall *Slaughterhouse-Five*.

II

Bokononism, a religion that freely acknowledges its status as a fiction, is one of the two lovely ironic inventions of *Cat's Cradle*. The other is *karass,* the doctrine of hidden soul families, which curiously resembles the Kabbalistic notion of *gilgul,* Isaac Luria's idea of the transmigration of souls. In Lurianic Kabbalah, soul families are united by the root of a common spark.

As an ironist, Vonnegut is too kindly to sustain comparison with Jonathan Swift, whose *A Tale of a Tub* is one of the ironic masterpieces of the ages. I prefer *Cat's Cradle* to Vonnegut's other fictions precisely because it seems so well aware of the limits of its irony. Barely below the surface of the book one can discover many of Vonnegut's nostalgias: a longing for the earthly paradise, an exultation of an ideal familial love, and the hopeless hope for a rational utopia, a redemptive reversal of the Faust myth, and a profoundly personal identification with the ironically successful prophet Jonah.

Bokononism is necessarily more an ironic humanism than it is a spirituality. Vonnegut, in my view, does not intend Bokononism as another pragmatic nihilism. Its secret is in *karass*, with the implication that almost anyone can belong to one's soul family. "Ye must love one another" is Vonnegut's authentic belief, which transcends irony.

An author who has been rewriting the book of Jonah all his life is probably aware that it is read aloud complete on the afternoon of the Jewish Day of Atonement. *Cat's Cradle* may seem too funny to be an atonement, but that is the achievement of Vonnegut's art. A Jonah who can move us to laughter is a valuable resource, perhaps our final ironist.

HOW TO WRITE
A GOOD ESSAY

By Laurie A. Sterling and Jennifer Banach

While there are many ways to write about literature, most assignments for high school and college English classes call for analytical papers. In these assignments, you are presenting your interpretation of a text to your reader. Your objective is to interpret the text's meaning in order to enhance your reader's understanding and enjoyment of the work. Without exception, strong papers about the meaning of a literary work are built on a careful, close reading of the text or texts. Careful, analytical reading should always be the first step in your writing process. This volume provides models of such close, analytical reading, and these should help you develop your own skills as a reader and as a writer.

As the examples throughout this book demonstrate, attentive reading entails thinking about and evaluating the formal (textual) aspects of the author's works: theme, character, form, and language. In addition, when writing about a work, many readers choose to move beyond the text itself to consider the work's cultural context. In these instances, writers might explore the historical circumstances of the time period in which the work was written. Alternatively, they might examine the philosophies and ideas that a work addresses. Even when writers explore a work's cultural context, though, papers must still address the more formal aspects of the work itself. A good interpretative essay that evaluates Charles Dickens's use of the philosophy of utilitarianism in his novel *Hard Times,* for example, cannot adequately address the author's treatment of the philosophy without firmly grounding this discussion in the book itself. In other words, any analytical paper about a text, even one that seeks to evaluate the work's cultural context, must also have a firm handle on the work's themes, characters, and language. You must look for and evaluate these aspects of a work, then, as you read a text and as you prepare to write about it.

WRITING ABOUT THEMES

Literary themes are more than just topics or subjects treated in a work; they are attitudes or points about these topics that often structure other elements in a work. Writing about theme therefore requires that you not just identify a topic that a literary work addresses but also discuss what that work says about that topic. For example, if you were writing about the culture of the American South in William Faulkner's famous story "A Rose for Emily," you would need to discuss what Faulkner says, argues, or implies about that culture and its passing.

When you prepare to write about thematic concerns in a work of literature, you will probably discover that, like most works of literature, your text touches on other themes in addition to its central theme. These secondary themes also provide rich ground for paper topics. A thematic paper on "A Rose for Emily" might consider gender or race in the story. While neither of these could be said to be the central theme of the story, they are clearly related to the passing of the "old South" and could provide plenty of good material for papers.

As you prepare to write about themes in literature, you might find a number of strategies helpful. After you identify a theme or themes in the story, you should begin by evaluating how other elements of the story—such as character, point of view, imagery, and symbolism—help develop the theme. You might ask yourself what your own responses are to the author's treatment of the subject matter. Do not neglect the obvious, either: What expectations does the title set up? How does the title help develop thematic concerns? Clearly, the title "A Rose for Emily" says something about the narrator's attitude toward the title character, Emily Grierson, and all she represents.

WRITING ABOUT CHARACTER

Generally, characters are essential components of fiction and drama. (This is not always the case, though; Ray Bradbury's "August 2026: There

Will Come Soft Rains" is technically a story without characters, at least any human characters.) Often, you can discuss character in poetry, as in T. S. Eliot's "The Love Song of J. Alfred Prufrock" or Robert Browning's "My Last Duchess." Many writers find that analyzing character is one of the most interesting and engaging ways to work with a piece of literature and to shape a paper. After all, characters generally are human, and we all know something about being human and living in the world. While it is always important to remember that these figures are not real people but creations of the writer's imagination, it can be fruitful to begin evaluating them as you might evaluate a real person. Often you can start with your own response to a character. Did you like or dislike the character? Did you sympathize with the character? Why or why not?

Keep in mind, though, that emotional responses like these are just starting places. To truly explore and evaluate literary characters, you need to return to the formal aspects of the text and evaluate how the author has drawn these characters. The twentieth-century writer E. M. Forster coined the terms *flat* characters and *round* characters. Flat characters are static, one-dimensional characters who frequently represent a particular concept or idea. In contrast, round characters are fully drawn and much more realistic characters who frequently change and develop over the course of a work. Are the characters you are studying flat or round? What elements of the characters lead you to this conclusion? Why might the author have drawn characters like this? How does their development affect the meaning of the work? Similarly, you should explore the techniques the author uses to develop characters. Do we hear a character's own words, or do we hear only other characters' assessments of him or her? Or, does the author use an omniscient or limited omniscient narrator to allow us access to the workings of the characters' minds? If so, how does that help develop the characterization? Often you can even evaluate the narrator as a character. How trustworthy are the opinions and assessments of the narrator? You should also think about characters' names. Do they mean anything? If you encounter a hero named Sophia or Sophie, you should probably think about her wisdom (or lack thereof), since *sophia* means "wisdom" in Greek. Similarly, since the name *Sylvia* is derived from the word *sylvan,* meaning "of the wood," you might want to evaluate that character's relationship with nature. Once again, you might look to the title of the work. Does Herman Melville's "Bartleby, the Scrivener" signal anything about Bartleby himself?

Is Bartleby adequately defined by his job as scrivener? Is this part of Melville's point? Pursuing questions like these can help you develop thorough papers about characters from psychological, sociological, or more formalistic perspectives.

WRITING ABOUT FORM AND GENRE

Genre, a word derived from French, means "type" or "class." Literary genres are distinctive classes or categories of literary composition. On the most general level, literary works can be divided into the genres of drama, poetry, fiction, and essays, yet within those genres there are classifications that are also referred to as genres. Tragedy and comedy, for example, are genres of drama. Epic, lyric, and pastoral are genres of poetry. *Form,* on the other hand, generally refers to the shape or structure of a work. There are many clearly defined forms of poetry that follow specific patterns of meter, rhyme, and stanza. Sonnets, for example, are poems that follow a fixed form of 14 lines. Sonnets generally follow one of two basic sonnet forms, each with its own distinct rhyme scheme. Haiku is another example of poetic form, traditionally consisting of three unrhymed lines of five, seven, and five syllables.

While you might think that writing about form or genre might leave little room for argument, many of these forms and genres are very fluid. Remember that literature is evolving and ever changing, and so are its forms. As you study poetry, you may find that poets, especially more modern poets, play with traditional poetic forms, bringing about new effects. Similarly, dramatic tragedy was once quite narrowly defined, but over the centuries playwrights have broadened and challenged traditional definitions, changing the shape of tragedy. When Arthur Miller wrote *Death of a Salesman,* many critics challenged the idea that tragic drama could encompass a common man like Willy Loman.

Evaluating how a work of literature fits into or challenges the boundaries of its form or genre can provide you with fruitful avenues of investigation. You might find it helpful to ask why the work does or does not fit into traditional categories. Why might Miller have thought it fitting to write a tragedy of the common man? Similarly, you might compare the content or theme of a work with its form. How well do they work together? Many of Emily Dickinson's poems, for instance, follow the meter of traditional hymns. While some of her poems seem to express traditional religious doctrines, many seem to challenge or strain against traditional conceptions of God and theology. What is the effect, then, of her use of traditional hymn meter?

WRITING ABOUT LANGUAGE, SYMBOLS, AND IMAGERY

No matter what the genre, writers use words as their most basic tool. Language is the most fundamental building block of literature. It is essential that you pay careful attention to the author's language and word choice as you read, reread, and analyze a text. Imagery is language that appeals to the senses. Most commonly, imagery appeals to our sense of vision, creating a mental picture, but authors also use language that appeals to our other senses. Images can be literal or figurative. Literal images use sensory language to describe an actual thing. In the broadest terms, figurative language uses one thing to speak about something else. For example, if I call my boss a snake, I am not saying that he is literally a reptile. Instead, I am using figurative language to communicate my opinions about him. Since we think of snakes as sneaky, slimy, and sinister, I am using the concrete image of a snake to communicate these abstract opinions and impressions.

The two most common figures of speech are similes and metaphors. Both are comparisons between two apparently dissimilar things. Similes are explicit comparisons using the words *like* or *as;* metaphors are implicit comparisons. To return to the previous example, if I say, "My boss, Bob, was waiting for me when I showed up to work five minutes late today—the snake!" I have constructed a metaphor. Writing about his experiences fighting in World War I, Wilfred Owen begins his poem "Dulce et decorum est" with a string of similes: "Bent double, like old beggars under sacks, / Knock-kneed, coughing like hags, we cursed through sludge." Owen's goal was to undercut clichéd notions that war and dying in battle were glorious. Certainly, comparing soldiers to coughing hags and to beggars underscores his point.

"Fog," a short poem by Carl Sandburg provides a clear example of a metaphor. Sandburg's poem reads:

The fog comes
on little cat feet.

It sits looking
over harbor and city
on silent haunches
and then moves on.

Notice how effectively Sandburg conveys surprising impressions of the fog by comparing two seemingly disparate things—the fog and a cat.

Symbols, by contrast, are things that stand for, or represent, other things. Often they represent something intangible, such as concepts or ideas. In everyday life we use and understand symbols easily. Babies at christenings and brides at weddings wear white to represent purity. Think, too, of a dollar bill. The paper itself has no value in and of itself. Instead, that paper bill is a symbol of something else, the precious metal in a nation's coffers. Symbols in literature work similarly. Authors use symbols to evoke more than a simple, straightforward, literal meaning. Characters, objects, and places can all function as symbols. Famous literary examples of symbols include Moby Dick, the white whale of Herman Melville's novel, and the scarlet *A* of Nathaniel Hawthorne's *The Scarlet Letter.* As both of these symbols suggest, a literary symbol cannot be adequately defined or explained by any one meaning. Hester Prynne's Puritan community clearly intends her scarlet *A* as a symbol of her adultery, but as the novel progresses, even her own community reads the letter as representing not just *adultery,* but *able, angel,* and a host of other meanings.

Writing about imagery and symbols requires close attention to the author's language. To prepare a paper on symbolism or imagery in a work, identify and trace the images and symbols and then try to draw some conclusions about how they function. Ask yourself how any symbols or images help contribute to the themes or meanings of the work. What connotations do they carry? How do they affect your reception of the work? Do they shed light on characters or settings? A strong paper on imagery or symbolism will thoroughly consider the use of figures in the text and will try to reach some conclusions about how or why the author uses them.

WRITING ABOUT HISTORY AND CONTEXT

As noted above, it is possible to write an analytical paper that also considers the work's context. After all, the text was not created in a vacuum.

The author lived and wrote in a specific time period and in a specific cultural context and, like all of us, was shaped by that environment. Learning more about the historical and cultural circumstances that surround the author and the work can help illuminate a text and provide you with productive material for a paper. Remember, though, that when you write analytical papers, you should use the context to illuminate the text. Do not lose sight of your goal—to interpret the meaning of the literary work. Use historical or philosophical research as a tool to develop your textual evaluation.

Thoughtful readers often consider how history and culture affected the author's choice and treatment of his or her subject matter. Investigations into the history and context of a work could examine the work's relation to specific historical events, such as the Salem witch trials in seventeenth-century Malden, Massachusetts, or the restoration of Charles to the British throne in 1660. Bear in mind that historical context is not limited to politics and world events. While knowing about the Vietnam War is certainly helpful in interpreting much of Tim O'Brien's fiction, and some knowledge of the French Revolution clearly illuminates the dynamics of Charles Dickens's *A Tale of Two Cities,* historical context also entails the fabric of daily life. Examining a text in light of gender roles, race relations, class boundaries, or working conditions can give rise to thoughtful and compelling papers. Exploring the conditions of the working class in nineteenth-century England, for example, can provide a particularly effective avenue for writing about Dickens's *Hard Times.*

You can begin thinking about these issues by asking broad questions at first. What do you know about the time period and about the author? What does the editorial apparatus in your text tell you? These might be starting places. Similarly, when specific historical events or dynamics are particularly important to understanding a work but might be somewhat obscure to modern readers, textbooks usually provide notes to explain historical background. These are a good place to start. With this information, ask yourself how these historical facts and circumstances might have affected the author, the presentation of theme, and the presentation of character. How does knowing more about the work's specific historical context illuminate the work? To take a well-known example, understanding the complex attitudes toward slavery during the time Mark Twain wrote *Adventures of Huckleberry Finn* should help you begin to examine issues of race in the text. Additionally, you might compare these attitudes to those of the time in which the novel was set. How might this comparison affect your interpretation of a work written after the abolition of slavery but set before the Civil War?

WRITING ABOUT PHILOSOPHY AND IDEAS

Philosophical concerns are closely related to both historical context and thematic issues. Like historical investigation, philosophical research can provide a useful tool as you analyze a text. For example, an investigation into the working class in Dickens's England might lead you to a topic on the philosophical doctrine of utilitarianism in *Hard Times.* Many other works explore philosophies and ideas quite explicitly. Mary Shelley's famous novel *Frankenstein,* for example, explores John Locke's tabula rasa theory of human knowledge as she portrays the intellectual and emotional development of Victor Frankenstein's creature. As this example indicates, philosophical issues are somewhat more abstract than investigations of theme or historical context. Some other examples of philosophical issues include human free will, the formation of human identity, the nature of sin, or questions of ethics.

Writing about philosophy and ideas might require some outside research, but usually the notes or other material in your text will provide you with basic information and often footnotes and bibliographies suggest places you can go to read further about the subject. If you have identified a philosophical theme that runs through a text, you might ask yourself how the author develops this theme. Look at character development and the interactions of characters, for example. Similarly, you might examine whether the narrative voice in a work of fiction addresses the philosophical concerns of the text.

WRITING COMPARISON AND CONTRAST ESSAYS

Finally, you might find that comparing and contrasting the works or techniques of an author provides a useful tool for literary analysis. A comparison and contrast essay might compare two characters or themes in a single work, or it might compare the author's treatment of a theme in two works. It might also contrast methods of character development or analyze an author's differing treatment of a philosophical concern in two works. Writing comparison and contrast essays, though, requires some special consideration. While they generally provide you with plenty of material to use, they also come with a built-in trap: the laundry list. These papers often become mere lists of connections between the works. As this chapter will discuss, a strong thesis must make an assertion that you want to prove or validate. A strong comparison/contrast thesis, then, needs to comment on the significance of the similarities and differences you observe. It is not enough merely to assert that the works contain similarities and differences. You might, for example, assert why the similarities and differences are important and explain how they illuminate the works' treatment of theme. Remember, too, that a thesis should not be a statement of the obvious. A comparison/contrast paper that focuses only on very obvious similarities or differences does little to illuminate the connections between the works. Often, an effective method of shaping a strong thesis and argument is to begin your paper by noting the similarities between the works but then to develop a thesis that asserts how these apparently similar elements are different. If, for example, you observe that Emily Dickinson wrote a number of poems about spiders, you might analyze how she uses spider imagery differently in two poems. Similarly, many scholars have noted that Hawthorne created many "mad scientist" characters, men who are so devoted to their science or their art that they lose perspective on all else. A good thesis comparing two of these characters—Aylmer of "The Birth-mark" and Dr. Rappaccini of "Rappaccini's Daughter," for example—might initially identify both characters as examples of Hawthorne's mad scientist type but then argue that their motivations for scientific experimentation differ. If you strive to analyze the similarities or differences, discuss significances, and move beyond the obvious, your paper should move beyond the laundry list trap.

PREPARING TO WRITE

Armed with a clear sense of your task—illuminating the text—and with an understanding of theme, character, language, history, and philosophy, you are ready to approach the writing process. Remember that good writing is grounded in good reading and that close reading takes time, attention, and more than one reading of your text. Read for comprehension first. As you go back and review the work, mark the text to chart the details of the work as well as your reactions. Highlight important passages, repeated words, and image patterns. "Converse" with the text through marginal notes. Mark turns in the plot, ask questions, and make observations about characters, themes, and language. If you are reading from a book that does not belong to you, keep a record of your reactions in a journal or notebook. If you have read a work of literature carefully, paying attention to both the text and the context of the work, you have a leg up on the writing process. Admittedly, at this point, your ideas are probably very broad and undefined, but you have taken an important first step toward writing a strong paper.

Your next step is to focus, to take a broad, perhaps fuzzy, topic and define it more clearly. Even a topic provided by your instructor will need to be focused appropriately. Remember that good writers make the topic their own. There are a number of strategies—often called "invention"—that you can use to develop your own focus. In one such strategy, called *freewriting*, you spend 10 minutes or so just writing about your topic without referring back to the text or your notes. Write whatever comes to mind; the important thing is that you just keep writing. Often this process allows you to develop fresh ideas or approaches to your subject matter. You could also try *brainstorming:* Write down your topic and then list all the related points or ideas you can think of. Include questions, comments, words, important passages or events, and anything else that comes to mind. Let one idea lead to another. In the related technique of *clustering,* or *mapping,* write your topic on a sheet of paper and write related ideas around it. Then list related subpoints under each of these main ideas. Many people then draw arrows to show connections between points. This technique helps you narrow your topic and can also help you organize your ideas. Similarly, asking journalistic questions—Who? What? Where? When? Why? and How?—can develop ideas for topic development.

Thesis Statements

Once you have developed a focused topic, you can begin to think about your thesis statement—the main point of your paper. It is imperative that you craft a strong thesis; otherwise, your paper will likely be little more than random, disorganized observations about the text. Think of your thesis statement as a kind of road map for your paper. It tells your reader where you are going and how you are going to get there.

To craft a good thesis, you must keep a number of things in mind. First, as the title of this subsection indicates, your paper's thesis should be a statement, an assertion about the text that you want to prove or validate. Beginning writers often formulate a question that they attempt to use as a thesis. For example, a writer analyzing the character Howard W. Campbell Jr. in Kurt Vonnegut's *Mother Night* might consider that the author presents Campbell in a curiously balanced manner. Campbell is depicted as neither wholly good nor evil, and his status as an innocent or guilty man remains ambiguous throughout the story. This may lead the writer to ask, Why does Vonnegut present Campbell in a balanced manner rather than portray him more definitively as either a wrongly accused patriot or an evil villain? While asking a question such as this is a good strategy to use in the invention process to help narrow your topic and find your thesis, a question cannot serve as your thesis because it does not tell your reader what you want to assert about theme. You might shape your thesis by instead proposing an answer to the question: In *Mother Night*, Kurt Vonnegut uses the character Howard W. Campbell Jr. to address philosophical subjects such as the dual nature of man, innocence and guilt, and personal responsibility and complicity. Campbell is presented as neither wholly good nor evil, and his status as an innocent or guilty man remains unclear throughout most of the story. Vonnegut's choice to refrain from portraying Campbell as a classic villain despite the ultimate revelation of his crime allows the author to demonstrate the complex and often ambiguous nature of morality and ethics, while making a statement about choice and responsibility. Minor characters such as the guards, George Kraft, Resi Noth, and even the Nazis are treated similarly, as complicated characters who are neither entirely innocent nor evil, while other formal elements of the text reinforce the concepts embodied in Campbell and mirrored in these minor characters. Ultimately, Vonnegut seems to conclude that we are not bound by an inescapable human nature reducible to good or evil; rather, we are defined by the conscious choices we make and the acceptance or avoidance of complicity in the face of wrongdoing. Notice that the thesis statement does not necessarily have to fit into one sentence. Notice too that this thesis provides an initial plan or structure for the rest of the paper. After demonstrating how Vonnegut introduces the philosophical subjects mentioned above through the character Howard W. Campbell Jr., you could use examples from the text to show how Vonnegut prevents readers from perceiving Campbell as either wholly good (and misunderstood) or evil. Next, you can advance your argument by demonstrating how Vonnegut keeps readers wondering about the status of Campbell as innocent or guilty throughout the story. You would need to explain how these details create a dialogue about the dual nature of man and the complexity and ambiguity of morality and ethics. You would then show how Vonnegut applies this same tactic in his treatment of the minor or supporting characters. By providing examples of how these characters are neither completely innocent and good nor evil, you will be demonstrating how they reinforce the ideas that Campbell represents. From here you would view the text more broadly, showing where these ideas are represented elsewhere in the text. Examining how the different elements of the novel— dialogue, form, imagery, and even the title—reinforce your view will help you to craft a strong thesis that will serve as a solid foundation for your argument. Consider, for instance, the reference to Johann Wolfgang von Goethe's *Faust* in the title of the novel and the excerpt of Mephistopheles's speech from *Faust* that appears in the editor's note of *Mother Night.* The references to darkness and light in this speech reflect the view of human nature that Campbell and the other characters embody. Finally, you will need to solidify your argument by showing that, in the absence of clearly defined evil, Campbell and the other characters are not bound by their nature but, rather, defined by the conscious choices they make and the acceptance or avoidance of complicity in the face of wrongdoing. Of course, this is only one possible method for exploring this topic. Other approaches may work just as well.

Second, remember that a good thesis makes an assertion that you need to support. In other words, a good thesis does not state the obvious. If you tried to formulate a thesis about the character Howard W. Campbell Jr. in Vonnegut's *Mother Night* by simply saying, Howard W. Campbell Jr. is an important character in *Mother Night,* you have done nothing but rephrase the obvious. Since Campbell is both the central character and the narrator of *Mother Night,* there would be no point in spending three to six pages supporting that assertion. Once you identify an important theme and pinpoint the primary question that your paper seeks to answer, you might try to develop a thesis from that point by asking yourself further questions: How do we feel about Campbell? Can we identify Campbell as a good person or an evil person? Why or why not? How can we make such a determination? Do we feel sympathy toward him or do we dislike him? Is he guilty? If so, what is he guilty of? What do the other characters have in common with Campbell? Why are these commonalities important? How do other formal elements of the text reinforce the concepts embodied in Campbell and mirrored in the other characters? What conclusion can be drawn from this? Such a line of questioning might lead you to a more viable thesis, like the one in the preceding paragraph, while helping you to organize your thoughts and develop a basic structure for your argument.

As the comparison with the road map also suggests, your thesis should appear near the beginning of the paper. In relatively short papers (three to six pages) the thesis almost always appears in the first paragraph. Some writers fall into the trap of saving their thesis for the end, trying to provide a surprise or a big moment of revelation, as if to say, "TA-DA! I have just proved that Vonnegut presents Howard W. Campbell Jr. as neither wholly good nor evil in order to demonstrate the dual nature of man, while the question of his innocence or guilt illuminates the complexity and ambiguity of morality and ethics. Through Campbell, the author suggests that people are not defined by their nature, reducible to good or evil; rather, they are defined by the choices they make and their acceptance or avoidance of complicity in the face of wrongdoing." Placing a thesis at the end of an essay can seriously diminish the essay's effectiveness. If you fail to define your essay's point and purpose clearly at the beginning, your reader will find it difficult to assess the clarity of your argument and understand the points you are making. When your thesis comes as a surprise at the end, you force your reader to reread your essay in order to assess its logic and effectiveness.

Finally, you should avoid using the first person ("I") as you present your thesis. Though it is not strictly wrong to write in the first person, it is difficult to do so gracefully. While writing in the first person, beginning writers often fall into the trap of writing self-reflexive prose (writing *about* their paper *in* their paper). Often this leads to the most dreaded of opening lines: "In this paper I am going to discuss. . . ." Not only does this self-reflexive voice make for very awkward prose, but it allows writers to boldly announce a topic while failing to present a thesis statement. An example might be a paper that begins as follows: `Slaughterhouse-Five, one of Vonnegut's most famous novels, was published during the Vietnam War. Billy Pilgrim, the story's central character, is kidnapped by aliens from the planet Tralfamadaore and becomes "unstuck in time," traveling backward and forward in his own life throughout the book. In this paper I am going to discuss how the novel challenges and deflates romanticized notions of war.` The author of this paper has done little more than announce a general topic for the paper (how the novel challenges and deflates romanticized notions of war), and the third sentence does not seem to hold any connection to the first or second sentence. While the third sentence might be the start of a thesis, the writer fails to present an opinion about how the novel challenges and deflates romanticized notions of war. What, specifically, does the novel tell us about war, the way that war has been depicted in the past, and the way that Vonnegut feels war should be depicted? Why is this significant? How does the author convey these viewpoints? To improve this "thesis," the writer would need to back up a couple of steps. Before crafting the thesis, the writer should examine the novel and draw conclusions about what the work tells us about war, the way that war has been depicted in the past, and the way that Vonnegut feels war should be depicted. After carefully examining key passages in the book, the writer might conclude that the novel presents the view that war has often been wrongfully and irresponsibly romanticized, while war should be presented as it truly is: gruesome, devastating, and incomprehensible. From here, the author could select the means by which Vonnegut communicates these ideas and then begin to craft a specific thesis. A writer who chooses to explore how Vonnegut challenges and deflates romanticized notions of war might, for example, craft a thesis such as this: `Inspired by the author's own experiences as a prisoner of war during the firebombing of Dresden in World War II, and published at the height` of one of the United States' most highly contested military conflicts, Kurt Vonnegut's *Slaughterhouse-Five* challenges and deflates romanticized notions of war. Unlike the glorified portrait of war often presented in popular media, Vonnegut's novel is purposely devoid of representations of glory, heroics, victory, and romance, replacing them instead with graver images of injury, post-traumatic illness, weakness, and death. The structure, plot, and even subtitle and dedication work symbiotically in the text to present a truthful picture of war. Vonnegut's most convincing tool, however, is his cast of characters: a clownish and pathetic chaplain's assistant and a tattered group of infantrymen who break apart the myth of the invincible hero-soldier. In detailing what becomes of these characters before, during, and after the war, Vonnegut drives home the point that there is nothing romantic about war; it is gruesome, devastating, and incomprehensible.

Outlines

While developing a strong, thoughtful thesis early in your writing process should help focus your paper, outlining provides an essential tool for logically shaping that paper. A good outline helps you see—and develop—the relationships among the points in your argument and ensures that your paper will flow logically and coherently. Outlining not only helps place your points in a logical order, but it also helps you subordinate supporting points, weed out irrelevant points, and decide if there are any necessary points that are missing from your argument. Most of us are familiar with formal outlines that use numerical and alphabetical designations for each point. However, there are different types of outlines; you may determine that an informal outline is a more useful tool for you. What is important, though, is that you spend time developing some sort of outline—formal or informal. If you do not spend sufficient time planning your supporting points and organizing the arrangement of those points, you will most likely construct a vague, unfocused outline that provides little, if any, help with the writing of your paper. Consider the following example:

Thesis: In *Mother Night,* Kurt Vonnegut uses the character
Howard W. Campbell Jr. to address philosophical subjects
such as the dual nature of man, innocence and guilt,
and personal responsibility and complicity. Campbell is
presented as neither wholly good nor evil, and his status
as an innocent or guilty man remains unclear throughout
most of the story. Vonnegut's choice to refrain from
portraying Campbell as a classic villain despite the
ultimate revelation of his crime allows the author to
demonstrate the complex and often ambiguous nature of
morality and ethics, while making a statement about
choice and responsibility. Minor characters such as the
guards, George Kraft, Resi Noth, and even the Nazis are
treated similarly, as complicated characters who are
neither entirely innocent nor evil, while other formal
elements of the text reinforce the concepts embodied
in Campbell and mirrored in these minor characters.
Ultimately, Vonnegut seems to conclude that we are not
bound by an inescapable human nature reducible to good
or evil; rather, we are defined by the conscious choices
we make and the acceptance or avoidance of complicity
in the face of wrongdoing.

    I. Introduction and thesis

   II. Minor or supporting characters who reflect the
       concepts embodied in Campbell
       A. The guards
       B. Resi Noth
       C. Mengel's view that everyone thought he or
          she was right during the war
       D. The Nazis

  III. Howard W. Campbell Jr.
       A. Allows the author to speak about
          philosophical subjects
          1. The dual nature of man
          2. Innocence and guilt

```
          3. Personal   responsibility   and
             complicity
       B. Is portrayed as neither wholly good nor
          evil
       C. Leaves us uncertain of his innocence or
          guilt throughout most of the story


   IV. Other evidence of the concepts embodied in
       Campbell
       A. The title of the novel


    V. Conclusion
```

This outline has a number of flaws. First, the major topics labeled with Roman numerals are not arranged in a logical order. If the purpose of the paper is to demonstrate that Vonnegut uses Howard W. Campbell Jr. to create a dialogue about philosophical issues and, ultimately, to conclude that we are defined by our conscious choices rather than some inescapable human nature reducible to good or evil, the writer should begin by discussing Howard W. Campbell rather than the supporting characters. Second, the thesis cites George Kraft as a relevant minor or supporting character, but the outline makes no mention of him. He should be added in the section titled "Minor or Supporting Characters" after the guards and before Resi Noth, since this is the order in which the supporting characters are listed in the thesis. Third, the writer includes Mengel's observation as one of the numbered items in section II, but A, B, and D refer to minor or supporting characters who mirror the concepts embodied by Campbell. While Mengel is a minor character, and his actions and thoughts may lend credence to your argument, his observation about others does not belong in this list. The writer could argue that Mengel's observation supports a view of morality and ethics as complex and ambiguous, but an observation is not an example of a minor or supporting character and, therefore, it should be omitted from this section. Mengel and the other guards might be listed individually in a subset under part A of the section titled "Minor or Supporting Characters," but any further subsections should demonstrate how each guard's own nature or actions—such as Mengel tightening the straps around Rudolf Franz Hoess's ankles at his execution—support the view listed above. Mengel's observation about others might be included more profitably under the major section titled "Other Evidence," along with further examples that do not fit under the other major headings. Vonnegut's own reflection that he might have been a Nazi if he had been born in Germany at that particular time, for example, found in the editor's note, is absent in the preceding outline but could also be included in "Other Evidence" along with Mengel's observation. A fourth problem is the inclusion of a part A in section IV. An outline should never include an A without a B, a 1 without a 2, and so forth. The final problem with this outline is the overall lack of detail. None of the sections provide much information about the argument that is to be presented, and it seems likely that the writer has not devoted sufficient thought to the content of the paper.

A better start to this outline might be as follows:

Thesis: In *Mother Night,* Kurt Vonnegut uses the character Howard W. Campbell Jr. to address philosophical subjects such as the dual nature of man, innocence and guilt, and personal responsibility and complicity. Campbell is presented as neither wholly good nor evil, and his status as an innocent or guilty man remains unclear throughout most of the story. Vonnegut's choice to refrain from portraying Campbell as a classic villain, despite the ultimate revelation of his crime, allows the author to demonstrate the complex and often ambiguous nature of morality and ethics, while making a statement about choice and responsibility. Minor characters such as the guards, George Kraft, Resi Noth, and even the Nazis are treated similarly, as complicated characters who are neither entirely innocent nor evil, while other formal elements of the text reinforce the concepts embodied in Campbell and mirrored in these minor characters. Ultimately, Vonnegut seems to conclude that we are not bound by an inescapable human nature reducible to good or evil; rather, we are defined by the conscious choices we make and the acceptance or avoidance of complicity in the face of wrongdoing.

I. Introduction and thesis

II. Howard J. Campbell Jr.: The central character
and narrator, he allows Vonnegut to create a
dialogue about certain philosophical issues
  A. Campbell is portrayed as neither wholly
good nor evil; accordingly, he represents
the dual nature of man.
    1. The book provides many examples of
Campbell's good nature.
      a. Campbell exhibits love for
his parents. He weeps when he
learns that they are dead.
      b. He loved his wife. We know this
based on accounts of their time
together as a "nation of two,"
accounts of his reaction upon
her presumed death, and his joy
when he believes they have been
reunited.
      c. In addition to the relationship
with his parents and wife,
Campbell does seem to develop
sincere relationships with
many of the minor characters,
including George Kraft, Resi
Noth, and even his guards.
      d. There is no emphasis on examples
of Campbell physically harming
another human being despite
his affiliation with the Nazi
party.
      e. He is described not only as
a playwright but also as a
sensitive poet, suggesting
that he possesses a certain
tenderness.

2. Vonnegut also provides evidence of a darker part of Campbell's nature in stark contrast to the good part of his nature.

    a. Campbell continues to create and disseminate Nazi propaganda despite his awareness of the horrendous atrocities associated with the Nazi party.

    b. He shoots Resi's dog when commanded to do so.

    c. He betrays his good friend by stealing his most prized possession.

    d. Vonnegut tells us that Campbell is a liar, leaving us unsure whether or not he can be trusted and believed.

B. Readers are also left uncertain of Campbell's innocence or guilt throughout most of the story. His predicament raises questions about right and wrong, highlighting the complexity and ambiguity of moral and ethical issues.

1. There are suggestions that Campbell might be innocent.

    a. Campbell tells us early in the story that he was recruited as an American agent, which raises questions about whether his actions are forgivable or whether the things he did could even be considered, in some way, honorable.

    b. At the conclusion of the story, Campbell claims to produce a letter from Frank Wirtanen confirming his status as an American spy. This seems to suggest not only that Campbell acted in accordance with a sense of duty and patriotism, but also that he is truthful and possibly innocent.

2. There are also suggestions, however, that Campbell is guilty.

   a. The very nature of the book—touted as Campbell's confessions—seems to indicate that Campbell wants to admit to some wrongdoing.

   b. Vonnegut tells us in advance that Campbell is a liar, suggesting that we cannot trust what he tells us. Therefore, his status as an American spy may be fiction, and his innocence should be questioned.

   c. Even Frank Wirtanen, who Campbell claims recruited him, accuses Campbell of wrongdoing.

III. Minor or Supporting Characters: The minor characters mirror the concepts embodied in Campbell, lending support to concepts such as the dual nature of man and the complexity and ambiguity of moral issues and emphasizing the significance of our ethical decisions and corresponding actions. They raise the same questions about good and evil, innocence and guilt, personal responsibility and complicity. They are depicted as neither wholly good nor evil, neither entirely innocent nor clearly guilty, and they are defined not by their nature but by their choices.

A. Campbell's guards: The guards are in a position to watch over accused war criminals; however, Vonnegut seems to suggest that they may be guilty of something themselves, either in their actions or by their complicity. Like Campbell, Vonnegut does not portray them as wholly good or evil, and so we sense the complexity of their moral dilemmas, the difficulty they must have faced in making these ethical decisions, and the significance of their choices.

1. Arnold Marx is a young guard who practices archaeology with his father. Despite his interest in history and the past, he is unaware of Hitler. His guilt seems to lie in his complacency and his ignorance.

2. Andor Gutman is an Estonian Jew who volunteered for the Sonderkommando, a group who led people to the gas chambers and carried their corpses out. He is ashamed of volunteering for this and admits that he is still unsure why he would have done such a thing.

3. Arpad Kovacs is a Jew who speaks animatedly of complacent individuals as briquets. In order to survive, he joined the Hungarian SS and was forced to turn people in and to murder.

4. Bernard Mengel is a Polish Jew who tightens the straps around a war criminal's ankles at his execution.

He compares it to tightening the straps on a suitcase, suggesting a disturbing lack of emotion and compassion.

B. George Kraft: Despite being revealed as a Russian agent, he seems to develop a sincere friendship with Campbell. His status as an agent likens him to Campbell and raises the question: Does his patriotism absolve him of the betrayal of his friend and any wrongdoing committed in the line of duty?

C. Resi Noth: Like Kraft, Resi also seems to have sincere feelings for Campbell. She goes so far as to claim that she loves him. Her status as an agent also causes us to consider if her actions might be considered justifiable, while the confession of her longtime love of Campbell raises complicated questions about what is permissible in the name of love and personal fulfillment.

D. The Nazis: As literary scholar Jerome Klinkowitz points out, Vonnegut has taken a unique approach in his portrayal of Nazis in *Mother Night:* He emphasizes their most human qualities rather than reducing them to manifestations of evil (*Vonnegut's America* 41).

   1. Campbell describes the Nazis as being like any other humans; they were members of his audience, and only in retrospect can he see them as anything other than human beings akin to any other.

   2. The Nazi characters who are named in the novel are not depicted in

a state of committing evil acts;
they are typically shown having
conversations, laughing, etc. They
seem unaware of their crimes and
even go so far as to deny them.

IV. Other evidence of the concepts embodied in
   Campbell: Many other aspects of the text
   underscore the idea of the dual nature of
   man, heightening our sense of the complexity
   and ambiguity of morality and ethics and
   emphasizing the importance of our ethical
   choices and actions.
   A. Title, Imagery, and Symbolism: The title
      of the novel references Mephistopheles's
      speech from Goethe's *Faust,* which
      presents a picture of the intertwined
      nature of darkness and light—a metaphor
      for the dual nature of man. It follows
      that if man is neither wholly good nor
      evil, man is not defined by his nature
      but rather by his choices. The editor's
      note, which presents the actual excerpt
      of Mephistopheles's speech, reinforces
      this concept.
   B. Dialogue: Mengel says that Campbell is
      the only person with a bad conscience
      about what he did in the war. He points
      out that everyone thought what he or
      she was doing was right, suggesting that
      morality may be a matter of point of view
      rather than a black-and-white issue of
      right and wrong.
   C. Metafiction: Referring to Campbell's
      predicament, Vonnegut reinforces the
      notion of the complexity and ambiguity of
      morality when he volunteers that he might

have been a Nazi also had he been born in Germany during this time in history.

V. Conclusion: In his portrait of Campbell and the reinforcement throughout the text of the notions embodied in Campbell, Vonnegut ultimately suggests that we are not defined by our nature, reducible to good or evil; we are defined, rather, by our conscious choices and the acceptance or avoidance of complicity in the face of wrongdoing.

    A. While Vonnegut acknowledges the dual nature of man, his ultimate choice not to portray Campbell and the other characters as villains suggests that we cannot blame our ethical missteps on human nature. The characters are not portrayed as evil people, and Vonnegut has deliberately revealed the good in them as well. Their guilt, therefore, lies in the conscious choices they have made and in their complicity in the face of wrongdoing.

    B. The explanation of the dedication in the editor's note confirms that Campbell recognizes his crime as "serving evil too openly and good too secretly" (xiii).

    C. The conclusion of the story reinforces this point. Campbell confesses that he is going to hang himself for what he calls "crimes against himself" (268).

This new outline would prove much more helpful when it came time to write the paper. An outline like this could serve as an even more useful tool if the writer fleshed out the argument by providing more specific examples from the text to support each point.

Once you have listed your main point and supporting ideas, develop this raw material by listing related ideas and material under each of those main headings. From there, arrange the material in subsections and order the material logically. For example, you might begin with one of the theses already cited: Inspired by the author's own experiences as a prisoner of war during the firebombing of Dresden in World War II, and published at the height of one of the United States' most highly contested military conflicts, Kurt Vonnegut's Slaughterhouse-Five challenges and deflates romanticized notions of war. Unlike the glorified portrait of war often presented in popular media, Vonnegut's novel is purposely devoid of representations of glory, heroics, victory, and romance, replacing them instead with graver images of injury, post-traumatic illness, weakness, and death. The structure, plot, and even subtitle and dedication work symbiotically in the text to present a truthful picture of war. Vonnegut's most convincing tool, however, is his cast of characters: a clownish and pathetic chaplain's assistant and a tattered group of infantrymen who break apart the myth of the invincible hero-soldier. In detailing what becomes of these characters before, during, and after the war, Vonnegut drives home the point that there is nothing romantic about war; it is gruesome, devastating, and incomprehensible. As noted previously herein, this thesis supplies a framework for the organization of your paper: You might start by introducing the origins of the book: *Slaughterhouse-Five* was written and published during the Vietnam War and is based on the author's experiences as a prisoner of war during the firebombing of Dresden in World War II. This information will situate readers by providing them with a general understanding of the context of the book, which you can address more fully in your conclusion. Next, you will need to demonstrate how Vonnegut challenges and deflates romanticized notions of war. Following the order of your thesis, you would show how the novel is devoid of typical romanticized representations of war and how it presents action and imagery in opposition to romanticized depictions of war. Then, you would show how the characters deflate romanticized notions of war by breaking apart the myth of the invincible hero-soldier. Finally, you will state your conclusion: that, together, these elements create a picture of war as gruesome, devastating, and incomprehensible. As suggested earlier, you might take your conclusion a step further by elaborating on context and relevance, explaining why Vonnegut's message was significant at the time of the book's initial publication and, most importantly, why it is still relevant today. Accordingly, in addition to the headings titled "Introduction" and "Conclusion," you might begin your outline with two topic headings: (1) Proof that the novel is devoid of romanticized notions of war and (2) How the characters deflate romanticized notions of war by breaking apart the myth of the invincible hero-soldier. Under each of those headings you could list corresponding ideas that support the particular point they appear beneath. Be sure to include references to parts of the text that strengthen your case.

An informal outline might look like this:

Thesis: Inspired by the author's own experiences as a prisoner of war during the firebombing of Dresden in World War II, and published at the height of one of the United States' most highly contested military conflicts, Kurt Vonnegut's *Slaughterhouse-Five* challenges and deflates romanticized notions of war. Unlike the glorified portrait of war often presented in popular media, Vonnegut's novel is purposely devoid of representations of glory, heroics, victory, and romance, replacing them instead with graver images of injury, post-traumatic illness, weakness, and death. The structure, plot, and even subtitle and dedication work symbiotically in the text to present a truthful picture of war. Vonnegut's most convincing tool, however, is his cast of characters: a clownish and pathetic chaplain's assistant and a tattered group of infantrymen who break apart the myth of the invincible hero-soldier. In detailing what becomes of these characters before, during, and after the war, Vonnegut drives home the point that there is nothing romantic about war; it is gruesome, devastating, and incomprehensible.

Introduction and Thesis

1. Proof that the novel is devoid of romanticized notions of war
   - Structure: Billy Pilgrim becomes unstuck in time. Therefore, there is no clear beginning, middle, or end of the story, which suggests that there will be no happy ending and no clear conclusion or resolution.
     - This nonlinear narrative allows us to witness the events leading up to, during, and after the firebombing of Dresden.
     - The structure, which reflects Billy's assertion that he can travel in time, suggests that he may be suffering from some type of post-traumatic illness.
   - Plot: Billy and his fellow soldiers are captured, become prisoners of war, and endure horrible conditions.
     - There is no evidence of heroics, glory, or victory; rather, readers encounter their opposites.
       - Many of the characters die: Colonel Wild Bob, Roland Weary, Ed Derby, etc.
       - There are several instances of characters in a state of surrender or captivity.
       - Many of the characters seem to lack a sense of loyalty; some betray one another.
       - There does not seem to be any positive effect of the soldiers' actions.
     - The plot lacks romance and is devoid of love stories.

- Billy confesses that he does not know why he married Valencia. He suggests that his marriage proposal to her is proof of his mental illness.
- Ed Derby's wife becomes a widow.

○ Glory is presented as an unfulfilled dream or fantasy.

- Roland Weary fantasizes about the Three Musketeers being recognized for their heroism, but the other two soldiers abandon him and are ultimately shot dead by German soldiers. Furthermore, Weary does not survive the war.
- Ed Derby, perhaps the most virtuous of the American soldiers, is executed; his dedication and heroism seem to be for naught.
- Colonel Wild Bob dies in the middle of delirious proclamations to a regiment that doesn't exist. In this book, victory on the battlefield is not a reality but a delusion.

- Even easily overlooked features such as the title and the dedication of the novel take on enormous significance.

○ The novel is dedicated in part to Mary O'Hare, the wife of one of Vonnegut's World War II buddies.

○ In the first chapter, Vonnegut reveals that Mary was concerned that he would write another book that falsely represents war.

   ○ Vonnegut reassures Mary that he will
     not do this and tells her that he
     will call the book "The Children's
     Crusade." This becomes the subtitle
     for the novel and a metaphor for the
     ideas about war presented in the book.

2. How the characters deflate romanticized notions
   of war and break apart the myth of the invincible
   hero-soldier
   • The characters are presented as pathetic
     and weak.
     ○ Billy Pilgrim is 21 years old and
       going bald. He is typically poorly,
       even absurdly, dressed and he is often
       weeping.
     ○ Roland Weary is a teenager and is
       likened to Tweedledum and Tweedledee,
       the bumbling twins of *Alice's Adventures
       in Wonderland.*
     ○ Paul Lazzaro is a little man concerned
       more with planning to exact revenge
       on his fellow American soldiers than
       fighting the enemy.
     ○ The German soldiers are also portrayed
       as pathetic and weak. They are youths and
       old folks, farmers rather than trained
       soldiers, cripples and injured men.
   • Any characters who possess the traits
     typically associated with a hero are
     defeated, and there is no further mention
     of heroes or victors in the text.
     ○ Ed Derby is executed by a firing
       squad.
     ○ The British soldiers are rendered
       impotent by their incarceration.

Conclusion

You would begin creating a formal outline using a similar process, though in the final stages you would label the headings differently and provide much greater detail. A formal outline for a paper that argues the thesis about *Slaughterhouse-Five* cited above—that the novel challenges and deflates romanticized notions of war—might look like this:

Thesis: Inspired by the author's own experiences as a prisoner of war during the firebombing of Dresden in World War II, and published at the height of one of the United States' most highly contested military conflicts, Kurt Vonnegut's *Slaughterhouse-Five* challenges and deflates romanticized notions of war. Unlike the glorified portrait of war often presented in popular media, Vonnegut's novel is purposely devoid of representations of glory, heroics, victory, and romance, replacing them instead with graver images of injury, post-traumatic illness, weakness, and death. The structure, plot, and even subtitle and dedication work symbiotically in the text to present a truthful picture of war. Vonnegut's most convincing tool, however, is his cast of characters: a clownish and pathetic chaplain's assistant and a tattered group of infantrymen who break apart the myth of the invincible hero-soldier. In detailing what becomes of these characters before, during, and after the war, Vonnegut drives home the point that there is nothing romantic about war; it is gruesome, devastating, and incomprehensible.

  I. Introduction and thesis

 II. Although the primary subject of *Slaughterhouse-Five* is war, the novel is devoid of many of the characteristics readers might expect of a work of this genre. What Vonnegut does reveal via the formal elements of the text, such as structure, plot, and even the title and dedication, deflates romanticized notions of war.

A. In the novel, Billy Pilgrim tells us that he has become "unstuck in time." This element of time travel, usually reserved for works of science fiction and not typically found in books about war (although works about war may oscillate between past and present in a less fantastical manner), plays an integral part in the translation of Vonnegut's ideas about war.

   1. The nonlinear structure of the story allows readers to witness the events leading up to, during, and after the firebombing of Dresden. Readers are, therefore, able to "witness" the devastating effects of the war on many of the characters.

   2. The fantastical element of time travel seems to suggest that Billy may be suffering from some kind of post-traumatic illness.

B. The basic plot of the novel is as follows: Billy and his fellow soldiers are captured by the Germans, become prisoners of war, and endure horrible conditions.

   1. There are few examples of heroic acts, glory realized, or victory in the book.

      a. Many of the characters lack a sense of loyalty. The soldiers that were with Weary and Billy abandon them. Fellow soldiers are often shouting at Billy. They do not allow him to sleep near them. Weary rescues Billy but then begins beating him up in his frustration.

       b. Many of the characters do not survive. Roland Weary dies of an infection from the clogs that he is forced to wear by the Germans. Colonel Wild Bob expires in a delirious state. Ed Derby is executed by a firing squad shortly before the end of the war.

       c. There is no evidence in the book of the positive effect of the soldiers' actions.

2. Although we have come to expect romance and love stories as part of any tale of war, there is no romance or love story to be found in *Slaughterhouse-Five*.

       a. Billy confesses that he does not know why he married his wife, Valencia. He says that his marriage proposal to her is proof of his mental illness. Valencia, presented as a foolish woman concerned with flatware patterns, represents the misguided view that war is romantic. "It was a simple-minded thing for a female Earthling to do to associate sex and glamour with war," says Billy (154). She is not a symbol of love but a symbol of ignorance and a reminder of Billy's fractured state.

       b. Ed Derby writes proud, loving letters to his wife, but she becomes a widow when he is executed for taking a teapot.

3. Any glory is presented as an unfulfilled dream or fantasy.

   a. Roland Weary fantasizes about the Three Musketeers being recognized for their heroics, but the other two soldiers abandon him and Billy and are subsequently shot and killed by German soldiers.

   b. Ed Derby, perhaps the most virtuous of the men, is executed by a firing squad for taking a teapot. His virtuousness is for naught.

   c. Colonel Wild Bob dies in the middle of a delirious proclamation to a regiment that no longer exists. Billy tells us he says that "they had nothing to be ashamed of, that there were dead Germans all over the battlefield who wished to God that they had never heard of the Four-fifty-first" (85). The victory he speaks about is a delusion.

C. The title and dedication also take on enormous significance, referencing the major concerns of the novel and reflecting Vonnegut's ideas about war.

   1. The novel is dedicated in part to Mary O'Hare, the wife of one of Vonnegut's real-life war buddies.

   2. The dedication was inspired by a conversation that took place during

a visit between Vonnegut and Mary's husband, Bernard, in the mid-1960s. When Vonnegut arrives, Mary is clearly angry. "She fixed herself a Coca-Cola, made a lot of noise banging the ice-cube tray in the stainless steel sink. Then she went into another part of the house. But she wouldn't sit still. She was moving all over the house, opening and shutting doors, even moving furniture around to work off her anger." (16–17)

3. Mary is concerned that Vonnegut will write another book that falsely represents the war. "You'll pretend you were men instead of babies, and you'll be played in the movies by Frank Sinatra and John Wayne or some of those other glamorous, war-loving, dirty old men. And war will look just wonderful, so we'll have a lot more of them. And they'll be fought by babies like the babies upstairs." (18)

4. Vonnegut promises that he will not represent the war in a romanticized fashion and tells her that he will call the book "The Children's Crusade." This becomes the subtitle for the book and a metaphor for Vonnegut's ideas about war as contained in the novel.

III. The characters best deflate romanticized notions of war by breaking down the myth of the invincible hero-soldier.

A. The characters are presented as weak, vulnerable, and pathetic.

   1. Billy Pilgrim is described as "preposterous." He is 21 years old and going bald. With no helmet, no coat, weapons, or boots, and a shoe with a broken heel, at the start of the novel Bill, looks "like a filthy flamingo" (42). He is also described as "cold, hungry, embarrassed, incompetent" (43). Later in the novel, readers encounter him dressed in a "blue toga and silver shoes, with his hands in a muff" (191). He appears like a clown, infuriating a surgeon in Dresden who believes Billy is deliberately making fun of war. The future Billy is no better off; he is often weeping.

   2. Roland Weary is also a young man. He is only 18 years old and "had been unpopular because he was stupid and fat and mean, and smelled like bacon no matter how much he washed" (44). Likened to Tweedledum or Tweedledee, the bumbling twins found in Lewis Carroll's *Alice's Adventures in Wonderland,* Weary was once responsible for the death of his entire gun crew when he gave away their position by firing a hasty shot at the enemy.

   3. Paul Lazzarro is a little man who is more concerned with planning to exact revenge on his fellow American soldiers than fighting the enemy. He is like a rabid dog or an injured

animal, lashing out at everyone around him.

4. The German soldiers are portrayed in the same light. They are youths and old folks, farmers not soldiers, crippled and injured civilians. "One of them," readers learn, "actually had an artificial leg, and carried not only a loaded rifle, but a cane" (190). Even the dog that appears with some German soldiers is revealed to be a female dog named Princess from a local farm.

B. Any characters that exhibit some of the qualities of a hero are defeated.

1. Ed Derby, a character who stands for the ideals commonly associated with a soldier—loyalty, courage, dedication, conviction—is executed by a firing squad for taking a teapot just before the conclusion of the war. His heroism seems to be useless.

2. The British soldiers, who do exhibit loyalty and dedication, are rendered impotent by their incarceration.

C. There is no further mention of heroes or victors in the story.

IV. Conclusion

A. The result is a view of war as gruesome, devastating, and incomprehensible.

B. In case readers are uncertain why this view might be important, Vonnegut incorporates passages from two historical sources: *Extraordinary Popular Delusions and the Madness of Crowds* by Charles Mackay, LL. D., published in 1841, and *Dresden—History, Stage and Gallery* by Mary Endell, published in 1908. Together they reinforce the necessity of seeing and depicting war truthfully.

1. Mackay's book enumerates on both the nature and the result of the Crusades: *"History in her solemn page informs us that the crusaders were but ignorant and savage men, that their motives were those of bigotry unmitigated, and that their pathway was one of blood and tears. Romance, on the other hand, dilates upon their piety and heroism, and portrays, in her most glowing and impassioned hues, their virtue and magnanimity . . . Now what was the grand result of all of these struggles? Europe expended millions of her treasures, and the blood of two million of her people; and a handful of quarrelsome knights retained possession of Palestine for about one hundred years!"* (20) The passage suggests that the losses were far greater than anything achieved.

2. Endell's book, meanwhile, presents the image of history repeating in its illustration of the prior destruction of Dresden in 1760 at the hands of the Prussians. It seems to be a reminder of how history may repeat itself if man does not take heed.

C. Vonnegut explains that *Slaughterhouse-Five* is so "jumbled and jangled . . . because there is nothing intelligent to say about a massacre" (24), but perhaps this is not entirely accurate, for Vonnegut has written his book just the same, and many authors of the same time period also wrote about war. Ultimately, through the act of writing the novel, Vonnegut is emphasizing the importance of how we remember and speak about war.

   1. Rachel McCoppin makes the observation that the truthful depiction of war was a common concern for many post-World War II writers during the 1960s (47). It is no surprise that war would have a prominent theme in literature during the time in which the book appears; it was presented to audiences during the Vietnam War, a highly contested conflict protested by large numbers of Americans.

   2. "Published at the height of the Vietnam War," Professor Thomas F. Marvin tells us, "*Slaughterhouse-Five* spoke powerfully to a generation exhausted and demoralized by the pointless brutality of modern warfare" (23).

D. While *Slaughterhouse-Five* utilizes certain elements of futility in an effort to speak truthfully about the purposelessness of war, there is true purpose in Vonnegut's book.

   1. Rachel McCoppin says: Vonnegut knows that *Slaughterhouse-Five* will be

unlikely to instigate much social or political change, yet the novel does its best to promote the idea that we are responsible for our actions and that a greater acknowledgement of this culpability may influence the future for the better. (58)

2. In its suggestion that romanticizing war is irresponsible; in its demand that we find new, more truthful ways of speaking about war; and, most importantly, in its promotion of the ideals of personal responsibility, the novel remains as relevant today as when it was published in 1969.

As in the previous sample outline, the thesis provided the seeds of a structure, and the writer was careful to arrange the supporting points in a logical manner, showing the relationships among the ideas in the paper.

Body Paragraphs

Once your outline is complete, you can begin drafting your paper. Paragraphs—units of related sentences—are the building blocks of a good paper, and as you draft, you should keep in mind both function and quality. Paragraphs help you chart and control the shape and content of your essay, and they help the reader see your organization and understand your logic. You should begin a new paragraph whenever you move from one major point to another. In longer, more complex essays, you might use a group of related paragraphs to support major points. Remember that, in addition to being adequately developed, a good paragraph is both unified and coherent.

Unified Paragraphs

Each paragraph must be centered on one idea or point, and a unified paragraph carefully focuses on and develops this central idea without including extraneous ideas or tangents. For beginning writers, the best way to ensure that you are constructing unified paragraphs is to include a topic sentence in each paragraph. This topic sentence should convey the main point of the paragraph, and every sentence in the paragraph should relate to that topic sentence. Any sentence that strays from the central topic does not belong in the paragraph and needs to be revised or deleted. Consider the following paragraph about how Vonnegut's portrayal of the guards reinforces the theme of the complexity and ambiguity of morality and ethics in *Mother Night:*

Although Howard W. Campbell Jr. is the central character in *Mother Night,* minor or supporting characters such as the guards also serve an important function, revealing significant information about key themes. For example, Vonnegut's collective portrayal of Campbell's guards reinforces the theme of the complexity and ambiguity of morality and ethics; the treatment of each of the guards raises questions about right and wrong, innocence and guilt, self-preservation and social responsibility. Campbell begins by introducing Arnold Marx. He tells us that Marx is a redheaded boy who guards him from six in the morning until noon each day. Although he is Jewish, remarkably, he does not know who Paul Joseph Goebbels is. He is, however, knowledgeable about a lesser-known historical figure named Tilgath-pileser the Third, a man he describes as "probably the most remarkable man the Assyrians ever produced" (4). Andor Gutman replaces Marx each day, keeping watch over Campbell until six o'clock. During his time as a prisoner at Auschwitz, Gutman volunteered for the Sonderkommando, a group that led prisoners to the gas chambers and carried their corpses out. Each evening, Arpad Kovacs, a Hungarian Jew, relieves Gutman. In order to survive, he joins the Hungarian SS. The last of Campbell's guards is a Polish Jew named Bernard Mengel, who compares tightening the straps around a war criminal's ankles at his execution to tightening the straps on his suitcase. He watches over Campbell from midnight until six in the morning.

Although the paragraph begins solidly and the second sentence provides the central idea of the paragraph, the author soon goes on a tangent. If the purpose of the paragraph is to demonstrate how Vonnegut's portrayal of the guards reinforces the theme of the complexity and ambiguity of morality and ethics, then the description of Marx's appearance and the notation of each guard's schedule are tangential here. Although details about the changing of the guards and the passage of time from morning to night and back to morning (or from light to darkness and back to light) may find a place elsewhere in the paper, such details should be deleted from this paragraph. The author needs to address more clearly how the portrayal of the guards reinforces the theme of the complexity and ambiguity of morality and ethics. All of the sentences in this paragraph should somehow tie in to this central point.

Coherent Paragraphs

In addition to shaping unified paragraphs, you must also craft coherent paragraphs that develop their points logically with sentences that flow smoothly from one to the next. Coherence depends on the order of your sentences, but order is not the only factor that lends coherence to the paragraph. You also need to craft your prose so that the reader can see the relationship among the sentences.

Consider the following paragraph about how the portrayal of Campbell's guards reinforces the theme of the complexity and ambiguity of morality and ethics in *Mother Night*. Notice how the writer addresses the same topic as above but fails to help the reader see the relationships among the points:

> Howard W. Campbell Jr. is the central character in *Mother Night*. Minor or supporting characters such as the guards also serve an important function, revealing important information about key themes. Vonnegut's collective portrayal of Campbell's guards reinforces the theme of the complexity and ambiguity of morality and ethics; the treatment of each of the guards raises difficult questions about right and wrong, innocence and guilt, self-preservation and social responsibility. Campbell begins by introducing Arnold Marx. He is Jewish.

He does not know who Paul Joseph Goebbels is. Marx is knowledgeable about a lesser-known historical figure named Tiglath-pileser the Third, a man he describes as "probably the most remarkable man the Assyrians ever produced" (4). Marx is studying to be a lawyer and he practices archaeology with his father. He is only eighteen years old and has never left Israel. Andor Gutman volunteered for the Sonderkommando, a group that led prisoners to the gas chambers and carried their corpses out. Andor does not know why he volunteered. "If you would write a book about that," he says to Campbell, "and give an answer to that question, that 'Why?'—you would have a very great book" (8). Arpad Kovacs joins the Hungarian SS in order to survive. Bernard Mengel compares tightening the straps around a war criminal's ankles at this execution to tightening the straps on his suitcase.

This paragraph demonstrates that unity alone does not guarantee effectiveness. The argument is hard to follow because the author fails to show connections between the sentences and to indicate how they work to support the overall point.

Several techniques are available to aid paragraph coherence. Careful use of transitional words and phrases is essential. You can use transitional flags to introduce an example or an illustration *(for example, for instance)*, to amplify a point or add another phase of the same idea *(additionally, furthermore, next, similarly, finally, then)*, to indicate a conclusion or a result *(therefore, as a result, thus, in other words)*, to signal a contrast or a qualification *(on the other hand, nevertheless, despite this, on the contrary, still, however, conversely)*, to signal a comparison *(likewise, in comparison, similarly)*, and to indicate a movement in time *(afterward, earlier, eventually, finally, later, subsequently, until)*.

In addition to transitional flags, careful use of pronouns aids coherence and flow. If you were writing about *The Wizard of Oz,* you would not want to keep repeating the phrase *the witch* or the name *Dorothy.* Careful substitution of the pronoun *she* in these instances can aid coherence. A word of warning, though: When you substitute pronouns for proper names, always be sure that your pronoun reference is clear. In a paragraph that discusses both Dorothy and the witch, substituting *she* could lead to confusion. Make sure that it is clear to whom the pronoun refers. Generally, the pronoun refers to the last proper noun you have used.

While repeating the same name over and over again can lead to awkward, boring prose, it is possible to use repetition to bolster your paragraph's coherence. Careful repetition of important words or phrases can lend coherence to your paragraph by reminding readers of your key points. Admittedly, it takes some practice to use this technique effectively. You may find that reading your prose aloud can help you develop an ear for the effective use of repetition.

To see how transitional aids are helpful, compare the following paragraph to the preceding one about how the portrayal of Campbell's guards reinforces the theme of the complexity and ambiguity of morality and ethics in *Mother Night*. Notice how the author works with the same ideas but shapes them into a much more coherent paragraph with a point that is clearer and easier to follow. Notice also how the concluding sentence unifies the thoughts and reveals the collective significance of the information provided:

> Although Howard W. Campbell Jr. is the central character in *Mother Night,* minor or supporting characters such as the guards also serve an important function, revealing significant information about key themes. For example, Vonnegut's collective portrayal of Campbell's guards reinforces the theme of the complexity and ambiguity of morality and ethics; the treatment of each of the guards raises difficult questions about right and wrong, innocence and guilt, self-preservation and social responsibility. Campbell's first guard, for instance, is a Jewish teenager named Arnold Marx who does not know who Paul Joseph Goebbels is. Because his professions are associated with ethics and history (he is studying to be a lawyer and practices archaeology with his father) and because Goebbels is well-known for his role in the extermination of countless Jews, Marx's ignorance is incriminating. To counter this, Vonnegut has Campbell

reveal that Marx is just a teenager. Because Marx was
only an infant during the World War II, readers may ask
themselves whether his ignorance is somehow forgivable.
Marx also happens to be knowledgeable about historical
subjects unknown to Campbell (and presumably to readers
as well). He tells Campbell about a historical figure
named Tilgath-pileser the Third, a man he describes
as "probably the most remarkable man the Assyrians
ever produced" (4). Marx's incredulity upon Campbell's
admission that he has never heard of Tilgath-pileser
the Third should inspire readers to question whether
it is Campbell or Marx who is ignorant. Like Marx, the
second guard, Andor Gutman, is also of Jewish heritage.
He was a prisoner at Auschwitz for two years and claims
that he "came this close to going up a smokestack
of a crematorium there" (7). During this time, he
volunteered for the Sonderkommando, a group that led
fellow prisoners to the gas chambers and carried their
corpses out. Gutman tells Campbell that he does not
know why he volunteered. "If you would write a book
about that," he says to Campbell, "and give an answer
to that question, that 'Why?'—you would have a very
great book" (8). His volunteering indicates that his
guilt lies in his complicity. The third guard, Arpad
Kovacs, also Jewish, refers to people like Gutman as
"briquets." He seems to be angered by complacency, and
yet Kovacs also seems to be guilty in his complicity.
Kovacs brags that he was responsible for the execution
of fourteen SS men, but we also know that the SS
was responsible for the murder of many more innocent
people. The knowledge that he posed as an Aryan and
joined the Hungarian SS in order to ensure his survival
makes the matter of his innocence or guilt much more
complicated. Finally, the Polish Jew Bernard Mengel
likens tightening the straps around a war criminal's
ankles at his execution to tightening the straps on
his suitcase. Campbell points out that Mengel did not

participate in the execution "with testimony," "[h]e did it with his two big hands" (16). Mengel is not complicit; instead he actively participates in the extermination of another human being. The dual roles of the guards as victim and victimizer, jailer and prisoner, coupled with the knowledge of the motivations behind each of their actions and the lingering questions about their innocence or guilt underscore the point that matters of morality and ethics are not black and white.

Introductions

Generally, your introduction should do two things: capture your reader's attention and explain the main point of your essay. In other words, while your introduction should contain your thesis, it needs to do a bit more work than that. You are likely to find that starting the first paragraph is one of the most difficult parts of writing the paper. It is hard to face that blank page or screen, and as a result, many beginning writers, in desperation to start somewhere, begin with overly broad, general statements. While it is often a good strategy to start with general subject matter and narrow your focus, do not begin with a broad sweeping statement such as Sight is an important theme in Slaughterhouse-Five. A sentence like this is nothing but empty filler. It begins to fill the blank page but does nothing to advance your argument. Instead, you should try to gain your readers' interest. Some writers like to begin with a pertinent quotation or with a relevant question. Alternatively, you might begin with an introduction of the topic you will discuss. If you are writing about sight in Slaughterhouse-Five, for instance, you might begin by noting that the author uses Billy's profession in optometry as a metaphor for sight and ways of seeing. Next, you can explain how the novel presents us with new ways of "seeing" complex philosophical issues. Another common trap to avoid is depending on your essay's title to introduce the author and the text you are writing about. Always include the work's author and title in your opening paragraph.

Compare the effectiveness of the following introductions:

1. Sight is an important theme. Billy's profession in optometry serves as a metaphor for sight and

ways of seeing. The novel ultimately functions as a corrective lens, suggesting new ways to "see" the world around us.

2. In *Slaughterhouse-Five*, Kurt Vonnegut uses Billy Pilgrim's profession in optometry to reference sight, while the philosophical content of the text moves us to consider a broader definition of sight defined as experience or the way in which we envision and understand the world. Through Billy's experiences, we are presented with unconventional ideas about subjects such as death, time, and free will. Ultimately, the novel itself can be likened to the corrective lenses that Billy prescribes for his patients, helping us to "see" in new and different ways.

The first introduction begins with a vague, overly broad sentence; cites unclear, undeveloped examples; and then moves abruptly to the thesis. Notice, too, how a reader deprived of the paper's title does not know the title of the story that the paper will analyze. The second introduction works with the same material and thesis but provides more detail and is consequently much more interesting. It begins by introducing the author and the text it will analyze, then moves on to discuss how Vonnegut creates a metaphor for sight, providing examples of this from the text, and shows how the philosophical concerns of the text move readers to consider a broader definition of sight as experience or the way in which we envision and understand the world around us. It concludes with the thesis: that the novel itself functions as a tool to promote new ways of seeing.

The paragraph below provides another example of an opening strategy. Again, it begins by introducing the author and the text it will analyze, and then it moves on to provide some necessary background information before revealing its thesis.

In Kurt Vonnegut's *Slaughterhouse-Five*, the author uses Billy Pilgrim's profession in optometry to reference sight, while the philosophical concerns of the text

move readers to consider a different kind of sight:
experience, or the way in which we see and understand
the world. Through Billy's experiences, readers are
presented with unconventional ideas about existential
subjects such as death, time, and free will. Death is
presented not as a conclusion but as a single moment
in a series of moments; time is not linear; and free
will is only an illusion. These new ways of seeing are
reflected in the views presented by the aliens from
Tralfamadore, who exhibit surprise that humans could
see things any other way. Ultimately, even the novel
itself can be likened to the corrective lenses that
Billy prescribes for his patients, helping readers to
"see" things in a new and different way.

Conclusions

No doubt you have heard the old adage about writing papers: "Tell us
what you are going to say, say it, and then tell us what you've said." While
this formula does not necessarily result in bad papers, it does not often
result in good ones. It will almost certainly result in boring papers and,
especially, boring conclusions. If you have done a good job establishing your points in the body of the paper, the reader already knows and
understands your argument. There is no need to merely reiterate. Do
not just summarize your main points in your conclusion. A boring and
mechanical conclusion does nothing to advance your argument or interest your reader. Consider the following conclusion to the paper about
war without romance in *Slaughterhouse-Five:*

> In conclusion, Vonnegut presents a view of war without
> romance. It is not filled with heroics; here, it is revealed
> to be gruesome, devastating, and incomprehensible.

Besides starting with a mechanical transitional device, this conclusion
does little more than summarize the main points of the outline (and it
does not even touch on all of them). It is incomplete and uninteresting.

Instead, your conclusion should add something to your paper. A good
tactic is to build upon the points you have been arguing. Asking "why?"

often helps you draw further conclusions. You might also speculate on other directions in which to take your topic by tying it into larger issues. You might do this by envisioning your paper as just one section of a longer essay. For example, in the paper on war without romance in *Slaughterhouse-Five,* you might not only summarize Vonnegut's point of view about the way that war was represented in media in the past but explain what relevance this has for readers today through some exposition of the book's message of personal responsibility. In the following conclusion to the paper on war without romance in *Slaughterhouse-Five,* the author discusses how Vonnegut's deflation of romanticized notions of war calls for a new, more truthful way of speaking about war, with emphasis on the significance of personal responsibility:

> Vonnegut says that *Slaughterhouse-Five* is so "jumbled and jangled . . . because there is nothing intelligent to say about a massacre" (24), but this is not entirely accurate, for Vonnegut has written his book, and many authors of the same time period also took up their pen to combat irresponsible depictions of war. Rachel McCoppin makes the observation that the truthful representation of war was a common subject for many post-World War II writers during the 1960s (47). It is no surprise that this would be a topic of such grave concern at this time, since one of the most highly contested conflicts in American history was taking place concurrently. "Published at the height of the Vietnam War," Professor Thomas F. Marvin tells us, "*Slaughterhouse-Five* spoke powerfully to a generation exhausted and demoralized by the pointless brutality of modern warfare" (23). So, while *Slaughterhouse-Five* allows itself to create a sense of futility in an effort to speak truthfully about the purposelessness of war, McCoppin explains that Vonnegut's efforts are not at all futile:
>
>> Vonnegut knows that *Slaughterhouse-Five* will be unlikely to instigate much social or political change, yet the novel does its best to promote the

> idea that we are responsible for our actions and
> that a greater acknowledgement of this culpability
> may influence the future for the better. (58)

In its suggestion that romanticizing war is irresponsible;
in its demand that we find new, more truthful ways
of speaking about war; and, most importantly, in its
promotion of the ideals of personal responsibility, the
novel remains as powerful and as relevant today as when
it was first published in 1969.

Citations and Formatting

Using Primary Sources

As the examples included in this chapter indicate, strong papers on literary texts incorporate quotations from the primary text or texts in order
to support their points. It is not enough for you to assert your interpretation without providing support or evidence. Without well-chosen
quotations to support your argument, you are, in effect, saying to the
reader, "Take my word for it." It is important to use quotations thought-
fully and selectively. Remember that the paper presents *your* argument,
so choose quotations that support *your* assertions. Do not let the author's
voice overwhelm your own. With that caution in mind, there are some
guidelines you should follow to ensure that you use quotations clearly
and effectively.

Integrate Quotations

Quotations should always be integrated into your own prose. Do not
just drop them into your paper without introduction or comment. Otherwise, it is unlikely that your reader will see their function. You can
integrate textual support easily and clearly with identifying tags—short
phrases that identify the speaker. For example:

> Paul Proteus says that calculus "is a wonderful thing."

While this tag appears before the quotation, you can also use tags
after or in the middle of the quoted text, as the following examples
demonstrate:

"Truer words were never spoken," said Fern.

"By and large," said Beatrice, "my contribution to the dignity of the family has been somewhat greater than yours."

You can also use a colon to formally introduce a quotation:

Anita's exasperation is evident: "Oh, honestly! What are you talking about?"

When you quote brief sections of a poem (three lines or fewer), use slash marks to indicate the line breaks in the poem:

As the poem ends, Dickinson speaks of the power of the imagination: "The revery alone will do, / If bees are few."

Longer quotations (more than four lines of prose or three lines of poetry) should be set off from the rest of your paper in a block quotation. Double-space before you begin the passage, indent it ten spaces from your left-hand margin, and double-space the passage itself. Because the indentation signals the inclusion of a quotation, do not use quotation marks around the cited passage. Use a colon to introduce the passage. Here are two examples:

The description of the landscape around the Ilium Works highlights the connection between past and present:

He was showing the cat an old battlefield at peace. Here, in the basin of the river bend, the Mohawks had overpowered the Algonquins, the Dutch the Mohawks, the British the Dutch, the Americans the British. Now, over bones and rotten palings and cannon balls and arrowheads, there lay a triangle of steel and masonry buildings, a half-mile on each side—the Ilium Works. Where men had

once howled and hacked at one another, and fought
nip-and-tuck with nature as well, the machines
hummed and whirred and clicked, and made parts
for baby carriages and bottle caps, motorcycles
and refrigerators, television sets and tricycles—
the fruits of peace.

By now, the reader should have a sense of the immense
changes that have taken place in the United States.

The whole of Dickinson's poem speaks of the imagination:

To make a prairie it takes a clover and one bee,
One clover, and a bee,
And revery.
The revery alone will do,
If bees are few.

Clearly, she argues for the creative power of the mind.

It is also important to interpret quotations after you introduce
them and to explain how they help advance your point. You cannot
assume that your reader will interpret the quotations the same way
that you do.

Quote Accurately

Always quote accurately. Anything within quotations marks must be the
author's exact words. There are, however, some rules to follow if you need
to modify the quotation to fit within your prose:

1. Use brackets to indicate any material that might have been
   added to the author's exact wording. For example, if you need
   to add any words to the quotation or alter it grammatically
   to allow it to fit within your prose, indicate your changes in
   brackets:

> Rumfoord tells Malachi that his wife
> "[Beatrice] hasn't seen [him] since [his] first
> materialization."

2. Conversely, if you choose to omit any words from the quotation, use ellipses (three spaced periods) to indicate missing words or phrases:

> Frank Wirtanen learned some things about Howard W.
> Campbell Jr. from his plays: "That [he] admire[s]
> pure hearts and heroes . . . That [he] love[s] good
> and hate[s] evil . . . and that [he] believe[s] in
> romance."

3. If you delete a sentence or more, use the ellipses after a period:

> The narrator presents a unique description
> of the class to which Winston Niles Rumfoord
> belongs:
>
> > The class was a true one because its limits
> > had been clearly defined for at least two
> > centuries—clearly defined for anyone with
> > an eye for definitions. From Rumfoord's
> > small class had come a tenth of America's
> > presidents, a quarter of its explorers, a
> > third of its Eastern Seaboard governors,
> > a half of its full-time ornithologists,
> > three-quarters of its great yachtsmen, and
> > virtually all of its underwriters of the
> > deficits of grand opera. It was a class
> > singularly free of quacks, with the notable
> > exception of political quacks. . . . Once
> > in office, members of the class became,
> > almost without exception, magnificently
> > responsible.

4. If you omit a line or more of poetry, or more than one paragraph of prose, use a single line of spaced periods to indicate the
omission:

```
To make a prairie it takes a clover and one bee,
.   .   .   .   .   .   .   .   .   .   .   .   .   .   .
And revery.
The revery alone will do,
If bees are few.
```

Punctuate Properly

Punctuation of quotations often causes more trouble than it should.
Once again, you just need to keep these simple rules in mind:

1. Periods and commas should be placed inside quotation marks,
even if they are not part of the original quotation:

```
Fern chastises Malachi: "For three months you
have made nothing but wrong decisions."
```

The only exception to this rule is when the quotation is followed
by a parenthetical reference. In this case, the period or comma
goes after the citation (more on these later in this chapter):

```
Fern chastises Malachi: "For three months you
have made nothing but wrong decisions, and you've
done what I would have said was impossible.
You've succeeded in more than wiping out the
results of almost forty years of inspired
guessing" (68).
```

2. Other marks of punctuation—colons, semicolons, question
marks, and exclamation points—go outside the quotation
marks unless they are part of the original quotation:

```
What does Vonnegut mean when he says that "lies
told for the sake of artistic effect . . . can
```

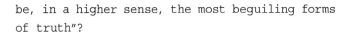

```
be, in a higher sense, the most beguiling forms
of truth"?
```

```
Campbell is curious: "What makes you think I
have a bad conscience?"
```

Documenting Primary Sources

Unless you are instructed otherwise, you should provide sufficient information for your reader to locate material you quote. Generally, literature papers follow the rules set forth by the Modern Language Association (MLA). These can be found in the *MLA Handbook for Writers of Research Papers* (seventh edition). You should be able to find this book in the reference section of your library. Additionally, its rules for citing both primary and secondary sources are widely available from reputable online sources. One of these is the Online Writing Lab (OWL) at Purdue University. OWL's guide to MLA style is available at http://owl.english. purdue.edu/owl/resource/557/01/. The Modern Language Association also offers answers to frequently asked questions about MLA style on this helpful webpage: http://www.mla.org/style_faq.

Parenthetical Citations

MLA guidelines call for parenthetical references in your text after quotations. When you are working with prose (short stories, novels, or essays), include page numbers in the parentheses.

```
Billy's mother has maintained her faith: "People would
be surprised if they knew how much in this world was
due to prayers" (131).
```

When you are quoting poetry, include line numbers:

```
Dickinson's speaker tells of the arrival of a fly:
"There interposed a Fly—/ With Blue—uncertain stumbling
Buzz—/ Between the light—and Me—" (12-14).
```

When you are citing classic drama, such as Shakespeare, your citation should include the act number, scene number, and the line numbers that you are citing separated by periods. For instance, if you were citing lines 24–26 from act 1, scene 2 of a classic play, your citation would appear as (1.2.24–26).

When you are citing modern or contemporary drama that does not follow a classical structure, you should include the appropriate page number or numbers, and you may also add a semicolon followed by any other identifiers, as available. These identifiers might be act numbers, scene numbers, or other forms of division, such as the "Blocks" used in Tennessee Williams's *Camino Real.* Since these works are usually found in more than one edition and are often collected in anthologies, this extra identifier will help your reader find the passage quickly and with ease in his or her own edition:

```
Gutman announces, "We have entered the second in a
progress of sixteen blocks on the Camino Real. It's five
o'clock. That angry old lion, the Sun, looked back once
and growled and then went switching his tail toward the
cool shade of the Sierras" (758; bl. 2).
```

The Works Cited Page
Parenthetical citations should be linked to a separate works cited page at the end of your paper. The works cited page lists works alphabetically by the authors' last names. An entry for the reference to Vonnegut's *Slaughterhouse-Five* would read:

```
Vonnegut, Kurt. Slaughterhouse-Five. New York: Dial,
    2005.
```

The *MLA Handbook* includes a full listing of sample entries, as do many of the online explanations of MLA style.

Documenting Secondary Sources
To ensure that your paper is built entirely upon your own ideas and analysis, instructors often ask that you write interpretative papers without any outside research. If, on the other hand, your paper requires research, you must document any secondary sources you use. You need to document direct quotations, summaries or paraphrases of others' ideas, and

factual information that is not common knowledge. Follow the guide-lines above for quoting primary sources when you use direct quotations from secondary sources. Keep in mind that MLA style also includes spe-cific guidelines for citing electronic sources. OWL's website provides a good summary: http://owl.english.purdue.edu/owl/resource/557/09/.

Parenthetical Citations

As with the documentation of primary sources, described above, MLA guidelines require in-text parenthetical references to your secondary sources. Unlike the research papers you might write for a history class, literary research papers following MLA style do not use footnotes as a means of documenting sources. Instead, after a quotation, you should cite the author's last name and the page number:

> "Many post-World War II authors, including Thomas Pynchon, Norman Mailer, Joseph Heller, and Vonnegut, were wary of the military" (McCoppin 47).

If you include the name of the author in your prose, then you would include only the page number in your citation. If it is the first time you are referencing the author, you should include his or her full name as well as a brief identifier. For example:

> According to literary scholar Rachel McCoppin, "Many post-World War II authors, including Thomas Pynchon, Norman Mailer, Joseph Heller, and Vonnegut, were wary of the military" (47).

After the first appearance, it is sufficient to reference the author by last name only.

> According to McCoppin, "Many post-World War II authors, including Thomas Pynchon, Norman Mailer, Joseph Heller, and Vonnegut, were wary of the military" (47).

If you are including more than one work by the same author, the paren-thetical citation should include a shortened yet identifiable version of the title in order to indicate which of the author's works you are citing. For example:

> Speaking of *The Sirens of Titan,* literary scholar Jerome Klinkowitz says: "The language is intentionally banal, reminiscent of the unaffected way Vonnegut's characters had spoken to one another in his magazine stories" (*Vonnegut Effect* 49).

Similarly, and just as important, if you summarize or paraphrase the particular ideas of your source, you must provide documentation:

> Jerome Klinkowitz recognizes that Vonnegut has taken a unique approach in his portrayal of Nazis in *Mother Night.* Vonnegut has emphasized their most human qualities rather than presenting them in the process of committing evil acts (*Vonnegut's America* 41).

Works Cited Page

Like the primary sources discussed above, the parenthetical references to secondary sources are keyed to a separate works cited page at the end of your paper. Here is an example of a works cited page that uses the examples cited above. Note that when two or more works by the same author are listed, you should use three contiguous em-dashes followed by a period in the subsequent entries. You can find a complete list of sample entries in the *MLA Handbook* or as part of a reputable online summary of MLA style.

WORKS CITED

Klinkowitz, Jerome. "Coming to Terms with Technique: *The Sirens of Titan, Mother Night, Cat's Cradle, and God Bless You, Mr. Rosewater.*" *The Vonnegut Effect.* Columbia, SC: U of South Carolina P, 2004. 46–74.

———. "Vonnegut's 1960s: Apocalypse Redone." *Kurt Vonnegut's America.* Columbia, SC: U of South Carolina P, 2009. 40–62.

McCoppin, Rachel. " 'God Damn It, You've Got to Be Kind':
    War and Altruism in the Works of Kurt Vonnegut." *New
    Critical Essays on Kurt Vonnegut.* Ed. David Simmons.
    New York: Palgrave Macmillan, 2009. 47-66.

Plagiarism

Failure to document carefully and thoroughly can leave you open to
charges of stealing the ideas of others, or plagiarism, and this is a very
serious matter. Remember that it is important to include quotation
marks when you use language from your source, even if you use just
one or two words. For example, if you wrote, The language in *The Sirens
of Titan* is reminiscent of the unaffected way the characters spoke
in his magazine stories, you would be guilty of plagiarism, since you
used Klinkowitz's distinct language without acknowledging him as the
source. Instead, you should write something like: Jerome Klinkowitz
observes that the dialogue in *The Sirens of Titan* "is reminiscent of the
unaffected way that Vonnegut's characters had spoken to one another in
his magazine stories" (*Vonnegut Effect* 49). In this case, you have properly credited Klinkowitz.

Similarly, neither summarizing the ideas of an author nor changing
or omitting just a few words means that you can omit a citation. In the
chapter titled "Coming to Terms with Technique" in *The Vonnegut Effect*
(cited in the sample above), Jerome Klinkowitz speaks about the use of
metafiction in *Mother Night:*

> Unraveling the truth is the substance of *Mother Night*,
> and fictive technique is the key to that unraveling.
> In its various levels of textuality, the novel is
> Kurt Vonnegut's first metafictive work, and a very
> sophisticated one at that. . . . At the very least,
> all this enfolding apparatus makes for a very personal
> narrative: from one perspective Campbell's; from another
> Vonnegut's own. (52)

Below are two examples of plagiarized passages:

> In *Mother Night,* readers find the first significant example of metafiction in Vonnegut's work. This device allows the author to create two distinct voices within one text, with one being his own. The incorporation of Vonnegut's own voice makes the work much more personal, strengthening the feeling of truth.

> In *Mother Night,* Vonnegut is concerned with unraveling the truth. In order to support this theme, the author creates a very personal narrative by using metafiction to incorporate his own voice. (*Vonnegut Effect* 52)

While the first passage does not use Klinkowitz's exact language, it does list the same ideas he proposes about metafiction and personal narrative in *Mother Night* without citing his work. Since this interpretation is Klinkowitz's distinct idea, this constitutes plagiarism. The second example has shortened his passage, changed some wording, and included a citation, but some of the phrasing is Klinkowitz's. The first passage could be fixed with a parenthetical citation. Because some of the wording in the second remains the same, though, it would require the use of quotation marks, in addition to parenthetical citation. The passage below represents an honestly and adequately documented use of the original passage:

> According to Jerome Klinkowitz, Vonnegut is concerned with "unraveling the truth" in *Mother Night.* In order to support this theme, the author creates "a very personal narrative" by using metafiction to incorporate his own voice. (*Vonnegut Effect* 52)

This passage acknowledges that the interpretation is derived from Klinkowitz while appropriately using quotations to indicate his precise language.

While it is not necessary to document well-known facts, often referred to as "common knowledge," any ideas or language that you take from someone else must be properly documented. Common knowledge generally includes the birth and death dates of authors or other well-documented facts of their lives. An often-cited guideline is that if you can find the information in three sources, it is considered common knowledge. Despite this guideline, it is, admittedly, often difficult to know if the facts you uncover are common knowledge or not. When in doubt, document your source.

Sample Essay

Victor Chang
Professor Thomas
English II
February 5, 2012

KURT VONNEGUT'S *SLAUGHTERHOUSE-FIVE*:
WAR WITHOUT ROMANCE

Inspired by the author's experiences as a prisoner of war during the firebombing of Dresden in World War II, and published at the height of one of the United States' most highly contested military conflicts, Kurt Vonnegut's *Slaughterhouse-Five* challenges and deflates romanticized notions of war. Unlike the glorified portrait of war often presented in popular media, Vonnegut's novel is purposely devoid of representations of glory, heroics, victory, and romance, replacing them instead with graver images of injury, post-traumatic illness, weakness, and death. The structure, plot, and even subtitle and dedication work symbiotically in the text to present a truthful picture of war. Vonnegut's most convincing tool, however, is his cast of characters: a clownish and pathetic chaplain's assistant and a tattered group of infantrymen who break apart the myth of the invincible hero-soldier. In detailing what becomes of these characters before, during, and after the war, Vonnegut drives home the point that there is nothing romantic about war; it is gruesome, devastating, and incomprehensible.

Although the primary subject of *Slaughterhouse-Five* is war, the novel is devoid of many of the characteristics readers might expect of a work of this genre. What Vonnegut does reveal via the formal elements of the text topples conventional notions of war. For instance, in the novel, Billy Pilgrim—a former chaplain's assistant during World War II—becomes "unstuck in time," traveling backward and forward in his own life. This element of time travel is usually reserved for works of science fiction and is not typically found in books about war (although works about war may oscillate between past and present in a less fantastical manner); here, it plays an integral part in the translation of Vonnegut's view of war. The nonlinear nature of the story makes it possible for readers to witness Billy's experiences leading up to, during, and after the firebombing of Dresden, in the process allowing them to witness the devastating effects of war on many other characters as well. Additionally, the fantastic nature of time travel seems to suggest that Billy may, in fact, be suffering from some kind of post-traumatic illness, an idea reinforced at the conclusion of the novel.

As the result of Billy's time travel, we see that Billy and his fellow soldiers are captured, become prisoners of war, and endure horrible conditions. This is the plot; there are few examples of heroic acts, and representations of glory and victory are glaringly absent. Many of the characters fail to exhibit any loyalty. Some betray and abandon one another. The soldiers that were with Weary and Billy, for instance, leave them behind. Fellow soldiers are often shouting at Billy; they do not allow him to sleep near them. In what initially seems like an act of heroism, Weary saves Billy by keeping him moving, but shortly thereafter, he begins beating Billy up in frustration.

Many of the characters do not survive, and consequently, their actions seem fruitless. Roland Weary dies of an infection from the clogs that he is forced to wear by the Germans. Colonel Wild Bob expires in a delirious state. Ed Derby is executed by a firing squad shortly before the end of the war. There is no evidence of the positive effects of the soldiers' actions.

While readers have come to expect romance and love stories as part of any tale of war, there is no romance and no love story to be found in *Slaughterhouse-Five*. Billy confesses that he does not know why he married his wife, Valencia; he considers his marriage proposal to Valencia proof of his mental illness. Valencia is presented as a foolish woman concerned with flatware patterns rather than the state of her sick husband. She does not stand as a symbol of love and romance but rather serves as a symbol of the prevalence of ignorance when it comes to perceptions of war. Her character perpetuates—with clear absurdity—the romanticized notion of war that Vonnegut seeks to counter. "It was a simple-minded thing for a female Earthling to do to associate sex and glamour with war," says Billy (154). Although Ed Derby and his wife embody romantic love, this love is rendered impotent when Derby is executed.

Furthermore, any glory referenced in the text is presented as an unfulfilled dream—a fantasy or delusion. Weary fantasizes about the Three Musketeers being recognized for their heroism during the war, but the men he envisions as the other two musketeers abandon him and are shot and killed shortly thereafter by German soldiers. Ed Derby, who is voted the leader of the American prisoners of war, is also executed by a firing squad shortly before the conclusion of the war for taking a teapot; his aspirations are for naught and his virtue seems to have been useless. The colonel known as Wild Bob dies in the midst of delirious proclamations to a regiment that no longer exists that the enemy is on the run. Billy tells us Wild Bob claims that "they had nothing to be ashamed of, that there were dead Germans all over the battlefield who wished to God that they had never heard of the Four-fifty-first" (85), but his notions of victory are simply part of a delusion, presumably caused by delirium immediately preceding his death.

In *Slaughterhouse-Five,* even minute details, such as the title and the dedication, play an enormous role in presenting a new, more truthful view of war. Vonnegut dedicates his book to Mary O'Hare, the wife of one of his fellow World War II soldiers, and Gerhard Muller, the German cab driver who takes Vonnegut and Mary's husband, Bernard, back to the slaughterhouse where they were held captive during the firebombing of Dresden. The dedication to Mary is particularly significant: In an early passage of the book, Vonnegut tells readers that the dedication to Mary was inspired by a conversation that the author had with her during a visit with her husband in the mid-1960s. Recalled in the first chapter of the novel, the conversation predicts what Vonnegut is up to in this book. When he arrives, Mary sets up a place for the author and her husband to talk. Subsequently, Vonnegut tells readers:

> She fixed herself a Coca-Cola, made a lot of noise banging the ice-cube tray in the stainless steel sink. Then she went into another part of the house. But she wouldn't sit still. She was moving all over the house, opening and shutting doors, even moving furniture around to work off her anger. (16–17)

The author reveals that Mary is concerned that he will write a book that falsely represents war—a book that will glamorize it—perpetuating the myths of romance in battle and the invincible hero-soldier.

> "You'll pretend you were men instead of babies, and you'll be played in the movies by Frank

Sinatra and John Wayne or some of those other glamorous, war-loving, dirty old men. And war will look just wonderful, so we'll have a lot more of them. And they'll be fought by babies like the babies upstairs." (18)

Her tirade gives way to a promise from Vonnegut that he will avoid such irresponsible, romantic representations of war. He promises her that he will name his book "The Children's Crusade," a phrase that ultimately becomes the subtitle of *Slaughterhouse-Five* and a metaphor for the ideas about war presented in the novel.

Keeping his promise, Vonnegut creates characters who appear so weak, vulnerable, and pathetic that they defeat any mythical, glorified notion of the hero-solider. Billy Pilgrim, for instance, the protagonist and sometimes narrator, is described as "preposterous." He is 21 years old and going bald. With no helmet, no coat, weapons, or boots, and a shoe with a broken heel, at the start of the novel he looks "like a filthy flamingo" (42). He is "cold, hungry, embarrassed, incompetent" (43). He is no better off as the novel progresses. In Dresden he is dressed in a "blue toga and silver shoes, with his hands in a muff" (191). He appears like a clown, infuriating a bystander who believes that Billy is deliberately mocking the idea of war. In passages that reflect Billy's experiences after the war, he is often weeping.

Other characters are portrayed as equally absurd and pathetic. Roland Weary is only 18 years old and "had been unpopular because he was stupid and fat and mean, and smelled like bacon no matter how much he washed" (44). Likened to Tweedledum or Tweedledee, the bumbling twins of Lewis Carroll's *Alice's Adventures in Wonderland*, Weary was once responsible for the death of his entire gun crew, killed when he gave away their position by firing a hasty shot at the enemy. Paul Lazzarro is a little man who is more concerned with planning to exact revenge on his fellow American soldiers than on defeating the enemy. He is like a rabid dog or a sick animal, lashing out at everyone around him. According to Howard W. Campbell Jr., an American who rose in the ranks of the German Ministry of Propaganda, American soldiers "were known everywhere to be the most self-pitying, least fraternal, and dirtiest of all prisoners of war" (166). Vonnegut deliberately refrains from contradicting this view. The American soldiers are portrayed as clowns and fools, and as the title of the novel suggests, they are akin to animals, pigs sent to slaughter. Readers find them scared, cornered, in boxcars like cattle, jailed. Significantly, the German soldiers are portrayed in much the same light. They are either very young or very old men, farmers not soldiers, physically impaired and injured civilians. "One of them," readers learn, "actually had an artificial leg, and carried not only a loaded rifle, but a cane" (190).

Meanwhile, any characters who do possess those characteristics traditionally associated with heroism—Edgar Derby, for instance, or the British soldiers—are immediately defeated, and with them the idea of the invincible hero-soldier is defeated too. Derby, a character who stands for the ideals commonly associated with a soldier—loyalty, courage, dedication, conviction—is executed by a firing squad shortly before the conclusion of the war. His virtue is useless. Likewise, the British soldiers, who are loyal to each other, who have maintained impeccable habits, and who seem united in their readiness to defeat the enemy, are rendered impotent by their captivity. These are not, as Mary O'Hare says, the Frank Sinatras or John Waynes of war movies. They are deeply flawed characters with weaknesses. They are susceptible, vulnerable, weak, and

prone to defeat. Remarkably, there is no further mention
of heroes or victors in the novel. The final result is
a view of war as undeniably gruesome, devastating, and
incomprehensible. The effects of the war are lasting.
Billy Pilgrim seems to exhibit symptoms of post-traumatic
illness. Bernard O'Hare, the author's real-life partner
in battle, is unable to drink hard liquor. They are the
lucky ones who have escaped death.

In case readers are still uncertain of the significance
of the view of war presented in *Slaughterhouse-Five*,
Vonnegut cites passages from two books: *Extraordinary
Popular Delusions and the Madness of Crowds* by Charles
Mackay, LL. D., published in 1841; and *Dresden—History,
Stage and Gallery* by Mary Endell, published in 1908.
Mackay's book discusses the nature and the result of
the Crusades:

> *History in her solemn page informs us that the
> crusaders were but ignorant and savage men, that
> their motives were those of bigotry unmitigated,
> and that their pathway was one of blood and tears.
> Romance, on the other hand, dilates upon their
> piety and heroism, and portrays, in her most
> glowing and impassioned hues, their virtue and
> magnanimity . . . Now what was the grand result of
> all of these struggles? Europe expended millions
> of her treasures, and the blood of two million of
> her people; and a handful of quarrelsome knights
> retained possession of Palestine for about one
> hundred years! (20)*

Endell's book, meanwhile, presents the image of history
repeating in its depiction of the destruction of Dresden
in 1760 at the hands of the Prussians. Together, the
passages suggest not only what we can learn about history
through books but how much can be lost and wasted if we

do not heed a warning about history repeating in the face of ignorance.

Vonnegut says that *Slaughterhouse-Five* is so "jumbled and jangled . . . because there is nothing intelligent to say about a massacre" (24), but this is not entirely accurate, for Vonnegut has written his book just the same, and many authors of the same time period also took up their pen to combat irresponsible depictions of war. Rachel McCoppin observes that the truthful depiction of war was a common subject for many post–World War II writers during the 1960s (47). It is no surprise that war would find such a prominent place as a topic of literature during this time; its prevalence coincided with one of the most highly contested conflicts in American history. "Published at the height of the Vietnam War," Professor Thomas F. Marvin tells us, "*Slaughterhouse-Five* spoke powerfully to a generation exhausted and demoralized by the pointless brutality of modern warfare" (23). So, while *Slaughterhouse-Five* allows itself to create a sense of futility in an effort to speak truthfully about the purposelessness of war, McCoppin explains that Vonnegut's efforts are not futile:

> Vonnegut knows that *Slaughterhouse-Five* will be unlikely to instigate much social or political change, yet the novel does its best to promote the idea that we are responsible for our actions and that a greater acknowledgement of this culpability may influence the future for the better. (58)

In its suggestion that romanticizing war is irresponsible; in its demand that we find new, more truthful ways of speaking about war; and, most importantly, in its promotion of the ideals of personal responsibility, the novel remains as powerful and as relevant today as when it was first published in 1969.

WORKS CITED

Marvin, Thomas F. "Literary Contexts." *Kurt Vonnegut: A Critical Companion.* Westport, CT: Greenwood, 2002. 13–24.

McCoppin, Rachel. "'God Damn It, You've Got to Be Kind': War and Altruism in the Works of Kurt Vonnegut." *New Critical Essays on Kurt Vonnegut.* Ed. David Simmons. New York: Palgrave Macmillan, 2009. 47–66.

Vonnegut, Kurt. *Slaughterhouse-Five.* New York: Dial, 2005.

HOW TO WRITE ABOUT
KURT VONNEGUT

When writing about Kurt Vonnegut and his body of work, you will use the same tactics that you would use when writing about any other author or works of literature: Identify an important feature or topic, begin gathering information about this topic, draft a thesis, support the thesis with evidence from Vonnegut's texts and other reliable sources, and finish with a conclusion that unifies your thoughts and demonstrates the significance of your observations. However, even before you take these steps, it is important to start with some research that provides you with a sense of context. This means consulting some secondary sources in order to learn about the author's background and the circumstances surrounding publication of the books, including the events of Vonnegut's life and times.

Kurt Vonnegut was born in Indianapolis, Indiana, in 1922 to German-American parents. He was one of three children. After high school, Vonnegut attended Cornell University, planning to major in chemistry. During this time, he also began writing for the school newspaper. However, after enlisting in the U.S. Army, he was transferred to the Carnegie Institute of Technology and the University of Tennessee for training in mechanical engineering. His mother committed suicide shortly after his enlistment, on Mother's Day, 1944. Only a few months later, on December 19, 1944, Vonnegut was captured by the Germans during the Battle of the Bulge in World War II. As a prisoner of war, he witnessed the firebombing of Dresden by the Allies in February of 1945, an event that decimated the city and killed a staggering number of soldiers and civilians. He would struggle to write about this event for more than a quarter of a century. Vonnegut was repatriated in May 1945. After the war, he returned home and married his childhood sweetheart, Jane Marie Cox. He began working for the City News Bureau of Chicago and studied anthropology at the University of Chicago, but his thesis was ultimately rejected (though the university would later award him a master's degree for his novel *Cat's Cradle* in 1971). Vonnegut and Cox moved to Schenectady, New York, and he took up a position working in public relations for General Electric, where his brother worked as a researcher. His first short story, "Report on the Barnhouse Effect," was published in 1950, and his first novel, *Player Piano,* soon followed in 1952. Vonnegut and Cox resided briefly in Barnstable, Massachusetts, where Vonnegut managed a car dealership and wrote short stories. His next novel, *The Sirens of Titan,* was not published until 1959. Vonnegut struggled with his writing during this time until he was offered a teaching position at the University of Iowa Writers' Workshop. Experimenting with form, he created works such as *Mother Night* and *Cat's Cradle, Slaughterhouse-Five* (the cumulative result of his efforts to write about the bombing of Dresden), and *Breakfast of Champions.* They would become his most popular and well-known works. The author later admitted that he had struggled with depression and mental health issues following the publication of *Slaughterhouse-Five.* He attempted suicide in 1984. Vonnegut and Cox had divorced years earlier, in 1979. They had three children together and had also raised his sister Alice's three children after she died of cancer and her husband was killed in an accident two days before her death. Vonnegut married the photographer Jill Krementz. They adopted one child together. The author continued to write novels, essays, and other works, but none were as successful as the novels published during the 1960s. Vonnegut also continued to speak out on political issues such as the Iraq war and details of American politics, promoting humanism as a solution for the ills of the world. He died in April 2007 due to irreversible brain injuries stemming from a fall at his home.

Like all works of literature, Vonnegut's novels are informed heavily by his own personal experiences. Knowledge of the author's background, therefore, lends insight into the portrayal of family and relationships, death and tragedy, war and mental illness in his texts. Not only does he fictionalize these experiences, but in several of his works, he goes so far as to speak directly (either within, as a character; or just outside of his novels in prefaces, editor's notes, and introductions) about some of the most grave of these experiences—the suicide of his mother, his own struggle with mental illness, and his time spent as a soldier and prisoner of war.

Just as the works reflect biographical context, Vonnegut's novels also evidence a broad cultural awareness. His works addressed the world wars and postwar living, the Great Depression, the Vietnam War, communism and the international arms race, the space age and the postindustrial revolution, civil rights issues, foreign relations, and, more generally, changes and shifts in American culture and living. With humor and absurdity, Vonnegut addressed the impact of historical events on the American public, citing changes in the American family, views on love and religion, and the overall quality of life. Subsequently, philosophical topics, such as the quest for purpose and meaning in a cultureless state and man's desire to understand death and suffering, became recurring themes in his works. By linking historical events and cultural changes to philosophical themes, Vonnegut effectively created a dialogue about the human experience that challenged our most basic preconceptions of time, memory, life, and death.

Even with these insights into Vonnegut's works, writing about the author's novels does come with some challenges. Some of the novels—such as *Slaughterhouse-Five* and *Breakfast of Champions*—may appear to lack structure and order, while narration and metafiction raise questions about truth in the works. Consider the relationship of form to theme. Ask yourself whether the works offer reliable narration. Are the characters reliable? In the novels, is Vonnegut reliable? If not, what is he really saying? Many of the novels also masquerade as that which they are not—*Player Piano* and *The Sirens of Titan* pose as works of science fiction, and *Mother Night* is presented as historical novel and memoir—therefore, as you evaluate each work, you will need to establish its true classification. Vonnegut's messages on philosophical subjects have also been a source of confusion for readers and scholars. Because of the dark subject matter and humorous tone of many of the texts, his message can be difficult to interpret. As you think about the philosophies and ideas, evaluate tone and point of view. How is the information presented? Again, is the information presented by a reliable source? Is there only one point of view offered or more than one? Does one point of view seem to stand out? Remember that a character's point of view—even if it seems to be dominant—is not necessarily equivalent to Vonnegut's own point of view. Consider, for instance, how humor and the absurd point out the folly of certain ideas. Likewise, remember that an author's treatment of a negative theme or a stereotype does not mean that the author supports or condones these views. In fact, authors often present viewpoints that are diametrically opposed to their own in order to facilitate a dialogue about a particular subject. For instance, the dark tone and subject matter of some of Vonnegut's novels evokes a sense of futility, but how does his act of writing the book counter or contradict futility and resignation? Through characters such as Kilgore Trout, Rabo Karabekian, and Beatrice Keedsler, and even Vonnegut himself, the power of art and literature becomes a central topic in his novels. His works create a dialogue about why we read and how we read, and they illuminate the power of art and literature to effect positive change.

As you consider Vonnegut's texts, you will note that there are a great number of similarities among them. Many of the works treat similar themes, and Vonnegut even reuses characters in certain works. Kilgore Trout appears more than once, as do Howard W. Campbell Jr. and many others. Some scholars have criticized the author for this, chastising him for recycling from his own works, but consider how these recurring features and elements provide insight into the meaning of his works and major themes. Likewise, observe differences in the texts and consider what they tell us about the author's development, cultural changes, or literary trends.

Finally, as you consult secondary works to find evidence to support your own argument, you may find that you do not agree with a particular scholar's point of view or even, more broadly, some popular conception of the author and his work. In this case, you might decide to write a paper that considers how the author, his works, or some element of his works is misunderstood. The interpretation of literary works is a fluid process, and the purpose of an essay such as yours is to contribute to a dialogue about the author's works, providing fresh insights and interpretations. Do not be afraid to provide your own observations or say something new. Just be sure to support your argument with cohesive, relevant, and well-organized evidence from Vonnegut's works.

TOPICS AND STRATEGIES

In the sections that follow, you will find a variety of suggested topics accompanied by questions and observations to assist you in the task of writing successfully about Kurt Vonnegut and his works. Remember that it is not a comprehensive list, and the statements and questions that appear after each suggested topic are merely a guide to help spark your own ideas about the work. A successful paper will present a strong thesis based upon your own original ideas and will be supported by relevant examples resulting from close readings of the text. A wide variety of interpretations will be possible as you consider each topic. Use the strategic questions and observations to stimulate your own thoughts about the text and to assist you in developing your thesis. Remember to read through the text more than once, making note of those elements that support your argument. It will be equally important to make note of those elements that contradict your thesis, as this will help you to refine your argument and present a stronger case.

Themes

While each of Kurt Vonnegut's novels is unique, an evaluation and analysis of theme makes it easy to find connections among the texts. Each work addresses topics of philosophical, psychological, and social concern, with many themes—fate and free will, progress and purpose, mental illness, the impact of science and technology, and the effects of consumer culture, to name only a few—appearing consistently throughout his oeuvre. As Vonnegut treats these major themes, he also creates a dialogue around a lengthy list of subtopics, including love, friendship, family, truth, identity, time, and death. Once you have identified the theme you wish to write about, you will need to consider first how this theme becomes visible in the texts. Second, you will need to determine what Vonnegut is saying about this particular subject. Consider how elements such as form, character, language, and symbolism reveal information about the theme you have chosen. Look for patterns of images, words, and concepts that reinforce a particular idea or point of view about your topic. If you are writing about more than one text, your paper should consider whether the works offer a consistent and unified point of view or whether they present a variety of viewpoints that reveal some shift or evolution in the author's treatment of the subject. If you can identify a dominant point of view among the texts, you might conclude that Vonnegut is making a clear and definitive statement about a particular theme. You could then construct your paper around a discussion and evaluation of the author's message and the means by which it is presented. If you observe that Vonnegut's point of view is varied, you may determine that the author means to pose questions and initiate dialogue instead. In this case, your paper should contemplate the author's reasons for initiating such a dialogue. Consider, for instance, how the questions and open-ended dialogue push readers to reconsider commonly held ideas or popular beliefs.

Sample Topics:

1. **Fate and free will:** Do Vonnegut's novels suggest that the fate of each human is predetermined or shaped by forces beyond his control, or are the characters in Vonnegut's novels able to effectively determine their own fates?

   Any of the novels treated in this guide may be used effectively in writing about this topic. Consider how the characters are controlled or, alternatively, exert control over their own lives. Evaluate characters such as Paul Proteus of *Player Piano,* Malachi Constant and Beatrice Rumfoord in *The Sirens of Titan,* and Dwayne Hoover and Kilgore Trout of *Breakfast of Champions.* What do the characters seem to have control over, and what are they unable to control? Consider the treatment of God, nature, moral choice, luck, and the accidental in these works. Are the characters' choices and actions ultimately futile, or are there indications that the characters are able to overcome outside influences and determine their own fates?

2. **Dehumanization and the effects of science and technology:** What message does Vonnegut deliver in his novels about dehumanization and the effects of science and technology?

Player Piano, The Sirens of Titan, and *Breakfast of Champions* will be particularly useful, although your research might extend to some of Vonnegut's works that have not been treated in this guide. Your paper should consist of a study of the characters that considers how they are dehumanized, what has caused this, and whether or not there is evidence of some greater good resulting from science and progress that trumps this effect. However, look for patterns of relevant imagery and symbolism as well, such as the motif of man as machine. Does Vonnegut seem to be saying that science and technology are inherently bad, or is he making more refined statements about the misplaced application of scientific invention and man's misguided search for meaning and purpose?

3. **Mental illness:** Explore mental illness as a recurring theme in Vonnegut's texts.

Although mental illness may not be mentioned literally in each of Vonnegut's novels, an argument can be made that there are suggestions of this theme in many of the texts. Consider how this subject becomes visible in Vonnegut's first novel, *Player Piano,* for instance. Likewise, scholars have contended that there are suggestions of some subtext about schizophrenia in the author's treatment of the characters and the theme of identity in *Mother Night.* Therefore, you might wish to begin by writing about the portrayal of mental illness in these texts, perhaps considering how the treatment of this theme corresponds to the treatment of this subject in later novels such as *Slaughterhouse-Five* and *Breakfast of Champions.* Look for literal representations of mental illness in the texts (revealed via language and character), but consider how elements such as imagery and symbolism also expose this theme. How does the form of each text complement the treatment of this theme? Discuss any commentary on the chemical nature of man in the novels, but consider, also, if there seems to be any relationship between the mental health of the characters and cultural circumstances. If a direct connection does seem to be present, you might explore how Vonnegut uses mental illness as a symbol or metaphor in the texts. What does the prevalence of mental illness among the characters suggest? Your paper should also tie in with some discussion of Vonnegut's own experiences with mental illness. How does knowledge of Vonnegut's connection to this topic affect our comprehension and reception of the texts in relation to this subject?

4. **The quest for meaning and purpose:** What do Vonnegut's novels suggest about man's quest for meaning and purpose?

Consider examples of the quest for meaning and purpose in the texts. This should extend into some exploration of representations of the quest for knowledge and truth. Is the result of this quest the same for each character? Evaluate examples of both the positive and negative implications of such quests in the texts. Are these quests ultimately fruitful? Do the characters seem to be fulfilled, finding what they are seeking? What provides the characters with a sense of meaning and purpose? Do the texts actually suggest what the meaning of life is? If not, do they at least establish where humans will fail to find meaning and purpose?

Character

While an analysis of a single character can support a paper, when you are addressing characterization in more than one work, you will need to look for distinct patterns, notable differences, or unique features that allow you to write about multiple characters in a unified and cohesive manner. A successful paper will show how the characters contribute to a single dialogue about a particular theme, informing readers about the true meaning of the works being considered. Any of the most striking features of characterization in Vonnegut's work could be explored effectively: the absence of heroes or villains; the use of tragicomic figures and protagonists; and the inclusion of nontraditional, often nonhuman, characters such as aliens and robots. There are also many motifs in characterization that could be explored: the soldier; the writer/artist/musician, and the mentally ill, to name just a few. An evaluation of the relationships between characters could also serve as a starting place for your paper. In this instance you would identify patterns that emerge in the treatment of the relationships between husbands and wives, friends, parents and children and consider what these patterns convey about love, family, friendship, and intimacy. Vonnegut's novels also contain many other interesting characterizations of people in larger groups. Consider the assemblage of characters in parades, crowds, armies, and granfalloons and the division of the characters by nationality, religion, and social class. Your paper might discuss what an analysis of one of these groupings reveals about society, human behavior, or a theme such as identity, faith and religion, war, prejudice, or allegiance.

No matter which element of characterization you choose to write about, it will be necessary to begin with some character analysis. As you evaluate each character, it will be helpful to consider some basic questions: How is the character portrayed? What is the significance of the words that the author uses to describe him or her? Why are details such as his or her name, profession, and appearance important? How do you feel about the character? Does your opinion of the character change as you read? What do the character's relationships reveal? What is suggested in dialogues or monologues presented by this character? How does the character inform us about other characters? How is this character like or different from other characters? Does the character seem representative of something—a particular idea or concept? By repeating this process, you will begin to see connections (or notable differences) among the characters and the texts that contain them. Use these observations to formulate your thesis.

Sample Topics:

1. **The tragicomic figure:** Evaluate Vonnegut's use of the tragicomic figure in his novels.

   The protagonists in Vonnegut's novels are often clownish and absurd, pathetic, suffering, and confused. Think of Billy Pilgrim, Dwayne Hoover, and even Vonnegut himself. How do these characters evidence characteristics associated with both tragedy and comedy? Consider details such as their appearance, their age, their struggles, their feelings and ideas. How do they respond to the other characters and to their surroundings? Do they triumph over anything? In addition to the protagonists in Vonnegut's novels, how do the supporting characters also reflect this archetype? Consider any relationship between the application of this character type and the genres of Vonnegut's works. You will also need to establish the connection between the use of the tragicomic figure and theme. Are these tragicomic characters symbolic of something?

2. **Kilgore Trout:** Kilgore Trout inhabits several of Vonnegut's novels. Explore the significance of his repeated presence in these works.

Consider the texts where Trout appears and perform an analysis of his character, evaluating details such as his appearance; gestures, actions, and ideas; and his relationship to the other characters. What is his role in each book? Consider how Trout is used symbolically in the texts. This will call for some evaluation of the relationship between his profession as a science fiction writer and the genre of science fiction. What does his character reveal about the usefulness of science fiction? How does his character assist in facilitating a dialogue about themes such as pollution, humanism, mental illness, the power and influence of art, and ways of seeing? What should readers conclude about Trout's ultimate fame and success in *Breakfast of Champions*? Finally, consider Trout's relationship to his creator. Is Trout somehow representative of Vonnegut? Are there any similarities between them? Why might these similarities be significant?

3. **Family:** What do Vonnegut's novels suggest about family?

Consider representations of family in the author's novels. Choose a few examples such as the Pilgrim family in *Slaughterhouse-Five;* the father and son relationships depicted in *Player Piano, Cat's Cradle,* and *The Sirens of Titan;* or the jarring portrayal of mothers in the novels. How are the relationships between family members characterized? What similarities are evident among representations of family in these texts? Are the relationships between family members loving and supportive? How do historical and cultural factors such as economic depression, postwar living, and industrialism seem to affect the construct and function of these families? Research the author's own family history. Does knowledge of Vonnegut's own background provide any new insights into his treatment of families in the novels?

4. **The soldier:** Analyze representations of the soldier in Vonnegut's novels.

Consider all representations of the soldier in *Player Piano, The Sirens of Titan, Mother Night,* and *Slaughterhouse-Five.* What similarities are evident among these characters? How are they described? Evaluate their age, appearance, level of training, and background. How does the collective treatment of the soldier in these novels contribute to a more extensive dialogue about war? What view of war do they represent? Explore Vonnegut's own experiences as a soldier. How does this connection provide insight into the characterization of soldiers in his books?

5. **People in groups:** What is revealed through the treatment of characters in groups in Vonnegut's novels?

You might choose to explore the portrayal of a single group among several texts or to look for a single connection among various groups. Begin by evaluating some of the groups in Vonnegut's novels, including karasses, duprasses, granfalloons, social classes, and people of like nationality and religion. Evaluate the composition of these groups and analyze the behavior and ideas of the people in these groups. What unites or divides the characters that form these groups? In *Player Piano* we find the characters divided or united by social class, in *The Sirens of Titans* crowds gather in the hopes of witnessing a miracle or receiving some message, in *Mother Night* the characters are bound by their complicity and moral missteps, and in *Cat's Cradle* the characters are divided according to nationality and religion. Look for patterns in the treatment of these groups. Consider how they inform us about topics such as allegiance, love and friendship, and prejudice.

6. **The absence of heroes or villains:** Explore characterization in Vonnegut's novels. Why is the absence of heroes and villains significant?

Begin by analyzing the characters, explaining how Vonnegut prevents readers from identifying the characters as heroes or villains. This means showing how Vonnegut has created a balanced or neutral portrait of his characters. In particular, it may be helpful to look for characters that would typically be identified as villains—such as the Nazis—and consider how Vonnegut presents an unexpected portrait of them. Consider how the treatment of the characters creates a dialogue about good and evil, identity, the dual nature of man, ethics and moral choice, and other subjects. Although many of the texts provide information about this subject, an evaluation of characterization in *Mother Night* will be especially useful.

History and Context

Although Vonnegut's works are often set within in a fictional time and space, they refer to very real historical events and cultural happenings. The novels reference both world wars as well as more recent conflict such as the Vietnam War and the cold war. They treat the Great Depression, the space age, the Industrial Revolution, and a period of postindustrial consumerism. The novels also establish a critical portrait of the United States that suggests the lost frontier and the changed American landscape, while exposing a dialogue about slavery and prejudice; civil rights; dissidence, protest, and revolution. Therefore, if you choose to write about history and context, there are many options available to you. You might perform an analysis of representations of a specific historical event or consider how Vonnegut's portrayal of American culture creates a portrait of modern living that demonstrates how historical events and cultural changes have influenced our ideas about family, religion, love, and romance. Alternatively, you might consider how Vonnegut's novels initiate a dialogue about race, gender, or social class. Is his treatment of these subjects in line with popular sentiment, or does he present an unexpected point of view? Because Vonnegut typically establishes a critical tone with respect to these subjects, essays on history and context will often overlap with a study of genre that looks at his use of black humor and the absurd and considers the function of his works as satire and cultural commentary.

As you write about history and context, it will be necessary to spend some time establishing the author's motivations for speaking about a past event or circumstance. Ask yourself how the author's treatment of past events ties in with more timely concerns. For instance, think about how references to Hiroshima in *Cat's Cradle* allow Vonnegut to speak about communism and the arms race or how the author's treatment of World War II in *Slaughterhouse-Five* expands into a dialogue about the Vietnam War and, more generally, the truthful representation of war in the media. Finally, remember to explain why these subjects are relevant today. Use caution: While you should incorporate relevant facts from outside sources and establish context with some discussion of the historical event or cultural factor you are writing about, you should ultimately allow Vonnegut's works to do most of the talking.

Sample Topics:

1. **War:** Evaluate the treatment of war in Vonnegut's novels.

> Consider the authentic conflicts referenced in the author's novels, such as World War II and the Vietnam War in *Slaughterhouse-Five* and World War II in *Mother Night*. Do the works seem to present a unified vision of these conflicts? You will also need to evaluate fictional representations of war and conflict, as in *Player Piano* and *The Sirens of Titan*. What kind of portrait of war does the author create? How are the soldiers depicted? Is there any heroism, glory, victory, or romance associated with war in the novels? You might rely heavily on an evaluation of *Slaughterhouse-Five* that focuses on its themes

of war without romance and the responsible representation of war in media. You might also cite the semiautobiographical nature of the texts, discussing Vonnegut's own experiences as a soldier and prisoner of war. How do these biographical details provide insight into the author's treatment of war in his novels? Another possibility is to tie your essay in with an evaluation of corresponding works of nonfiction by Vonnegut. How do these nonfiction texts provide insight into the treatment of war in Vonnegut's fiction?

2. **Consumerism and the postindustrial revolution:** What kind of portrait do the novels create about consumerism and the postindustrial revolution? What are the effects of industry and consumer culture?

   Works such as *Player Piano, The Sirens of Titan, Slaughterhouse-Five,* and *Breakfast of Champions* will be most useful. Begin by considering how Vonnegut creates a sense of a culture of postindustrial consumerism in these texts. This will depend primarily on an analysis of characters, imagery, and language. What are the positive and negative effects of the Industrial Revolution, and how does the author characterize postindustrial life in the United States? Consider how consumerism affects not only the characters but the American landscape. How does consumerism alter mankind's relationship with nature? What message does the author ultimately seem to be delivering about consumerism? Are the characters fulfilled by wealth? Do they find happiness and contentment with their possessions? What impact does postindustrial consumerism have on culture? Consider Vonnegut's sentiments on this topic in the preface to *Breakfast of Champions.*

3. **Vonnegut's portrait of the United States:** Evaluate the portrait of the United States generated by Vonnegut's novels.

   Consider all representations of American history, culture, and living in Vonnegut's novels, from the accounts of American history in *Player Piano* to the descriptions of the landscape and the portrayal of the state of American living in *Breakfast of Champions.* Do the texts reveal a positive portrait or a critical one? Your essay should conclude by linking this subject to present-day cultural issues in the United States. Your essay should explain why the portrait of the United States revealed in the novels was significant at the time of the book's initial publication and why it is still relevant today.

Philosophy and Ideas

Each of Vonnegut's novels explores complex philosophical issues such as fate and free will, morality and ethics, identity, truth, and religion, but the author does not always provide conclusive statements about these topics. With this in mind, you might write an essay that considers how Vonnegut's novels highlight the complexity and ambiguity of a certain philosophical issue. Begin by considering how a discussion of these intangible and abstract ideas is generated within the text. Next, evaluate point of view. If the texts raise questions about your subject, consider how the author's treatment inspires us to rethink or reconsider typical ideas and beliefs. How do the characters contribute to a discussion of these philosophies and ideas? As you write about the philosophies and ideas treated in Vonnegut's works, it will be particularly important to pay attention to tone. Evaluate the author's use of humor and the absurd. Ask yourself how Vonnegut uses humor and the absurd to negate an idea or to show the folly of a particular viewpoint. Alternatively, how does he generate a sympathetic or empathetic response from readers by avoiding the use of humor and the absurd in places, instead creating a sense of the tragic? Finally, consider the relationship of form to the philosophical subjects treated in each text. Notice how the form of *Breakfast of Champions,* for instance, creates a sense of disorder and chaos that mirrors its key themes and how the nonlinear storytelling in *Slaughterhouse-Five* contributes to our understanding of the author's treatment of subjects like time, death, and memory.

Sample Topics:

1. **Religion and faith:** What statement does Vonnegut make about religion and faith through his novels?

Consider all representations of religion and faith in the novels. What kind of view of Christianity is offered in *Slaughterhouse-Five* and *Cat's Cradle*? What insight does the author
provide into the subject of religion through the use of fictional
religions in his texts? Consider, for instance, the Church of
God the Utterly Indifferent in *The Sirens of Titan* and Bokononism in *Cat's Cradle*. Does Vonnegut present a literal and
realistic portrayal of religion in the novels, or does he create
an absurd and symbolic portrait of religion? Does religion
seem to offer the characters truth, happiness, or comfort? Do
the novels suggest that religion and faith are useful? If not,
do the works suggest what might take the place of religion in
modern times? How, for instance, do the works create a dialogue about humanism? You might also discuss Vonnegut's
own personal thoughts on religion, but be careful to use only
firsthand information such as interviews.

2. **Death:** Evaluate the treatment of death in Vonnegut's novels.

Begin by considering representations of death in the author's
novels. Are there many deaths represented or few? Which
characters die, and what causes their deaths? Are the deaths
portrayed as tragic or matter of fact? How do the other characters respond to these deaths? Is there any representation
of grief or mourning in these books? Is there any indication of glory, heroism, or redemption associated with these
deaths? Consider Vonnegut's employment of elements of science fiction in treating this topic. In *Slaughterhouse-Five*, for
instance, how do the aliens from Tralfamadore offer a new
way of understanding death? Does the author seem to be suggesting that humans should adopt their way of thinking? Is
Vonnegut ultimately creating a fatalistic portrait through his
characterization of death and human response to it? Consider
the relationship between the treatment of this subject and the
author's own experiences with death, including the untimely
death of several family members, the suicide of his mother, and
the stunning number of deaths of fellow soldiers and civilians

that the author witnessed in wartime. How do these personal experiences contribute to the view of death presented in Vonnegut's novels?

3. **Absurdism:** Consider the relationship between Vonnegut's novels and the philosophy of absurdism. Is it accurate to classify his novels as absurdist texts?

It will be necessary to begin by researching the philosophy of absurdism, particularly its origins and how it is defined. Explore relevant writings of the nineteenth-century philosopher Søren Kierkegaard, as well as the roots of existentialism. Consider Albert Camus's treatment of this subject in his essay "The Myth of Sisyphus." You will also need to consider historical and cultural context by evaluating the link between the development of this philosophy and the circumstances of postwar living. Next, return to Vonnegut's works. How do his novels reflect mankind's tendency—and failure—to find meaning and value in life? Do his novels suggest how individuals should respond to this failure? Look to the characters of the novels. How do they embody this philosophy? Finally, you will need to decide whether the texts are ultimately in line with this philosophy or whether they ultimately reject absurdism. In other words, establish whether the characters find meaning or whether the text proposes some alternative philosophy that negates the philosophy of absurdism.

Form and Genre

Genre is often a straightforward subject, but with Vonnegut's works it acquires much more depth. Vonnegut's novels resist classification within a single genre; instead, his works are unique hybrids of popular genres such as science fiction and fantasy, historical work, memoir, spy novel, satire, apocalyptic and dystopic tale, comedy and tragedy. While genre is often passive—simply the classification that a work belongs to—Vonnegut uses plays on genre as a device to effectively deliver messages about key themes. Consider, for instance, how he allows his works to masquerade as science fiction (as with *Player Piano* and *The Sirens of Titan*) or as historical fiction and memoir (as with *Mother Night*). Although the works cited take on characteristics of these genres, how do they also resist classification within these genres? And how do the fantastic elements and parodies of realistic genres illuminate or dispel certain truths? Since most of the works present a critical commentary, another option is to consider his works as satire. Collectively, what kind of commentary do the novels present? Your paper should reveal the topics that the novels satirize and the ultimate message that the satire reveals with respect to these subjects. An analysis of an element of form such as narration, point of view, structure, recycling and repetition, or metafiction can also serve as the foundation for your paper. Ask questions: Does the narrative method remain consistent among the texts, and is the narration reliable? How does the structure of each novel complement or reinforce its thematic content? What is the purpose of the use of metafiction in the texts, and is it used traditionally? Consider how your interpretation of Vonnegut's works would be different if these elements were absent or were applied differently. Ultimately, an essay of this kind should illuminate the relationship of form to theme. You might choose to write an essay that evaluates the effectiveness of a particular element of form or one that shows how an element of form is used in a new or different way than previously seen in literature. This could be accomplished by comparing certain novels with standout elements of form—*Slaughterhouse-Five* and *Breakfast of Champions,* perhaps—to earlier works by Vonnegut, to works by other authors that preceded these novels, or even to works by other authors that were published contemporaneously.

Sample Topics:

1. **Science fiction:** Explore the role of science fiction in the works of Vonnegut.

   This essay should not only consider whether Vonnegut's works belong to the genre of science fiction; it should consider how science fiction becomes a subject and symbol within the texts. Establish where readers find elements of science fiction in the novels by looking to character and setting and by evaluating the ideas presented in these works. Consider alien characters such as the Tralfamadorians, the harmoniums, and the robot Salo. What seems to be their purpose in the stories they inhabit? What do they reveal to readers that the human characters do not? Explore the significance of the interplanetary setting of *The Sirens of Titan*. How does science fiction open up a dialogue about new ways of thinking and the way we respond to that which is alien or foreign to us? How does it facilitate and shape a dialogue about themes such as time, death, war, purpose, and friendship? Evaluate the character Kilgore Trout, paying attention to his ideas as revealed in dialogue, internal monologue, narration, and accounts of his stories. His characterization in *Slaughterhouse-Five* and *Breakfast of Champions* will be most helpful. What effect does science fiction have on the other characters in Vonnegut's novels? What effect does it have on you as a reader? Consider, also, Vonnegut's frustrations with being characterized as a science fiction writer. Why is this detail significant? What insight does it provide into Vonnegut's relationship to this genre and the repeated appearance of elements of science fiction in his work?

2. **Black humor and the absurd:** Analyze the use of black humor and the absurd in Vonnegut's novels.

Consider some examples of humor and the absurd in the texts. What effect do these passages have on you as a reader? What kind of response do they elicit? Does the tone created by the use of humor and the absurd complement or contradict the themes and points of view presented in these texts? What does the humor illuminate for readers? How does the use of humor and the absurd contribute to the satirical nature of Vonnegut's work? Is the inclusion of humor and the absurd reflective of any particular idea or philosophy promulgated by the novels?

3. **Evolution of form:** Is a clear evolution of form evident in Vonnegut's novels over the course of his career?

Begin by considering the form of Vonnegut's first novel, *Player Piano*, and continue on, perhaps ending with *Breakfast of*

Champions. Consider the overall structure and organization of each story. How is the story divided? Is the plot presented in a linear fashion? Consider the openings and conclusions of these books. Is a classic rising-action/climax/falling-action structure evident? Refine your evaluation by considering sentence structure, rhythm, repetition and recycling, and the author's use of metafiction. Do any clear changes in form begin to emerge? If so, does there seem to be some relationship between the evolution of form and the treatment of theme in the corresponding texts? Consider how form in storytelling also becomes a subject within Vonnegut's novels, as in *Mother Night, Slaughterhouse-Five,* and *Breakfast of Champions.* In each of these texts, what do the dialogues about this subject reveal about the author's process and his decisions about form?

4. **Fiction as autobiography:** Consider the novels as semiautobiographical texts. What insights do they provide about the author?

   How do the novels function as at least partial self-portraits of Vonnegut? You will need to begin with some reading about the author, considering major biographies and interviews. What elements of the author's own life are visible in his novels? How does Vonnegut reveal these in his texts? How do the characters correspond to the author? Do any of the characters actually resemble Vonnegut? Consider Vonnegut's role as a character in his own novels. What is the purpose of including himself as a character? Does the personal nature of his books lend credibility to his fiction? How else does it shape and influence reader response?

5. **Metafiction:** Evaluate the use of metafiction in Vonnegut's novels.

   Consider all examples of metafiction in the texts, evaluating prefaces and introductions, dedications, interruptions in the delivery of plot, and the author's appearances as a character in his own works. If you are unfamiliar with metafiction, it may be helpful to begin by reading William H. Gass's 1970 essay "Philosophy and the Form of Fiction." Does Vonnegut employ metafiction traditionally in all of his works in order to create a self-conscious reflection on the texts? Consider, in particular, his distinctive use of metafiction in *Mother Night*. How does the author's application of metafiction change or develop throughout his career?

Language, Symbols, and Imagery

Many of Vonnegut's phrases—especially, "So it goes" and his famous call to attention of "Listen" in *Slaughterhouse-Five*—have stuck with readers many years after they first appeared in print, becoming popular jargon. Vonnegut's works are also filled with memorable imagery. In his novels, he balances telling with showing, establishing a visual language that provides major insights into key themes. Because both the imagery and the language of Vonnegut's novels have drawn the attention of censors throughout his career, an essay might effectively confront the controversial nature of this material, making a case for its effectiveness or necessity. There are also many symbols in Vonnegut's works that are worthy of exploration: Birds, games, and music appear throughout his oeuvre. Remember that symbols are not only images. Characters, settings, genres, and even literary devices can also function symbolically. For instance, Vonnegut uses contrast in his novels to expose important similarities and differences, but, when it is applied to characters, the contrast also represents the dual nature of man, reflects the foreign and the unknown, and helps to create a sense of the passage of time. Likewise, the author uses repetition—mirrored in representations of echolalia in several of the novels—to reinforce key ideas, but the repetition itself could also be evaluated as a symbol that corresponds to a dialogue about mental illness, acceptance, futility, the cyclical nature of life, and other subjects.

Sample Topics:

1. **Language:** Evaluate language in the works of Vonnegut.

   Your paper should explain why Vonnegut's use of language is effective, memorable, or notable. Consider word choice, arrangement, and sentence structure. Analyze dialogue and information presented by the narrators. What is the purpose of his use of repetition? How does the inclusion of cursing, profanity, and vulgarity in the texts contribute to our understanding of certain recurring themes? Evaluate the author's use of fictional language such as the language of Bokononism. Why does the author employ a fictional language rather than one that readers are familiar with? Are Vonnegut's choices with respect to language ultimately good ones?

2. **Setting as symbol:** Evaluate setting as symbol in Vonnegut's novels.

Consider the settings of Vonnegut's novels, including Ilium, Midland City, outer space, San Lorenzo, and the lost frontier or changed American landscape. Are these sites authentic or familiar to us? As a backdrop for each story, what kind of mood do they create? Consider how these places are described by evaluating imagery and word choice. Are they primarily industrial or natural? How do the characters relate to these sites? Think about the opening sections of *Player Piano* and *Breakfast of Champions*. Consider details of setting including the architecture described in *The Sirens of Titan* or the mountain and the island in *Cat's Cradle*. How do these sites reflect the thematic concerns of the texts that they appear in? Is there some observable commonality among the various settings—some similarity in intent and purpose?

3. **Contrast:** Explore Vonnegut's use of contrast as a revelatory device.

In order to write about this subject, you would need to look for pairings of opposites in the texts. Although many of the novels might be referenced in this essay, *Player Piano, Mother Night,* and *Cat's Cradle* could serve as an effective trio. You may look, first, for opposites among the imagery, but consider how the author also uses contrast in characterization. Consider how this contrast allows him to present ideas in opposition or multiple points of view within a single text. How does he use contrast to speak about philosophical subjects or historical or cultural concerns? Think, for instance, how contrast in *Mother Night* exposes a dialogue about the dual nature of man or how the author employs imagery in opposition, such as the mechanical and the natural, the old and the new in *Player Piano,* to create a sense of the changed American landscape. How does he use this device in *Cat's Cradle* to speak about the foreign?

Comparison and Contrast Essays

When considering an author's entire oeuvre, the options for comparison and contrast essays are virtually limitless. Of course, you might compare or contrast an element within a single work, but there is much that can be gained from a consideration of several works together. For instance, a comparison of an early novel to later ones might reveal consistency in the treatment of a particular theme that lends clarity to the author's message, or it could expose significant changes or developments in the author's process with respect to form and style. Comparison and contrast essays can also extend to a consideration of works by other authors by asking how Vonnegut enters into a dialogue with works of the past or how Vonnegut's novels have influenced authors that followed him.

As you prepare to write your essay, remember not to choose too many works for comparison or contrast. Citing too many works will leave your reader confused and overwhelmed. Choose texts that best correspond to your topic. Likewise, not all of the similarities or differences you observe between texts will be relevant to your paper. Observe the similarities and differences and then edit the information you find. You will find that certain works lend themselves to a group comparison better than others. For instance, many of Vonnegut's novels contain elements of science fiction, so one option would be to compare the works that possess characteristics of science fiction, using your observations to discuss how genre is used to speak about key themes. However, since so many of the author's works contain elements of science fiction, an alternative would be to compare these works to a novel that does not incorporate elements of science fiction, such as *Mother Night*. In other words, begin by considering how a few works are similar—Do they treat similar themes, share certain elements of characterization, or make use of a particular symbol?—but then note any differences you find. Observe how these similarities and differences illuminate the most meaningful features of each work. How are apparently similar texts actually dissimilar or unique? How do the differences reveal some shift in Vonnegut's process, style, or treatment of theme? Do not simply state the obvious by noting what makes works alike or dissimilar. Your paper should illuminate some major point that is not obvious without such a comparison.

Sample Topics:

1. **A single element across Vonnegut's works:** Compare a single element across Vonnegut's works.

   Consider the formal elements of Vonnegut's works. Choose an element that stands out among his texts. You might choose a theme that Vonnegut addresses in more than one work, a recurring symbol or motif, some pattern in characterization, or a striking feature of form. Explain how the element is treated similarly or dissimilarly in each text. No matter which topic you choose to explore, remember to explain what these similarities or differences reveal about Vonnegut's work. What message does this comparison reveal? How does a consideration of this element in more than one text make the author's ideas clearer?

2. **The works of Vonnegut and the works of another author:** What does a comparison of these works reveal about the texts under consideration and about patterns or developments in literary history?

   You might compare a single work or a few works by Vonnegut to the work of another author who published during the same time period, or you might compare Vonnegut's work to the work of an author who preceded or succeeded him, discussing influence as well as trends and developments in literature. Some ideas are to contrast Vonnegut's works to the work of a science fiction writer; compare the treatment of war in Vonnegut's novels and the works of other modern authors; evaluate the form of various works; compare Vonnegut's language to that of Ernest Hemingway or Norman Mailer; discuss how Vonnegut's works show evidence of the influence of Romanticism or Victorian literature; compare Vonnegut's novels to works of satire or social commentary by other authors; evaluate the use of humor and the absurd in Vonnegut's texts and the works of another author such as Mark Twain and George Orwell; or discuss Vonnegut's unexpected application of genre by comparing some of his works to the works of a contemporary author such as Jonathan Lethem. Limit your comparison to a few works and be sure not to simply present a list of similarities. Your essay should demonstrate how an evaluation of one work shapes and informs our understanding of another. What new insights does a comparison provide into each of the works you have considered and the authors under consideration? What does this comparison reveal about the relationship among works of literature? How does a comparison of the works document some cultural changes or shifts in popular ideology?

Bibliography and Resources

Allen, William Rodney, ed. *Conversations with Kurt Vonnegut.* Literary Conversations Series. Jackson, MS: U of Mississippi P, 1999.

———. *Understanding Kurt Vonnegut.* Understanding Contemporary American Literature. Columbia, SC: U of South Carolina P, 2009.

Amis, Martin. "Kurt Vonnegut: After the Slaughterhouse." *The Moronic Inferno and Other Visits to America.* New York: Penguin, 1991. 132–37.

Berryman, Charles. "After the Fall: Kurt Vonnegut." *Critique* 26.2 (1985): 96–102.

Blackford, Russell. "Physics and Fantasy: Scientific Mysticism, Kurt Vonnegut, and *Gravity's Rainbow.*" *Journal of Popular Culture* 19.3 (Winter 1985): 35–44.

Bloom, Harold, ed. *Kurt Vonnegut.* Modern Critical Views. Philadelphia: Chelsea House, 2000.

Bodtke, Richard. "Great Sorrows, Small Joys: The World of Kurt Vonnegut, Jr." *Crosscurrents* 20 (Winter 1970): 120–25.

Boon, Kevin A., ed. *At Millennium's End: New Essays on the Work of Kurt Vonnegut.* Albany, NY: State U of New York P, 2001.

Boon, Kevin A. *Chaos Theory and the Interpretation of Literary Texts: The Case of Kurt Vonnegut.* Lewiston, NY: Edwin Mellen, 1997.

Bosworth, David. "The Literature of Awe." *Antioch Review* 37 (1979): 4–26.

Broer, Lawrence R. "Pilgrim's Progress: Is Kurt Vonnegut Jr. Winning His War with Machines?" *Clockwork Worlds: Mechanized Environments in Science Fiction.* Ed. Richard D. Erlich and Thomas P. Dunn. Westport, CT: Greenwood, 1983: 137–61.

———. *Sanity Plea: Schizophrenia in the Novels of Kurt Vonnegut.* Second edition. Tuscaloosa, AL: U of Alabama P, 1994.

Buck, Lynn. "Vonnegut's World of Comic Futility." *Studies in American Fiction* 3 (Autumn 1975): 181–98.

Burhans, Clinton. "Hemingway and Vonnegut: Diminishing Vision in a Dying Age." *Modern Fiction Studies* 21 (1975): 173–92.

Ciardi, John. "Manner of Speaking." *Saturday Review* 30 September 1967: 16, 18.

Clancy, L. J. "If Accident Will: The Novels of Kurt Vonnegut." *Meanjin Quarterly* 30 (1971): 37–45.

Crichton, J. M. "Sci-Fi and Vonnegut." *New Republic* 26 April 1969: 33–35.

Davis, Todd F. *Kurt Vonnegut's Crusade; or, How a Postmodern Harlequin Preached a New Kind of Humanism.* Albany: State U of New York P, 2006.

DeMott, Benjamin. "Vonnegut's Otherworldy Laughter." *Saturday Review* 1 May 1971: 29–32, 38.

Dimeo, Stephen. "Novel into Film: So It Goes." *The Modern American Novel and the Movies.* Ed. Gerald Peary and Roger Shatzkin. New York: Ungar, 1978. 282–92.

Engel, David. "On the Question of Foma: A Study of the Novels of Kurt Vonnegut, Jr." *Riverside Quarterly* 5 (February 1972): 119–28.

Fiene, Donald M. "Elements of Dostoevsky in the Novels of Kurt Vonnegut." *Dostoevsky Studies* 2 (1981): 129–42.

Friedman, Melvin J. "Dislocations of Setting and Word: Notes on American Fiction Since 1950." *Studies in American Fiction* 5 (1977): 79–98.

Gass, William H. "Philosophy and the Form of Fiction." *Fiction and the Figures of Life.* Jaffrey, NH: Godine, 2000. 3–26.

Giannone, Richard. "Violence in the Novels of Kurt Vonnegut." *Thought* 56 (1981): 58–76.

———. *Vonnegut: A Preface to His Novels.* Port Washington, NY: Kennikat, 1977.

Gill, R. B. "Bargaining in Good Faith: The Laughter of Vonnegut, Grass, and Kundera." *Critique* 25 (1984): 77–91.

Goldsmith, David H. *Kurt Vonnegut: Fantasist of Fire and Ice.* Bowling Green, OH: Bowling Green U Popular P, 1972.

Grossman, Edward. "Vonnegut in His Audience." *Commentary* July 1974: 40–46.

Hansen, Arlen J. "The Celebration of Solipsism: A New Trend in American Fiction." *Modern Fiction Studies* 19 (Spring 1973): 5–15.

Harris, Charles B. *Contemporary American Novelists of the Absurd.* New Haven, CT: College and University Press Services, Inc., 1971. 51–75.

Hendin, Josephine. *Vulnerable People: A View of American Fiction since 1945.* New York: Oxford UP, 1978.

———. "Writer as Culture Hero." *Harpers* July 1974: 82–87.

Hipkiss, Robert A. *The American Absurd: Pynchon, Vonnegut, and Barth.* Port Washington, NY: Associated Faculty Press, 1984. 43–73.

Hume, Kathryn. "Kurt Vonnegut and the Myths and Symbols of Meaning." *Texas Studies in Literature and Language* 24 (1982): 429–47.

———. "Vonnegut's Self-Projections: Symbolic Characters and Symbolic Fiction." *Journal of Narrative Technique* 12.3 (Fall 1982): 177–90.

Irving, John. "Kurt Vonnegut and His Critics." *New Republic* 22 September 1979: 41–49.

Kazin, Alfred. *Bright Book of Life: American Novelists and Storytellers from Hemingway to Mailer.* Boston: Atlantic-Little, Brown, 1973.

———. "The War Novel from Mailer to Vonnegut." *Joseph Heller's Catch-22: A Critical Edition.* Ed. Robert M. Scotto. New York: Dell, 1973.

Kennedy, R. C. "Kurt Vonnegut, Jr." *Art International* 15 (May 1971): 20–25.

Ketterer, David. *New Worlds for Old: The Apocalyptic Imagination, Science Fiction and American Literature.* Garden City, NY: Anchor, 1974.

Klinkowitz, Jerome. *Kurt Vonnegut.* London: Methuen, 1982.

———. "Kurt Vonnegut, Jr. and the Crime of His Times." *Critique* 12 (1971): 38–53.

———. *Literary Disruptions: The Making of Post-Contemporary American Fiction.* Urbana, IL: U of Illinois P, 1980.

———. *Structuring the Void: The Struggle for Subject in Contemporary American Fiction.* Durham, NC: Duke UP, 1992.

———. *The Vonnegut Effect.* Columbia, SC: U of South Carolina P, 2004.

———. *Vonnegut in Fact: The Public Spokesmanship of Personal Fiction.* Columbia, SC: U of South Carolina P, 1998.

Klinkowitz, Jerome and Donald L. Lawler, eds. *Vonnegut in America: An Introduction to the Life and Work of Kurt Vonnegut.* New York: Delacorte Press-Seymour Lawrence, 1977.

LeClair, Thomas. "Death and Black Humor." *Critique* 17.1 (1975): 5–40.

Leeds, Marc. *The Vonnegut Encyclopedia: An Authorized Compendium.* Westport, CT: Greenwood, 1995.

Leeds, Marc and Peter J. Reed. *Kurt Vonnegut: Images and Representations.* Westport, CT: Greenwood, 2000.

Marvin, Thomas F. *Kurt Vonnegut: A Critical Companion.* Westport, CT: Greenwood, 2002.

Marx, Leo. *The Machine in the Garden: Technology and the Pastoral Ideal in America.* New York: Oxford UP, 2000.

May, John R. *Toward a New Earth: Apocalypse in the American Novel.* Notre Dame, IN: U of Notre Dame P, 1972: 172–200.

———. "Vonnegut's Humor and the Limits of Hope." *Twentieth Century Literature* 18.1 (1972): 25–36.

McNelly, Willis E. "Science Fiction the Modern Mythology." *SF: The Other Side of Realism.* Ed. Thomas D. Clareson. Bowling Green, OH: Bowling Green U Popular P, 1971. 193–98.

Merrill, Robert, ed. *Critical Essays on Kurt Vonnegut.* Boston: G. K. Hall, 1990.

Morse, Donald E. *Novels of Kurt Vonnegut: Imagining Being an American.* Westport, CT: Praeger, 2003.

———. *Kurt Vonnegut.* San Bernardino, CA: Starmont House, 1992.

Mustazza, Leonard, ed. *The Critical Response to Kurt Vonnegut.* Westport, CT: Greenwood, 1994.

———. *Forever Pursuing Genesis: The Myth of Eden in the Novels of Kurt Vonnegut.* Cranbury, NJ: Associated UP, 1990.

Myers, David. "Kurt Vonnegut, Jr.: Morality-Myth in the Antinovel." *International Fiction Review* 3 (1976): 52–56.

Nadeau, Robert. *Readings from the New Book on Nature: Physics and Metaphysics in the Modern Novel.* US: U of Massachusetts P, 1981. 121–98.

Nelson, Joyce. "Vonnegut and Bugs in Amber." *Journal of Popular Culture* 7 (1973): 551–58.

Pauly, Rebecca M. "The Moral Stance of Kurt Vonnegut." *Extrapolation* 15 (1973): 66–71.

Pieratt, Asa B., Julie Huffman-Klinkowitz, and Jerome Klinkowitz. *Kurt Vonnegut: A Comprehensive Bibliography.* Hamden, CT: Archon Books, 1987.

Rackstraw, Loree. *Love as Always, Kurt: Vonnegut as I Knew Him.* Cambridge, MA: Da Capo, 2009.

Reed, Peter J. and Marc Leeds, eds. *The Vonnegut Chronicles: Interviews and Essays.* Westport, CT: Greenwood, 1996.

Rovit, Earl. "Some Shapes in Recent American Fiction." *Contemporary Literature* 15.4 (Autumn 1974): 550–65.

Rubens, Philip M. "Nothing's Ever Final: Vonnegut's Concept of Time." *College Literature* 6.1 (Winter 1979): 64–72.

Samuels, Charles Thomas. "Age of Vonnegut." *New Republic* 12 June 1971: 30–32.

Scholes, Robert. *The Fabulators.* New York: Oxford UP, 1967.

Scholl, Peter A. "Vonnegut's Attack upon Christendom." *Christianity and Literature* 22 (1971): 5–11.

Schriber, Mary Sue. "Bringing Chaos to Order: The Novel Tradition and Kurt Vonnegut, Jr." *Genre* 10 (1977): 283–97.

Schultz, Max F. "The Unconfirmed Thesis: Kurt Vonnegut, Black Humor, and Contemporary Art." *Critique* 12.3 (1971): 5–28.

Seelye, John. "What the Kids Are Reading." *New Republic* 17 October 1970: 23–26.

Segal, Howard P. *Future Imperfect: The Mixed Blessings of Technology in America.* Amherst: U of Massachusetts P, 1994.

Simmons, David. *The Anti-Hero in the American Novel: From Heller to Vonnegut.* American Literature Readings in the 21st Century. New York: Palgrave Macmillan, 2008.

Simmons, David, ed. *New Critical Essays on Kurt Vonnegut.* American Literature Readings in the 21st Century. New York: Palgrave Macmillan, 2009.

Tanner, Tony. *City of Words: American Fiction 1950–1970.* New York: Harper & Row, 1971.

Uphaus, Robert W. "Expected Meaning in Vonnegut's Dead-End Fiction." *Novel* 8.2 (Winter 1975): 164–74.

Vonnegut, Kurt, and Lee Stringer. *Like Shaking Hands with God: A Conversation about Writing.* New York: Seven Stories Press, 1999.

Wymer, Thomas L. "Machines and Meaning of Human in the Novels of Kurt Vonnegut, Jr." *Mechanical God: Machines in Science Fiction.* Ed. Thomas P. Dunn and Richard D. Erlich. Westport, CT: Greenwood, 1982: 41–52.

Ziegfield, Richard E. "Kurt Vonnegut on Censorship and Moral Values." *Modern Fiction Studies* 26 (1980): 631–35.

PLAYER PIANO

READING TO WRITE

When preparing to write about a work published early in an author's career, following the natural inclination to compare it with the works that succeeded it can serve as a useful tactic. In the process of identifying how an early work compares with later ones, you will be uncovering the most significant characteristics of each and detecting important trends or developments in the author's oeuvre. Accordingly, a comparison of *Player Piano*—Vonnegut's first published novel—and those works produced later in his career yields an abundance of topics worthy of exploration. Certainly the themes of progress and human purpose and the concern with technology and consumer culture evidenced in the text are recognizable to those who have read the author's later works. This might lead to a paper that discusses how *Player Piano* marks the genesis of a preoccupation with the dangers of scientific progress that would last throughout Vonnegut's career or one that shows how the treatment of consumer culture in this first novel compares to the treatment of the same subject in a later work such as *Breakfast of Champions.* Alternatively, one could compare the treatment of relationships in *Player Piano* to the treatment of relationships in the author's other novels. For example, the relationship between Paul Proteus and his wife, Anita, could easily be likened to the relationship between Billy Pilgrim and Valencia in *Slaughterhouse-Five,* and one can certainly find many similarities in the father-son relationships presented in *Player Piano* and Vonnegut's second novel, *The Sirens of Titan.* Collectively, these observations could serve as the foundation of a paper that shows how patterns in Vonnegut's treatment of relationships reveal a deeper dialogue about family, intimacy, or love.

A consideration of the discrepancies between *Player Piano* and Vonnegut's later novels can be equally profitable. Many of the elements that readers have come to associate with Vonnegut's work—nonlinear narrative; abbreviated sentence structure and repetition; metafiction; black humor; and treatment of the absurd, to name a few—are either absent or not quite fully developed in this first novel. This might inspire you to write about the evolution of Vonnegut's style over the course of his career or to perform an analysis of the varied usage of a single element among a few of the texts. No matter which approach you take, you will need to begin by asking questions about the formal elements of the texts you choose: How are the characters alike or different? Do the works share similar narration or form? Do readers find like imagery and language? What themes do the works have in common? How does the treatment of these elements differ or remain consistent among the texts? Most importantly, remember that it is not sufficient to simply list similarities or differences. You will need to explain why these similarities or differences are significant, focusing on how these observations provide readers with new insight into *Player Piano* and its meaning.

If *Player Piano* is the first work by Vonnegut that you have encountered, or if you prefer a more focused approach, you may wish to limit your paper to an examination of this single work. Again, a thorough analysis of any formal element found in the novel will work well, or you might choose to write about context. In the first instance you would employ the same process outlined above: Identify a key feature such as a significant character or relationship, a certain type of imagery, noteworthy language, or a compelling theme; look for patterns or variations in the treatment of this single element within the text; investigate these patterns or variations by asking questions; and, finally, using evidence gathered from the text itself, explain why these patterns or variations are significant. If you choose to write about context, like a photographer using a wide-angle camera lens, you would begin by considering the work from a broader perspective. Think about the time period in which the book was written and published. What significant cultural events were taking place at that time? What had happened or was happening in the author's own life around the time that the book was written? Where do we find these contextual elements reflected in the text, and how does the author present them to readers? In interviews, Vonnegut revealed that *Player Piano* was inspired by his own observations about the growing presence of machines and technology while working in public relations for General Electric during the late 1940s. Using this fact as a starting point, writers interested in the link between fiction and reality could explore *Player Piano* as a semiautobiographical work, making a case for this classification by providing additional evidence of the direct influence of Vonnegut's own life experiences in the text, or as cultural commentary and social satire, showing how the book presents a critique of a drastically altered and still rapidly changing American landscape. Continuing along this line of thought, while *Player Piano* is drawn from the author's real-life experiences and observations, it is still a novel. In other words, Vonnegut chose to write fiction rather than a memoir or a work of nonfiction. Specifically, *Player Piano* is a novel that contains distinct elements of fantasy and science fiction; so one might also choose to write about this aspect of the work, explaining how Vonnegut uses fantasy to help readers see their reality in a new way. In each of these instances, you would be writing about genre, or the classification of the work.

If, after completing a pass of the novel, you have still not settled on a topic, simply return to the beginning. Consider the title and review the opening passages. While there are some exceptions, the opening of a novel almost always reveals (or at least begins to suggest) the key elements and concerns of the work. Again, you should observe characters, look for important imagery and language, and note patterns of ideas that begin to surface in this part of the text. A consideration of symbolism—what a particular character, place, or object represents—can serve as an excellent starting place for your paper. By identifying a major symbol, analyzing its treatment in the novel, and explaining its significance, you will be uncovering key themes, and in the exploration of the relationship between symbol and theme, you will discover the ideas that will help you to develop your thesis. Once you have identified a symbol, begin by asking and answering some basic questions. In the case of *Player Piano*, the title references one of the major symbols of the novel. If you decided to write about this symbol, it would be helpful to ask: What is a player piano? What does the player piano call to mind? Certainly, we equate it with music but, more specifically, the player piano produces sound automatically without a human musician. Therefore, in its ability to produce music, it represents something very human and emotional, but it is also something automated, technological, and even ghostly. As you analyze a symbol, remember that you may need to move beyond the primary text, consulting secondary sources or reference works for further information. In this case, for example, it is helpful to have a general understanding of the history of the player piano and its place in American culture. Therefore, encyclopedia entries, reference works, and texts such as Brian Dolan's *Inventing Entertainment: The Player Piano and the Origins of an American Musical Industry* and James Parakilas's *Piano Roles: A New History of the Piano* will be valuable. As you consult these sources, look for details such as when the player piano was invented and why its invention was significant. Ask yourself how the information you uncover corresponds to the application of the symbol in the novel and the major thematic concerns of the text you are writing about. Broaden your line of questioning. Have you seen many player pianos? What does this say about their popularity and their success as a consumer good? Why is the failure or success of the piano as a consumer good relevant? In answering questions such as these, you should begin to see some connection to the major themes of the novel: progress, purpose, and the impact of technological advancement on humankind.

Equipped with an understanding of the symbol and what it represents, you should have enough preliminary information to begin drafting your paper. However, you will need to return to the novel to find evidence that supports your thesis and refines your argument. Make note of passages where the symbol appears in the text. In chapter 3, for example, speaking of Paul Proteus, the narrator tells us: "His back was against an old player piano" (25). A short time later, an uncomfortable Paul leans against the keyboard and "a faint discord [comes] from the piano, hum[s] to nothingness" (30). Counter to the discord produced by Paul, a ragtime song plays when Rudy Hertz pops in a coin. In chapter 9 we find the piano being used again, operated not by a coin, but played by human hands—those of the "frenzied pianist" Ed Finnerty. Details such as who operates the piano and the sounds that each causes it to make were chosen with intention and should not be overlooked. Do not simply examine passages that feature the piano literally either. Keep in mind that your goal is to analyze and evaluate the symbolic value of the player piano and to uncover what it tells us about the themes of the book. If, for example, you propose that the player piano represents a drastically altered United States by serving as a symbol of the dehumanizing effects of scientific progress and automation, you will need to consult the text to see where else these ideas are referenced. A review of the opening passages reveals several noteworthy examples. Like the player piano, the setting introduced in chapter 1 also references automation and shows evidence of dehumanization resulting from "production without man-power" during a postwar period of industrialism (1):

> Ilium, New York is divided into three parts.
>
> In the northwest are the managers and engineers and civil servants and a few professional people; in the northwest are the machines; and in the south, across the Iroquois River, is the area known locally as Home-stead, where almost all of the people live.
>
> If the bridge across the Iroquois were dynamited, few daily routines would be disturbed. Not many people on either side have reasons other than curiosity for crossing.
>
> During the war, in hundreds of Iliums over America managers and engineers learned to get along without their men and women, who went to fight. It was the miracle that won the war—production with almost no manpower. (1)

Later in this same chapter, Paul Proteus looks out over an old battlefield:

> Now over bones and other rotten palings and cannonballs and arrow-heads, there lay a triangle of steel and masonry buildings, a half-mile on each side—the Ilium Works. Where men had once howled and hacked at one another, and fought nip-and-tuck with nature as well, the machine hummed and whirred and clicked, and made parts for baby carriages and bottlecaps, motorcycles and refrigerators, television sets and tricycles—the fruits of peace. (3)

Notice, again, how the imagery references automation and industrialism, while the incorporation of historical references in both passages (here, a Native American battlefield; earlier, a river named the Iroquois) begins to suggest a portrait of a drastically altered American landscape. Look for other passages that echo these ideas. Consider, for instance, the conversation about the Industrial Revolution that takes place between Paul Proteus and his secretary, Katharine Finch, the reference to the tape that "could make the essence of Rudy Hertz produce one, ten, a hundred or a thousand of the shafts" (11), or Paul Proteus's reference to the sound of the machinery as "the music of Building 58" (11). Of course, these are only a few examples from chapter 1; there are numerous other examples in the chapters that follow. From here you would repeat this process, identifying passages in the book that support your thesis and uncovering the connections between them in order to create a unified and coherent paper. With plenty of evidence from the text to support your thesis, you will be able to make a strong case and finish with a powerful conclusion.

TOPICS AND STRATEGIES

In the sections that follow, you will find a variety of suggested topics accompanied by questions and observations to assist you in the task of writing successfully about *Player Piano.* Remember that it is not a comprehensive list, and the statements and questions that appear after each suggested topic are merely a guide to help spark your own ideas about the work. A successful paper will present a strong thesis based upon your own original ideas and will be supported by relevant examples resulting from close readings of the text. A wide variety of interpretations will be possible as you consider each topic. Use the strategic questions and observations to stimulate your own thoughts about the text and to assist you in developing your thesis. Remember to read through the text more than once, making note of those elements that support your argument. It will be equally important to make note of those elements that contradict your thesis, as this will help you to refine your argument and present a stronger case.

Themes

Player Piano centers on the dramatic interplay between man and machine. It should not be surprising then that there is evidence of a similar dual dynamic among the major themes of the novel. In this work Vonnegut enters into a dialogue about progress and purpose, pairing social and cultural concerns with emotional and philosophical ones. The relationship between progress and purpose could serve as the subject for a successful essay. Either of these topics could be explored individually as well. Of course, progress and purpose are only two of the subjects addressed in *Player Piano*; the novel also presents many secondary themes that could be explored profitably. Because these themes are revealed to readers via the formal elements of the text, you will find that writing about them demands that you also speak about form and genre, language, symbols, imagery, and characters. Once a general topic is evident, consider how each individual element of the text lends itself to a deeper examination of this subject. In other words, you should not only explain what you believe Vonnegut is saying about a particular topic but how his work transmits this information to readers. Finally, remember that an author may not always offer conclusive statements about a particular subject; the text may pose questions and provoke dialogue instead. Accordingly, more than one viewpoint may be presented in a single text. For instance, if you choose to write a paper about progress in *Player Piano*, you might note that some of the characters seem to be happy with the technological advancements that have taken place, while others find them to be dangerous and dehumanizing. Therefore, you might make a case for technological advancement in the novel by discussing the many references to the role of invention in American history found in the text, supporting this with an evaluation of a corresponding character such as the ingenious Bud Calhoun. A paper could promote a contrary viewpoint by emphasizing the class conflict in Ilium and analyzing a character like Ed Finnerty, who gives voice to the negative consequences of technological advancement. Notably, at the end of the story, even the surviving members of the revolution are happy to find a once-loathed Orange-O machine. This detail might lead you in a third direction, inspiring you to ask: Does Vonnegut purposely refrain from defining progress as good or bad and, if so, why? As you read, think about how the novel invites readers to consider broader definitions of progress not limited to technological or industrial advancement. For instance, how do the dangers of technological progress illuminated in the story point to the author's desire for a dialogue about a different, more fundamental kind of progress—progress in humanity, in our relationships and the treatment of one another? Notice how this topic can lead into a dialogue about the cultivation of a deeper sense of human purpose. The examples herein and the corresponding suggestions below show how a general topic can yield many variations on a single theme. Remember: While you may be exploring a so-called gray area, your own position should be clear, and you should use plenty of evidence from the text to build your argument and support your claims.

Sample Topics:

1. **The dehumanizing effects of technological advancement:** What message does *Player Piano* present about the dehumanizing effects of technological advancement? Are these effects unavoidable, necessary, or valuable even? Or is Vonnegut's novel a warning?

   Begin by looking for examples of the dehumanizing effects of technological advancement in the novel. Of course, a good place to start will be with the characters, who would be the bearers of these effects. Which characters seem to be negatively impacted by technological advancement? How do they seem to be dehumanized? What characteristics reveal this? Consider details of the characters' interactions with one another, including their dialogue. The first exchange between Paul Proteus and his wife, Anita, for instance, yields important information on this subject, but readers also find relevant information among characters such as Ed Finnerty, Katharine Finch, some of the employees of the Ilium Works, and the residents of Homestead. After you have shown how various characters seem to be dehumanized as the result of technological advancement, look for key symbols and imagery that reinforce this notion of dehumanization, such as the player piano and the machinery at the Ilium Works. Finally, you will need to determine whether there is any evidence that these effects are necessary or valuable in some way. Do we find evidence of the positive impact of technology anywhere in the novel? Use the answer to this question as a basis for your conclusion, explaining what you believe the author is ultimately saying about this topic, while showing how the text supports this view.

2. **Progress:** Evaluate the theme of progress in *Player Piano*.

Although this topic is similar to the one presented above, it allows a writer to consider a broader, more comprehensive definition of progress—one not limited to technological advancement. While *Player Piano* addresses technological advancement, consider other examples of progress (or lack of progress) in the novel. What types of progress does the book enumerate on? Using examples from the text to support your claims, explain how progress should be defined. Think, for instance, about the evolution of the characters in the novel. Do they show any evidence of progress? If so, how? Which of the characters do we associate with the idea of progress? Is point of view important? How does Paul Proteus's vision of progress, for instance, compare to Lasher's or Kroner's ideas of progress? Do these points of view ultimately reveal some coherent message about progress, or do they simply inspire a more complicated and multifaceted dialogue about this topic? This will require that you establish whether the novel ultimately provides a balanced presentation of progress or a biased one. Does one point of view dominate the text?

3. **Purpose:** What does the novel tell us about the human need for purpose?

While some of the information mentioned in association with the two topics above may also be useful here, this third topic allows a writer to adopt a philosophical and psychological approach. Because you will be talking about emotion and human need, writing about this subject demands that you rely primarily on the characters to construct your argument. Many of the characters in the novel seem to be struggling with feelings of uselessness. Why? Is this feeling particular to a certain gender or social class, or is it universally evident? What does this tell readers? Consider, for instance, the reaction that Edgar's wife has upon hearing the confession of his infidelity; the repeated implications that women could be replaced by machines; Katharine's status as the only woman at the Ilium Works; or the revelation that Anita is unable to have children. Think about Ed Finnerty and Paul Proteus. How do their struggles relate to issues of purpose? Finally, it will be helpful to consider The Ghost Shirt Society. Does the revolution ultimately provide the characters involved with the sense of fulfillment and purpose they desire? If not, where, according to the novel, does a sense of fulfillment and purpose come from? Professional advancement? Financial success? Social engagement? Love and friendship? Or does the novel suggest that the diminished nature of human purpose is simply an unavoidable side effect of living in modern society? A consideration of Vonnegut's interest in humanism and its relationship to this topic might also provide an illuminating and centering point of focus for this paper.

Character

In *Player Piano,* the protagonist Paul Proteus is forced to choose between preserving the legacy built by his father or taking a more difficult path in order to do right and feel a sense of purpose. Accordingly, he embarks on an existential journey common to protagonists in literature. While an analysis of Proteus's character or his existential struggle could serve as a fruitful essay topic, the novel also presents a unique look at human interaction and the influence that people have on one another. For this reason, the other characters are equally compelling. Vonnegut manages to address issues of race, gender, social class, age, and nationality through a diverse cast of supporting characters. He also presents an interesting take on the relationships between husband and wife, father and son, boss and employee, exposing what unites and divides us. Whether you choose to write about a major character or a supporting character, you will need to consider what ties your character to the others or what separates them. For example, in analyzing the relationship between characters of various generations in the novel—Paul Proteus and his father, Proteus and the younger generation of employees at the Ilium Works, or Proteus and Kroner—you would need to ask questions such as: How do these characters relate to one another? Do they understand each other? Is there something fundamental that bridges the age gap? Are their differences significant—representative of some cultural change—or are the characters united in some way that reinforces Kroner's assertion that little really changes over the years? Notice how the relationship between the characters of varied ages begins to illuminate key themes of the texts, conjuring subjects such as time, change, and topics of historical and cultural significance. Observe how each character influences your own interpretation of the story and the themes it presents. Finally, remember to consider a broad definition of character: Information can sometimes be imparted to readers via a character mentioned but not actually appearing in the story (like Paul Proteus's father); or a nontraditional (i.e. nonhuman) "character" such as an animal, alien, robot, or ghost. What are readers to make of Checker Charley, for instance, and the reaction to his "death"? Likewise, we find the Shah of Bratpuhr speaking to the machine known as EPICAC XIV as if it were a human being. What is the significance of this scene? An analysis of the interaction between the human characters and nonhuman "characters" could present an interesting and enlightening discourse that reveals as much about the novel's key themes as a consideration of the story's protagonist.

Sample Topics:

1. **Paul Proteus:** Analyze this character.

> Paul Proteus is a complex character, and much of the novel is devoted to his existential struggles. When we first encounter him in the novel, how is he described? Is this portrayal accurate? Truthful? Tongue-in-cheek? Would you say that he is a "typical" protagonist? Consider details such as his profession and what the novel tells us about his personal life, including his relationship to the other characters. Consider his character as a whole, but do not fail to note more unassuming details. For instance, why might Vonnegut have chosen to name Proteus after the shape-changing monster in Homer's *Odyssey*? How does he change throughout the novel? Does he have control over his actions and, ultimately, over his fate? How does he perceive the others around him and how do they perceive him? Does your perception of this character change or remain consistent throughout the story? Do readers come to know Pro-

teus by way of his own reflections and observations or by way of the other characters or a combination of both? This requires some thought about narration and point of view. What does Paul share in common with the other characters? Finally, does Paul's character function symbolically in any way? Is his journey particular to him, or is it representative of some universal experience?

2. **The Shah of Bratpuhr and Ewing J. Halyard:** What is the significance of the pairing of the Shah of Bratpuhr and Ewing J. Halyard in the novel?

Begin by revisiting passages that feature these two characters. What do readers learn from their interactions? Does their pairing create a sense of unity or does it foster a feeling of contrast? What does each character seem to represent? How do scenes that feature Halyard and the Shah inform readers' understanding of the text and its key themes? Are the scenes serious or humorous? Consider how the characters expose issues of difference, prejudice, and point of view. Think also about the fact that their communication is mediated by a translator. What does this reveal about communication and understanding? How does the pairing of these characters provide perspective about diplomacy and international relations? If you find this last question particularly interesting, you might choose to construct your paper around a consideration of genre, exploring the work as social commentary or satire.

3. **Women:** Evaluate the portrayal of women in the novel.

Consider the female characters of the novel such as Paul Proteus's wife, Anita; his secretary, Katharine Finch; "Mom" Kroner; Barbara and Martha in the saloon; and Edgar's wife. How are these characters alike? Are there distinct differences among them? Can they be described as "typical" female characters? What feelings do the characters exhibit? What kind of details does Vonnegut reveal about each of these characters?

What kind of functions do they perform? How do they speak? Do not overlook their relationship to the male figures in the story. Does the treatment of the female characters perpetuate gender stereotypes or counter them? Finally, do you feel that Vonnegut is making a statement about the role or function of women in modern society? If so, what is he saying?

4. **Kroner:** Analyze this character.

Kroner is Paul Proteus's boss and one of the highest-ranking men in Ilium. Why is it important that Vonnegut depicts Kroner as a father figure to Paul and the other employees? Consider details such as Kroner's ownership of a Victorian mansion and his views on gender roles, automation, progress, and change. What beliefs does Kroner embody? Are his views consistent and complementary? How do his views on gender, for instance, compare to his vision of progress? Does Vonnegut create a sense of irony through this character? If so, what purpose does this serve? What does Kroner's pairing with Baer reveal about Kroner's character, and how do these revelations contribute to our overall understanding of the themes of the novel?

History and Context

All stories must take place within a certain space and a certain period of time. Even science fiction, which may present a world we have never experienced or one that does not really exist, is framed within a certain space and time. Whether a setting and time period are wholly fictional or whether they closely resemble reality, they offer us clues to understanding what the author has to say. An author may write about the time period in which he is living, his view of a time or event of the past, or he may speculate about the future. Vonnegut chose to set *Player Piano*, published in 1952, in a fictionalized United States of the future, a fantastic setting that allowed him to enter into a dialogue about timely and real social and cultural issues. The novel was written after the conclusion of World War II when people were still reeling from the Great Depression and when tensions from the cold war and the Korean War were running high. It was also a time of rapid technological advancement and changing values. Accordingly, though fictional, *Player Piano* references a particular time in American history when the working class struggled in the face of a newly industrialized economy. Despite the book's futuristic setting, references are also made to facets of early American history such as Native American culture and invention, while the defunct farm purchased by Paul Proteus serves as a symbol of the decline of the agricultural industry in the United States. The novel also speaks of some other interesting components of American history, namely, dissidence and revolution. In creating a portrait of a cultural landscape shaped by the American Revolution and in its portrayal of the new revolution of the fictional Ghost Shirt Society and references to Henry David Thoreau's real-life act of dissidence, an interesting question is raised: Is *Player Piano* itself the product of an act of dissidence? If you believe the answer is yes, you may wish to consider how *Player Piano* fits within a powerful and long-standing tradition of American protest literature.

Sample Topics:

1. **Capitalism:** How does the novel reveal a dialogue about capitalism? What does Vonnegut's viewpoint on this subject seem to be?

   It will be helpful to begin by defining capitalism for your readers and providing some brief contextual information. Once you have established context, return to the novel. Where do readers find examples or symbols of capitalism in *Player Piano*? Is private enterprise represented in the novel? If so, do these businesses seem to be successful? Does Vonnegut seem to be implying that capitalism is good or bad? Consider topics such as social class, value, wealth, status, and industrialism. You may wish to tie your essay in with a discussion of ideas about socialism or communism found in the novel as well. Can the governmental role in socialism be compared to the role that the government seems to be playing in *Player Piano*? Consider the portrayal of businesses, the Reconstruction and Reclamation Corps, and the army. How do these contribute to a dialogue on capitalism? Your paper should explain why Vonnegut would have been interested in talking about capitalism at the time the book was written. Most importantly, your conclusion should explain why the dialogue generated in Vonnegut's book is still relevant today.

2. **Historical references:** *Player Piano* is set in the future, and yet Vonnegut incorporates countless historical references in the text. Why? Analyze the use of historical references in the novel.

This is primarily an analysis of the historical references in the novel with a focus on their relationship to theme. Consider all of the historical references presented in the text. There are references to old battles, Native American culture, Thomas Edison, the Battle of Little Bighorn, the Holocaust, and the Industrial Revolution, to name only a few. Why do you think Vonnegut would have wanted to reference these in a novel set in the future? You may choose to focus on a single historical reference, establishing its relationship to the major themes of the text, or to theorize about the use of historical references as a whole. Does the incorporation of historical references seem to create a sense of change or a lack of change with the passing of time? Or both? And what does this tell us about history, time, and our own role in shaping history?

3. **Division by social class:** What kind of commentary does *Player Piano* present about the division of people by social class?

The novel begins with an explanation of how the characters are divided into different social classes. There are managers and engineers, the humans who live in Homestead, and machines. They are divided physically by geographical boundaries, but your paper should also consider how they are divided in their experiences and in their philosophy and ideas. Think about characters like Ed Finnerty and Paul Proteus, who sometimes cross over into Homestead, or inhabitants of Homestead who seem to sympathize with engineers and managers. Why is this crossing of boundaries significant? What is the significance of

Paul Proteus's assertion that his wife, Anita, would have been a member of the class in Homestead had he not married her? Finally, it will be important to explain why social class would have been an important subject at the time the book was written. What is the relationship between the emphasis of this subject in the novel and the social and cultural climate at the time of the book's creation?

4. **Dissidence and revolution:** Explore dissidence and revolution in the novel.

The most obvious example of dissidence in the novel comes via the revolution initiated and enacted by The Ghost Shirt Society, but how does the revolution turn out? Can we say that it was successful? Is Lasher the only character with realistic expectations of revolution? Does the actual outcome of the revolution matter, or does the novel suggest that the significance of an act of protest lies simply in its attempt to cultivate hope? Consider the reference to Henry David Thoreau's imprisonment and his dialogue with Ralph Waldo Emerson in the novel. Why would Vonnegut choose to reference a real-life act of dissidence in a work of fiction? What effect does this have? Move away from the novel briefly and consult secondary sources, considering other examples of dissidence in American history and the effects of these acts. How has American history been shaped and influenced by acts of dissidence, protest, and revolution? Where do we find evidence of this in the novel? Finally, should *Player Piano* be considered a work of protest and the output of an act of dissidence? Does the book challenge some institution, doctrine, or established or popular beliefs? If so, is it successful? Why or why not?

5. **The Industrial Revolution and the changed American landscape:** How does the novel create a portrait of a changed American landscape resulting from industrialization? What is this United States like? Is it an improved place?

Both literal and figurative representations of a changed American landscape can be found in the text. Consider imagery and symbolism, paying attention to descriptions of the physical landscape including the mechanized city of Ilium and the defunct farm purchased by Paul Proteus. Also, look for relevant examples of dialogue such as the passionate ravings of Ed Finnerty and the exchange between Paul Proteus and Katharine Finch in which they discuss the Industrial Revolution. It will also be necessary to explore how the characters themselves reflect a changed nation. How does Bud Calhoun, for example, serve as a representative of a changed United States? Consider his role as an inventor. Is his ingenuity rewarded, or is it rendered useless by technological advancements? You will need to consider where the ideas he embodies are represented elsewhere in the text. For example, what are readers to make of the once defunct workshop of Edison that is again churning with machinery? How does Rudy Hertz reflect a changed American culture? Finally, consider corresponding symbols (such as the player piano) and relevant motifs (such as the ghost motif utilized in the story). Does the evidence gathered indicate that this is an improved United States? If so, how is it improved? If not, how has it been altered for the worse?

Philosophy and Ideas

When writing about philosophical concepts in a text, the bulk of your work lies in making abstract, often unnamed, concepts "visible," exposing where they are found in the text and explaining what the author has to say about these concepts. After identifying a significant philosophical subject, you should establish how the characters, imagery, language, and other elements of the novel bring these abstract concepts to readers' attention. For example, in addition to its consideration of progress and purpose (explored in the previous sections), the novel presents a look at another interesting concept: dystopia. This concept, coined by the philosopher John Stuart Mill, has been explored by many authors including Aldous Huxley, George Orwell, Ray Bradbury, and Yevgeny Zamyatin, but how is Vonnegut's vision of dystopia different? In considering an author's individual treatment of a philosophical topic, many other subtopics will also begin to emerge. The same elements that allow us to consider *Player Piano* as a dystopic work also illuminate themes such as humankind's relationship to nature, conflict and destruction, freedom, and faith. Any of these subtopics could serve as the subject of a dynamic and engaging paper.

Sample Topics:

1. **Dystopia:** Is *Player Piano* truly a dystopic novel?

First, you will need to provide an explanation of the concept of dystopia in order to provide some context for your readers. This will require some research into the philosophy of John Stuart Mill and a general understanding of the cultural influence of this philosophy not only throughout history but within literature. What characteristics does *Player Piano* share with other dystopic works? Since you will need to avoid turning your paper into a list of shared characteristics, once you have established these similarities, consider if there is any evidence that *Player Piano* contradicts, challenges, or redefines traditional conceptions of dystopia. What are readers to make of Vonnegut's use of humor and his incorporation of the absurd, for instance?

2. **Faith:** Evaluate the treatment of faith in *Player Piano.*

Although religious faith is not among the major themes of the novel, think about where examples of faith, or a lack of faith, are found in the text. Do readers learn anything about faith from the Shah of Bratpuhr? Are there many examples of religious faith in the text? Or does the novel suppose that religious faith is supplanted in modern times by other forms of faith, such as faith in modern technology or faith in our fellow man? In writing about this subject, it will be helpful to consider context, including the time period in which the book was written. Is Vonnegut's vision of faith personal, or is the treatment of faith in *Player Piano* representative of some pervasive cultural sentiments about faith related to postwar life and shifts in cultural mores at the time the book was written?

Form and Genre

Modern and contemporary works of literature are often not easily classifiable. They do not typically fit neatly within a single genre; often they are hybrids of various genres or subgenres. *Player Piano* is a prime example of this. While Vonnegut's first novel can be broadly classified as fiction and, specifically, as a novel, it has also been studied as satire, as a semiautobiographical work, as an example of black humor, as a dystopic work, and as a work of fantasy and science fiction. As you attempt to classify a text, you must rely on the text itself rather than on superficial elements such as cover art, cover and jacket copy, and other marketing devices that may be wholly misleading. Remember that a study of genre will also necessitate a look at the form of the work. This aspect of a work can be easily overlooked, but the structure and order of a work imparts valuable information about a text and the ideas it represents. For example, a consideration of *Player Piano* as a dystopic novel (as discussed in the previous section) leads into a study of its form that provides tremendous insight into the major themes of the text. *Player Piano* resists the classic rising-action/climax/falling-action structure typically found in works of literature. There is no definitive beginning, middle, and end to *Player Piano,* nor is there a clear resolution. This structure—or deconstruction of structure—is deliberate and cultivates a sense of disorder and unease that complements the subject matter and key themes of the text.

Sample Topics:

1. **Science fiction:** Is *Player Piano* a work of science fiction?

   Following its initial publication, *Player Piano* was rereleased and marketed as science fiction, a commercially popular genre during the early 1950s. This led to Vonnegut being branded as a science fiction writer—a label that the author rejected throughout his career. Writing about this topic, therefore, calls for you to consider why Vonnegut might have disapproved of this label. Begin by thinking about how one determines if a work fits under the heading of science fiction. What characteristics are typically associated with this genre? Are they present in *Player Piano*? Look beyond the obvious. While the novel presents certain elements of science fiction such as a futuristic setting and nonhuman "characters," is it concerned with subjects that are typically central to works of science fiction?

2. **Satire and social commentary:** How does the novel function as satire or social commentary? What social issues does it address?

First, consider the typical characteristics of satire and social commentary. How does Vonnegut use elements such as irony, sarcasm, and wit to speak about issues of social significance in *Player Piano*? You will need to consider imagery, language, setting, and character. Next, you will need to think about the work's social or cultural relevance. What social issues does the book address? How do the aforementioned elements of the text generate a dialogue about these topics? What does Vonnegut, ultimately, seem to be saying?

Language, Symbols, and Imagery

Imagery, setting, and the specific words or phrasing that an author uses can easily be overlooked, but these details yield important information that is key to understanding a text. Consider the rote "I love you[s]" exchanged by Paul and Anita, the mechanical imagery that dominates the text, and descriptions of the city of Ilium and the Ilium Works. Each of these details plays a critical role in shaping a reader's interpretation and understanding of the novel. The Reading to Write section showed how a single symbol can assist in uncovering the major themes of the text. It will also be helpful to look for motifs—patterns of symbols and ideas—within the text. Consider, for instance, the ghost motif that runs throughout the novel, including Hertz's assertion that watching the piano play is like seeing a ghost, Anita's comment that Paul Proteus looks like he has seen a ghost, and the Ghost Shirt Society, named after an extinct Native American tribe. How does this motif create a dialogue about the past and that which is dead or defunct?

Sample Topics:

1. **Contrast in *Player Piano*:** How does Vonnegut use contrast as a revelatory device?

   In the novel, readers find contrasting pairings such as man and machine, the natural and the technological, the historical and the futuristic. What is revealed through these pairings? What themes do these pairings illuminate? How does the use of contrast echo the feeling of division that is found throughout the novel among the characters in terms of class, generation, geography, and philosophy? Is the contrast only meant to highlight differences, or does this device actually serve some unifying purpose?

   In addition to contrasting imagery in the novel, consider how Vonnegut cultivates a sense of contrast via characterization and dialogue. Would readers experience the text in the same way if this contrast was absent?

2. **Uniforms and costumes:** In *Player Piano,* Vonnegut pays particular attention to how his characters are dressed. Examine the significance of uniforms and costumes in the story.

   Revisit scenes that reference uniforms, costumes, and the way that characters are dressed. You will find that there are many such examples throughout the novel. Think about the Shah of Bratpuhr, Luke Lubbock, Halyard, the men at the Meadows, Paul's change of clothes when he travels to Homestead, the descriptions of Finnerty's appearance, and the parades. The scenes where Halyard strips out of his clothes and Luke Lubbock changes into his uniform will be particularly helpful. How do the characters seem to be defined or transformed by their clothing? What is the clothing representative of? What does this reveal about identity?

3. **The lie detector test:** At the end of the novel, Paul Proteus takes a lie detector test. Evaluate the significance of this scene.

The lie detector scene could be used as the foundation for a paper that contends that machinery is not flawless and cannot trump human thought, or it could be used to approach a philosophical topic such as the nature of truth. Of course, these are only two options. In the first instance you would need to show how this scene ties in with the major themes of the novel: progress, purpose, and the dehumanizing effects of technological advancement. Look for other imagery and symbols that reinforce this view. In the second instance, you would consider the outcome of the lie detector test. What does it convey about the complexity or ambiguity of truth? Is the lie detector reliable?

Comparison and Contrast Essays

The similarities between characters and events create an informative, unifying force within a text, but differences also inform us in ways that similarities cannot. Division is a dominant force in *Player Piano,* and Vonnegut reinforces the feeling of division and disorder by utilizing contrast as a revelatory device, pairing contrasting imagery and presenting sentiments in opposition, such as the use of humor and the absurd in the presentation and discussion of grave or complex issues. Just as Vonnegut uses this tactic to reveal important information about his major concerns, so too can you employ contrast to illuminate your own ideas about the text. Considering differences within a text or between two texts will help you to avoid the pitfall of simply listing similarities between works without citing what makes a work distinctive.

Sample Topics:

1. *Player Piano* **and Vonnegut's later novels:** Compare and contrast the novel with one or two of Vonnegut's later novels.

   Player Piano functions as social satire like *Cat's Cradle;* it addresses consumer culture and the effects of progress like *Breakfast of Champions;* it features a father-son relationship akin to the one found in *The Sirens of Titan.* Once you have chosen the subject of your paper and the works you would like to compare, consult the texts and ask yourself if the works reflect the same approach or a unique approach in the treatment of your subject element. You can choose almost any element of the text as long as you remember that the purpose of your paper is to identify why these similarities or differences are important. What do the similarities and differences reveal about each text, the author's development, or the author's viewpoints on a particular subject? Finally, what new insights does this provide about *Player Piano*?

2. *Player Piano* **and Aldous Huxley's** *Brave New World* **and/or Yevgeny Zamyatin's** *We:* Compare and contrast these works.

In interviews, Vonnegut acknowledged the link between *Player Piano,* Huxley's *Brave New World,* and Zamyatin's *We.* Consider what these works have in common. Look at formal elements such as setting, form, characters, language, and imagery. If the works seem to address the same subject or adopt a similar form, consider why Vonnegut would have been interested in addressing this same subject or adopting this form. Certainly, authors are not interested in simply repeating what another author has already said, so what might Vonnegut's motivations be? In other words, the key to writing this essay successfully will lie in your ability to identify what makes Vonnegut's book different despite the many similarities among these three texts.

3. **Postwar life in** *Player Piano* **and the works of Ernest Hemingway and/or F. Scott Fitzgerald:** How does the treatment of postwar life in *Player Piano* compare to the treatment of postwar life in the works of Hemingway or Fitzgerald?

First you will need to choose the texts that you wish to compare with *Player Piano.* You will probably want to limit this to a few texts so that you (and your readers) are not overwhelmed. Next, you will need to demonstrate how each of the texts creates a portrait of postwar life. How do the texts treat issues of social class, wealth, dignity, happiness, purpose, love, gender roles, sexuality, and mental illness? Do the texts seem to present a shared vision? Look to the formal elements of the text. How did each author convey his ideas about postwar life? How do they each treat character? How do the structure, language, and form of each text compare or differ? Finally, since Vonnegut's novel is the central work of your paper, it may also be helpful to establish what *Player Piano* contributes to a dialogue on postwar life that the other works do not.

Bibliography and Resources for *Player Piano*

Dolan, Brian. *Inventing Entertainment: The Player Piano and the Origins of an American Musical Industry.* Lanham, MD: Rowman & Littlefield, 2009.

Hicks, Granville. "The Engineers Take Over." Review of *Player Piano,* by Kurt Vonnegut. *New York Times on the Web.* 17 August 1952. Retrieved 10 August 2010. <http://www.nytimes.com/1952/08/17/books/vonnegut-player.html>.

Hoffman, Thomas P. "The Theme of Mechanization in *Player Piano.*" *Clockwork Worlds: Mechanized Environments in Science Fiction.* Ed. Richard D. Erlich and Thomas P. Dunn. Westport, CT: Greenwood, 1983. 125–35.

Hughes, David Y. "The Ghost in the Machine: The Theme of *Player Piano.*" *America as Utopia.* Ed. Kenneth M. Roemer. New York: Burt Franklin, 1981. 108–14.

Klinkowitz, Jerome. "Coming to Terms with Theme: Early Stories and *Player Piano.*" *The Vonnegut Effect.* Columbia, SC: U of South Carolina P, 2004. 20–45.

Marvin, Thomas F. *Kurt Vonnegut: A Critical Companion.* Westport, CT: Greenwood, 2002. 25–42.

Morse, Donald E. "No Survivors: The Early Novels." *Kurt Vonnegut.* Rockville, MD: Starmont House, 1992. 31–58.

———. "Sensational Implications: Kurt Vonnegut's *Player Piano* (1952)." *The AnaChronist* 6 (2000): 303–14.

———. "We Are Marching to Utopia: Kurt Vonnegut's *Player Piano.*" *The Utopian Fantastic: Selected Essays from the Twentieth International Conference on the Fantastic in the Arts.* Ed. Martha Bartter. Westport, CT: Praeger, 2004. 23–32.

Mustazza, Leonard. "The Machine Within: Mechanization, Human Discontent, and the Genre of Vonnegut's *Player Piano*." *Papers on Language and Literature* 25.1 (1989): 99–113.

Parakilas, James. *Piano Roles: A New History of the Piano*. New Haven, CT: Yale UP, 2002.

Ross, Andrew. "Don't Shoot the Piano Player." *Nice Work if You Can Get It: Life and Labor in Precarious Times*. New York: New York UP, 2009. 163–73.

Scholes, Robert. "A Talk with Kurt Vonnegut, Jr." *The Vonnegut Statement*. Ed. Jerome Klinkowitz and John Somer. New York: Delacorte, 1973. 90–118.

Segal, Howard P. "Vonnegut's *Player Piano*: An Ambiguous Technological Dystopia." *No Place Else: Explorations in Utopian and Dystopian Fiction*. Ed. Martin H. Greenberg, Joseph D. Olander, and Eric S. Rabkin. Carbonville, IL: Southern Illinois Press, 1983. 162–81.

Thomas, P. L. "*Player Piano* and *Galapagos*: The Evolution of Science and Technology." *Reading, Learning, Teaching Kurt Vonnegut*. New York: Peter Lang, 2006. 107–30.

Vonnegut, Kurt. *Player Piano*. New York: Dial, 2006.

THE SIRENS OF TITAN

READING TO WRITE

The first edition of *The Sirens of Titan,* published by Dell in 1959, featured classic science fiction cover art and headline copy that read: "A remarkable and terrifying novel of how life might be for the space travelers of the future." Later editions were packaged with similar space-themed covers and copy. Readers could, therefore, reasonably expect that *Sirens* would be a classic work of science fiction, and yet, while the book contains some of what readers may have been expecting—a futuristic setting, aliens and robots mingling with humans, and an interplanetary war—a close reading of the text reveals something unexpected. Consider the opening of the novel:

Everyone now knows how to find the meaning of life within himself.

But mankind wasn't always so lucky. Less than a century ago men and women did not have easy access to the puzzle boxes within them.

They could not name even one of the fifty-three portals to the soul.

Gimcrack religions were big business.

Mankind, ignorant of the truths that lie within every human being, looked outward—pushed ever outward. What mankind hoped to learn in its outward push was who was actually in charge of all creation, and what creation was all about.

Mankind flung its advance agents ever outward, ever outward. Eventually it flung them out into space, into the colorless, tasteless, weightless sea of outwardness without end.

It flung them like stones.

These unhappy agents found what had already been found in the abundance on Earth—a nightmare of meaninglessness without end. The bounties of space, of infinite outwardness, were three: empty heroics, low comedy, and pointless death.

Outwardness lost, at last, its imagined attractions.

Only inwardness remained to be explored.

Only the human soul remained *terra incognita.*

This was the beginning of goodness and wisdom.

What were people like in olden times, with their souls as yet unexplored? (1–2)

The passage—the first of the book—reveals that *Sirens* will not be concerned with alien subjects but with a philosophical subject of universal human concern: the meaning of life. Accordingly, while the narrator speaks about space travel, it is only to explain to readers that the book is not about the physical journey into space but, rather, the journey into space as a *symbol* of humankind's (misdirected) search for purpose and meaning. Space exploration is described as a wasted experience born of ignorance and characterized by "empty heroics, low comedy, and pointless death"—surprising sentiments to be found in a work masquerading as science fiction!

Without a close reading of the text, readers might easily have been misled. Vonnegut's play on genre (using elements of science fiction to undermine popular beliefs about science and progress) serves as a reminder that a good reader must move beyond appearances and delve deeper than the surface. In order to understand the true meaning of what you are reading, remember to consider not only what Vonnegut is saying but how he presents these ideas. Observe the symbols and imagery that appear and think about the choice of language used. In the passage cited above, for instance, minimal imagery is presented—only the emptiness of space—and the passage is composed of words like *unhappy, low, meaningless, pointless, nightmare,* and *ignorant.* Together, they ensure that the author's message—revealed in the first sentence—is clear: Scientific pursuits, such as space travel, will not provide us with answers about the meaning of life. Meaning is found within.

A consideration of how *Sirens* fulfills or challenges readers' expectations exposes a wealth of ideas for exploration. Performing an analysis of an example of this within the text can be a great way to narrow your topic and begin developing your thesis. By fulfilling our expectations, an author may underscore a particular point of view, shaping and solidifying a reader's interpretation and reception of the text. For example, a work that demonstrates the positive impact of love on its characters promotes and validates a view of love as meaningful and fulfilling. Alternatively, by undermining our sense of the expected, an author may compel readers to rethink traditional views and beliefs and to ask questions. Certainly, nothing captures our attention better than a surprise!

Vonnegut's play on genre—a science fiction novel that decries space exploration and highlights the folly of scientific advancement—is only one example of readers' expectations being trifled with. There are countless other instances of this throughout the text. For instance, if one considers how topics such as religion, the stock market, and war are presented in the book, one would quickly find that Vonnegut challenges convention rather than presenting traditional views of these subjects. An analysis of the treatment of all three of these topics together could, therefore, serve as the basis for a paper that explores *Sirens* as a work of satire. A consideration of the unexpected among the characters of the novel is also an excellent place to begin cultivating material for your essay. The charismatic Winston Niles Rumfoord, depicted as stylish, charming, and clairvoyant, is revealed to be incapable of true love or friendship and, ultimately, not in control of his own fate. The alluring title "characters"—the sirens of Titan—turn out not to be characters at all but peat statues submerged at the bottom of a pool. And, arguably, it is the alien robot Salo, rather than any human character, who reflects the fullest, deepest range of human emotions. Certainly, an evaluation of the unexpected elements of any of these characters could support an entire paper. Another method is to take a more global approach, considering how the characters' expectations are undermined. Malachi and Beatrice, at the start of the story, are surprised that they cannot alter their fate; Rumfoord is surprised to find out that he is susceptible to the accidental and the roller-coaster turns of life experienced by the other characters; and Salo is surprised to discover that the message he carries is not meaningful.

If you do choose to write about patterns of overturned expectations in the text, remember that you need to do more than simply cite examples of this. Your paper should consider why Vonnegut would have wanted to challenge his readers in this way. When you locate a relevant example in the text, try asking some questions. For example, by overturning the expectations of both his characters and his readers, Vonnegut creates a sense of universal experience and evokes from readers a sense of sympathy and understanding. Why would this be important in light of the major themes of the text? In the pattern of overturned expectations revealed internally through characterization and plot and mirrored externally in the reader experience, is Vonnegut, perhaps, making a statement about human expectation itself? These are just a few of the questions that can be used as a starting place for an insightful and engaging paper.

TOPICS AND STRATEGIES

In the sections that follow, you will find a variety of suggested topics accompanied by questions and observations to assist you in the task of writing successfully about *The Sirens of Titan*. Remember that it is not a comprehensive list, and the statements and questions that appear after each suggested topic are merely a guide to help spark your own ideas about the work. A successful paper will present a strong thesis based upon your own original ideas and will be supported by relevant examples resulting from close readings of the text. A wide variety of interpretations will be possible as you consider each topic. Use the strategic questions and observations to stimulate your own thoughts about the text and to assist you in developing your thesis. Remember to read through the text more than once, making note of those elements that support your argument. It will be equally important to make note of those elements that contradict your thesis, as this will help you to refine your argument and present a stronger case.

Themes

Works of literature typically have a central theme—a primary topic of concern that can usually be identified easily within the text. Often these central themes encompass broad, complex subjects. For instance, the initial passage of *The Sirens of Titan*, cited above, reveals the major theme of the novel: the meaning of life. Once you have begun to view the novel as a work about this subject, it can be overwhelming knowing how to begin writing about it. How do we talk about the intangible—about existence, religion, death, fate, or free will? Your challenge as a writer lies in talking about abstract ideas in concrete terms. Begin by consulting the text. Observe how Vonnegut has represented these subjects and translated his ideas. Information about abstract subjects is transmitted to readers through the formal elements of the text. Consider imagery, language, symbolism, plot, and characters. Once you have noted how these elements work together to reveal a dialogue about the central theme, there are two ways to approach your paper: You can start with a broad topic—such as the meaning of life—and deconstruct it by identifying related subtopics that inform us about the parent theme; or you can work in reverse, starting with a more refined subtopic or secondary theme—such as wealth, for example—and exploring in depth how it informs us about the broader concerns or central theme of the text. Writing about the meaning of life calls for some reflection on purpose and, subsequently, about the things that provide (or fail to provide) a sense of purpose and meaning. An exploration of the meaning of life in *The Sirens of Titan*, therefore, opens up to a broader dialogue about religion, wealth, love, and friendship. Finally, do not fall into the trap of simply citing a long list of formal elements. Identifying how a single formal element corresponds to theme may be a more effective strategy. The Reading to Write section above showed how Vonnegut uses genre—particularly, classic elements of science fiction—to generate a dialogue about the meaning of life, but this is only one option. Each formal element of the text plays a part in informing us about key themes.

Sample Topics:

1. **The meaning of life:** What does *The Sirens of Titan* suggest is the meaning of life? Does the novel answer this question conclusively?

   Writing on this subject calls for you to consider what gives the characters—or fails to give the characters—a sense of purpose. Consider the opening of the novel. What sentiments does the narrator present to readers about this topic? For instance, after Rumfoord materializes, the narrator says that the riot "was an exercise in science and theology—a seeking after clues by the living as to what life was all about." Are the people in the crowd satiated? Outside of this scene, how does each of the characters reveal information about this subject? Think, for example, of Boaz's relationship with the harmoniums, Chrono's relationship with the Titanic bluebirds, and the transformation of Bee and Malachi. What gives each of these characters a sense of purpose? Is it the same for each character? Consider any characters who seem devoid of a sense of purpose, since a more interesting question may be what fails to provide the characters with a sense of purpose. An analysis of Rumfoord would be particularly useful here. How does his character bring the other characters (and readers) to a better understanding of what is meaningful?

2. **Wealth:** Analyze the treatment of wealth in the novel. What statement does the book make about the relationship between wealth and fulfillment?

Several of the main characters begin as wealthy people but lose their riches. Malachi is identified as the richest man in the world. Winston Niles Rumfoord is also rich, using his wealth to travel in space. His wife, Beatrice, subsequently loses her wealth. In addressing this topic, it will be most helpful to adopt a before-and-after approach. What do we know about the characters when they are first introduced and still in possession of their wealth? Are they likable characters? Do we empathize with them? Consider the introduction of these characters and your response to them at the start of the story. This calls for some focus on the first chapter of the novel. Does their wealth seem to bring them happiness or fulfillment? How do these characters change upon the loss of their wealth? Is there something else that becomes important in lieu of money? How do the values of each character change? Do their views on life change? Consider how this riches-to-rags concept informs readers about the major theme of the novel. You might also consider why this may have been an important theme at the time the novel was written. This means considering the book from a historical and cultural perspective. What was happening historically around the time the book was written? Think about representations of war, economic depression, and the stock market in the story. How do these representations create a link to important historical events and issues that correspond to this topic?

3. **Love and friendship:** Analyze and evaluate the treatment of love and friendship in the novel.

Writing about this topic calls, primarily, for a consideration of the relationships among the characters in the story. There are many interesting relationships depicted in the novel: Malachi and Stony Stevenson; Unk and Boaz; Malachi, Beatrice, and Chrono; Salo and Rumfoord; and even Rumfoord and his dog Kazak; and Boaz and the harmoniums. Studying these relationships, consider how love and friendship are represented and defined within the novel. Does the novel present traditional examples of love and friendship? How do representations of love and friendship change over the course of the story? Is romantic love represented in the story? You may wish to focus on a single relationship, demonstrating how it serves as the embodiment of Vonnegut's views of love and friendship, or you could explore more than one relationship, identifying important patterns that emerge and explaining their significance. Consider, also, any characters who are unable to have relationships built upon love and friendship. How do these characters contribute to a dialogue on these subjects?

4. **Time:** Explore the treatment of time in the novel.

The novel contains countless symbols and representations of time. At the opening of the story, readers find references to Malachi's watch, and Beatrice's desire for people to be prompt is emphasized. Malachi understands Beatrice's desire for punctuality to be a manifestation of what it means to "exist as a point." What does he mean by this? Their child's moniker—Chrono—references time, while his role as son also references the passage of time through the suggestion of youth and the passing of generations. Consider other examples, such as Rumfoord's impermanence as the result of being caught in a chrono-synclastic infandibulum, Skip's museum, and the skeletons of animals that appear throughout the novel. What are readers to make of Rumfoord's assertion that everything that ever has been always will be and everything that ever will be has always been? How does Salo view time? Does his perception of time differ from that of the other characters? Why is this important? Consider, also, the structure of the novel. Rumfoord indicates that he has known Malachi previously, which means that the story is nonlinear in nature. How does the form of the novel relate, then, to issues of time, including the related issues of permanency, mortality, and death? How does this tie in with the central theme of the novel: man's search for meaning in life?

Character

The Reading to Write section discussed how *The Sirens of Titan* provides an escape from the typical, challenging readers' expectations in countless ways. Within characterization, Vonnegut does employ some classical motifs—such as journey and transformation—but in employing such motifs, he utilizes nontraditional pairings of humans, animals, aliens, and robots. Among these pairings, it becomes important to consider whether readers find traditional representations of friendship, family, intimacy, and love. Remember to think about all of the characters, even those who appear minimally or who do not appear at all—such as Stony Stevenson, the sirens of Titan, and Malachi's father. These characters provide important and revealing information; they also influence the other characters in undeniable ways. Since control and change become important subjects in the story, consider what motivates the characters and how they change or fail to change. We learn the most about the characters through representations of their interactions with one another—how they relate to one another as friends, family, comrades, and, simply, as fellow living creatures. In *Sirens*, Vonnegut creates an interesting portrait of group interaction. Readers find armies, crowds, and congregations. Accordingly, search for commonalities—that which binds or unites the characters. Consider, for instance, the messenger motif in *Sirens*. The characters all seem to be hoping for some message, but in the meantime they are also bearers of messages. Just as the characters are messengers to each other, the characters are messengers to us, revealing important information about the author's greatest concerns and the major ideas of the text.

Sample Topics:

1. **Malachi Constant:** Analyze this character.

Malachi—the protagonist of the story—takes on many incarnations throughout the novel. Consider him as the Hollywood playboy that readers encounter at the start of the story; as the mind-controlled, but resistant soldier Unk; as the Space Wanderer; as father; as friend; as messenger; and as Messiah. Note minutia such as the meaning of his name as well as more emphatic facets of his character, such as his relationships with the other characters. Most importantly, how does Malachi change or evolve over the course of the story? How do you feel about him initially, and how do your feelings about him change as the story progresses? What do readers learn from Malachi's evolution? Most importantly, is Malachi's character representative of something? Does he function as an allegorical figure? Explain.

2. **Journey and transformation:** Evaluate the motif of journey and transformation among the characters.

An exploration of this motif calls for you to focus your attention on the evolution of the characters over the course of the novel. The journey and subsequent transformation of characters is a familiar motif in literature. Sometimes an author sets his characters on a physical journey; other times a character does not travel physically but, rather, embarks on a philosophical or existential journey. In this book, many of the characters are indeed subjected to a physical journey, but it is one that is also symbolic of a philosophical or existential journey. You may wish to focus on the journey and transformation of a single character—such as Malachi, Bee, or Boaz—explaining how the example you have chosen is representative of the classical journey and transformation motif, or you might wish to write about journey and transformation as a motif among the characters as a whole. Consider the relationship of the characters to plot. How are the characters initially represented? What happens to them throughout the story? How are they affected by their experiences? How do they change not only as individuals but in their relationships with one another? In answering this question it would be helpful to consider the friendship of Unk and Boaz, the love of Malachi and Bee, or Chrono's relationship with the Titanic bluebirds. Although your main focus should remain on character, think also about how other formal elements reinforce this motif. Think about symbolism and setting. How does the interplanetary setting complement the motif of journey and transformation? If you choose to focus on the journey and transformation of the characters as a group, you will need to consider what the characters share in common. What is the collective outcome of their journeys?

3. **Salo:** Analyze this character.

Although Salo is mentioned earlier in the novel, his true introduction comes at the end of the story in the final chapter titled "The Gentleman from Tralfamadore"—a curious title for a chapter about an alien robot! Consider how Salo is described, paying close attention to the particular language used. He is an alien and a robot, but is Salo described with mechanical or alien terms or with human terms? Why are Salo's various habits significant? What emotions does he display? Consider Salo's response to Rumfoord's accusation that he is a "machine": a despondent Salo "kills" or disassembles himself. What is the effect of a nonhuman character doing this? What impact does it have on you as a reader? Finally, explore the significance of his final scene with Malachi at the conclusion of the story.

4. **The messenger:** Analyze the motif of the messenger in the novel.

Begin by considering where readers find representations of the messenger motif within the text. You will find that there are many representations of messengers—and those awaiting a messenger—throughout the story. For instance, Malachi indicates that his name means faithful messenger. He also indicates that he is waiting for a message, considering if there is "someone up there" watching over and communicating with him. The reverends are messengers and their congregations are receivers of the message. Rumfoord also functions as a messenger, and people wait anxiously for his materialization to see what message he brings. The harmoniums act as messengers to Unk and Boaz. Ransom Fern reveals his hope that the letter from Malachi's father contains some important message to be shared. Salo is a messenger, but he also awaits a message since his spaceship broke down. The messenger motif is even applied to inanimate objects. Monuments are revealed to be bearers of messages. Remember to consider other less obvious examples of the messenger motif. For instance, how is history itself represented as a messenger? After you have explored examples of this motif in the text, you will need to explain why representations of the desire for a message and our ability to deliver messages are significant. What kind of message do the characters seem to hope for? Is their desire fulfilled? How do the characters' experiences correspond to our own desires for messages and create a dialogue about our own ability to influence others not only through words but actions?

5. **The sirens of Titan:** Evaluate the significance of the sirens of Titan. Why might Vonnegut have chosen to name his story after them?

Although the sirens of Titan are the title "characters," at the end of the story they are revealed to be nothing more than statues made out of peat, submerged at the bottom of a pool. Study initial descriptions of the characters. How are they introduced to readers and to Malachi? Consider how Vonnegut treats the sirens as characters and then breaks down readers' (and Malachi's) expectations. Why is this important? What do the sirens represent? How do they correspond to the major themes of the text?

History and Context

Whether they are identifiable as realist works or historical fiction, or as surreal or absurdist tales within the realm of fantasy or science fiction, all works function within a specific historical and cultural context. Even if a text cannot be identified as political fiction, protest literature, or war novel, it still reflects historical or cultural concerns. The text may put forth some conclusive, powerful statement by emphasizing a particular point of view, or it may raise questions and call for social, political, or cultural change. Despite its interplanetary setting and alien characters, *The Sirens of Titan* references several real-life historical events, creating a commentary on postwar/post-Depression living and ideology. But, if this information is not presented literally, how can readers find this in the text? The most "visible" evidence lies in the setting: a narrator tells us that the book is set in a fictional postwar era "between the Second World War and the 3rd Great Depression" dubbed "the nightmare ages." These two reference points that punctuate the setting—war and a period of severe economic depression—are deeply significant. They provide relatable points of reference, functioning as clues that illuminate the connection between the themes of the text and real life. They provide context and create a dialogue. How did life change following World War II and the Great Depression? How was the political landscape altered, and what impact did these events have on people's everyday lives, including their beliefs, lifestyles, and priorities? Look for examples of this in the text. A particularly interesting and notable character in this dialogue is Winston Niles Rumfoord, modeled after a well-known historical figure—Franklin D. Roosevelt—who was elected president of the United States at the height of the Great Depression and remained president throughout World War II. A paper could focus on this character, exposing where the subjects, characteristics, and viewpoints that he represents can be found elsewhere among the setting, symbols, imagery, and themes treated in the text. References to historical figures and events do more than create a link to the past; they can inspire us to think philosophically about our own lives—about meaning and purpose, ethics and morality, fate and free will, choice and responsibility. Therefore, you might choose to write a paper that centers on the relationship between history and philosophy. How do the historical figures and events referenced in the text, for instance, contribute to a dialogue about purpose and the meaning of life?

Finally, while the story is not ultimately about space exploration, the book is inhabited by a variety of characters—Rumfoord, the reverends, and even the narrator—who present differing viewpoints about space travel and our attempts at progress through scientific exploration. Consider whether one particular viewpoint dominates the text. If you choose to write about this subject, your paper should include some background about the American space age, including some explanation of the motivation for exploration in space and the result of these endeavors. Ultimately, however, you need to consider the relationship of this information to the major concerns of the novel. Again, linking the historical with the philosophical can be helpful in creating a dynamic and engaging paper that does more than regurgitate historical facts. Remember: No matter which topic you choose to write about, the most important question you can seek to answer in your paper is why your readers should be interested and concerned with the historical or cultural issues represented in the text and what value and relevance they have for readers today.

Sample Topics:

1. **Winston Niles Rumfoord and Franklin D. Roosevelt:** Explore the correlation between Rumfoord and Roosevelt. Why might Vonnegut have chosen to use FDR as the basis for one of the main characters of *Sirens*?

   In interviews, Vonnegut revealed that the character Winston Niles Rumfoord was indeed modeled after President Franklin D. Roosevelt, who lived from 1882 to 1945 and who served as the thirty-second president of the United States from 1933 to 1945. This is a major revelation that provides an immense amount of contextual information, shedding light on the meaning of the novel and its major thematic concerns. First, you will need to acquaint yourself with Rumfoord. Consider the passages where he appears. Note how he is described, and observe his relationship to the other characters, his ideas, and how the other characters relate to him. Next, you will need to do some research about Franklin D. Roosevelt. There are many books available on this subject. Jeffrey W. Coker's *Franklin D. Roosevelt: A Biography* of the Greenwood Biographies series could be useful, as could other books that provide historical context, such as Richard D. Polenberg's *The Era of Franklin D. Roosevelt, 1933–1945: A Brief History with Documents*. You will need to consider the character of Roosevelt as well as historical context, including the details of his life and times. What kind of person was Roosevelt? As the thirty-second president of the United States, what role did he play in American and world politics, and what impact did he have upon American culture? What issues were relevant during his presidency? Do we find them represented in the text? Where do we find these elements and characteristics mirrored in Rumfoord, and how do they relate to the themes of the text? How does knowledge of the relationship between Rumfoord and Roosevelt inform or alter your understanding of the novel and the issues it represents?

2. **The age of space exploration:** Although readers are warned by the narrator that space travel is not the actual concern of *The Sirens of Titan*, does the novel impart some final opinion of space travel and the American space age?

Consider the time in which the book was written and published. What scientific developments were taking place at this time, and why would space travel have been an important topic? You may wish to begin with a brief introduction to the age of space travel and the role of the United States in the space race, providing some historical context that focuses on the time period when the book was written. Next, return to *Sirens*. In the first chapter of the novel, the narrator tells readers that there is nothing good to say about the exploration of space, but the president in the novel touts a new age of space travel that, he believes, is indicative of progress. He suggests that those who disagree are simply afraid of change. Does the rest of the book support the view promoted by the president or the view provided by the narrator? What do the "fundamentalist" preachers in the novel think about space travel? Consider the sermon given by Reverend Bobby Denton. Many of the characters in the novel experience interplanetary travel: Rumfoord, Beatrice, Malachi, and Salo. What is the outcome of their travels? Does there seem to be any positive outcome or effect of their time in space?

3. **War:** Analyze the treatment of war in the novel.

The war depicted in the novel may not seem, at first, like a typical war, but does it somehow create a realistic portrait of war? Consider the recent wars and other conflicts that the United States had been involved in before the creation of the novel: World War II, the Korean War, and the cold war, for example. Also, consider Vonnegut's own experiences of war as a soldier and a prisoner of war. How do his experiences seem to shape and inform the text? What is the purpose of the war in the novel? How are the soldiers portrayed? Are they willing to fight? Are they glorified, presented as heroes? What is the outcome of the war? Does the novel indicate that any good comes from war?

Philosophy and Ideas

In considering the central theme of *Sirens*—the meaning of life—many subtopics emerge: purpose, fate, free will, determinism, the accidental, luck, and religion, to name a few. The meaning of life could be adopted as the primary subject of your paper, but any of these subthemes will also work well. Look for where these ideas are represented in the text and try to determine whether one point of view dominates the text or whether Vonnegut provides balanced and varied points of view. This information will reveal whether he is making a conclusive statement or raising questions and generating an unfinished dialogue about a particular topic. Since many of these subtopics are related to issues of choice and control, you might look to the characters first. At the start of the story, Rumfoord predicts Malachi and Beatrice's fate, but, in the end, all of the characters—even Rumfoord—succumb to accidents, the unpredictable, and the unexpected. An interesting question for exploration becomes: What, if anything, do the characters have control over? And, if the characters cannot, ultimately, determine their own fate, what is it that controls them and shapes their destiny?

Sample Topics:

1. **Fate and free will:** Are the characters, ultimately, able to exercise free will and alter their fate?

   Consider the characters' choices and motivations, what they are forced to do, and what they choose to do. Think about Beatrice's roller coaster analogy and Rumfoord's assertion that even if the characters knew their fate they would still have to act it out. At the conclusion of the novel, does Rumfoord seem to be correct? Early in the novel, Malachi and Beatrice try to alter their fate following Rumfoord's prediction, but they are not successful. Despite this, are there other factors or areas of their life that they are able to control? What are readers to make of the representations of luck and accidents in the novel? If you determine that the characters do not truly have free will and the ability to determine their own fate, consider whether the book provides any indication of what actually controls them. You might consider whether the book creates a sense of futility. If so, does Vonnegut present any countering notion that suggests humankind's resistance to futility? Consider Unk's actions, for instance, or Beatrice's decision to write a book late in life. Is their resistance reflective of a disbelief in predetermination, or is it simply a resistance to that which they cannot deny?

2. **Religion:** What does the book have to say about religion and faith?

Examine the various references to faith and religion in the text such as the Church of God the Utterly Indifferent and religious figures such as Reverend Denton and Reverend Redwine. How is Rumfoord like God? Consider the crowd's interest in miracles, Malachi as Messiah, the twelve-sided building in chapter 3 representing twelve religions, and Noel Constant's use of the Bible to get rich. Evaluate the notion that the universal will to become creates universes but is not found on Earth. What is the significance of the biblical references such as the mention of Jonah, the Tower of Babel, Saint Francis of Assisi, Saint Augustine, and the parting of the Red Sea? At the end of the story, Chrono makes shrines. How do his parents react to this? Does the novel ultimately present some view of whether religion is good, bad, or at least useful?

Form and Genre

As noted in The Reading to Write section, the most interesting characteristic of *Sirens* may be its ability to masquerade as science fiction. Vonnegut uses elements of science fiction to undermine the very ideas typically presented in this genre. Therefore, considering how the book both fulfills and undermines our expectations of genre can be the start of an engaging and insightful paper. You might ask some initial questions such as: How does the book break with convention and redefine genre? How can genre itself be employed as a tool to reveal themes? Alternatively, you could analyze the structure and form of the book, showing how they mirror the key concerns of the text, or you could consider another unexpected feature of the book: fictional quotations and references. Think about how these quotations and references create a dialogue about truth and authenticity. Finally, as you think about genre and form, it may be profitable to consider context—not only historical and cultural context but literary context. You might write a paper that tells readers how the genre and form of the work make it like or unlike other works created during the same time period. Since many postwar novelists chose to create realist texts, Vonnegut's use of elements of fantasy, science fiction, and the absurd deserves a closer look.

Sample Topics:

1. **Science fiction:** Evaluate *Sirens* within the context of the genre of science fiction.

> You will need to determine whether or not *The Sirens of Titan* can and should be defined as science fiction. What elements of science fiction does Vonnegut employ? What is the effect of these elements? While classical science fiction elements may be easy to see, look for places where the book diverges from traditional science fiction. Consider theme and context. Why would elements of science fiction be an effective vehicle for the treatment of the themes represented in the text? How might the genre of science fiction itself function as a symbol and metaphor within the context of this book?

2. **Authenticity:** Vonnegut uses fictional quotations and cites fake historical references within the text. Why?

> Consider the references that appear in the text, such as passages from the book that analyzes Rumfoord's social class, the children's encyclopedia that explains the chrono-synclastic infandibulum, the three intelligent commentaries on war, and the many examples cited in chapter 9. *Sirens* is clearly a work of fiction, so you will need to explain why Vonnegut incorporates these references. What effect do these references have on you as a reader? Do these elements bolster the feeling that what we are reading is true? In what genre do readers typically find such references? What message might this send readers not only about the way that we remember and write about historical events and issues but about what we are willing to accept as truth? What does this device, ultimately, tell us about truth in literature? Is the incorporation of these references suggestive of a kind of pervasive cultural propaganda? Where else in the

book does Vonnegut address issues of what is real and what is fake, or truth and authenticity?

3. ***The Sirens of Titan* as satire:** Analyze the novel as a satirical work.

First, you will need to establish how the work can be identified as satire. Look for examples of wit, humor, irony, and parody in the text. Next, evaluate the text to determine what issues the book satirizes. In satirizing these issues, is Vonnegut making some broad statement, or does he create distinct commentaries on each topic he treats? Would you contend that satire is an effective means for transmitting his message? Why or why not?

4. **Form:** Analyze the form of the novel.

Consider the structure of the work. Is there a clear beginning, middle, and end? Is there a clear conclusion or resolution of issues at the end of the tale? Does the book suggest a linear or nonlinear sense of time? Think about the pace of the work or the speed at which the plot is revealed. How does the setting enable this pace and why are these details significant? How do all of these factors correspond to the major themes of the story?

Language, Symbols, and Imagery

Although the novel contains many symbols—the fountain, the painting of Beatrice, Rumfoord's transparency and state of coming and going, to name a few—the most interesting symbol may be the most easily overlooked because of its pervasiveness: the setting itself. In *Sirens*, outer space becomes a metaphor for the unexplored frontier, that which is foreign to us, and the unknown. It is a catalyst for the characters' journey and transformation as well as a symbol of the search for meaning outside of ourselves. But, as you write about setting, remember that it is not only the grand, interplanetary location that is important; remember to also consider small details. The architecture that serves as a backdrop for the story is chosen purposefully and described carefully. Even inanimate objects play an important role in the story, reminding readers that meaning can be found where we least expect it.

Sample Topics:

1. **Setting as symbol:** How does the setting itself function as a symbol?

   Where and when does the story take place? Is this a setting that is familiar to readers, or is it a foreign setting? Does most of the action take place in one site? Consider the architecture presented in the story: Magnum Opus, the Rumfoord mansion in Newport, and Rumfoord's Taj Mahal on Titan. In the opening scenes of the novel, Vonnegut employs very deliberate imagery: walls, locks, and iron doors. What do these represent? What kind of feeling do they evoke from you as a reader? How do these elements correspond to the major themes of the text?

2. **The fountain:** Analyze the symbolic significance of the fountain.

   Consider where and when the fountain appears in the story. Who sees the fountain? Is it functioning? Analyze its shape and design. At the start of the story, Malachi notes that the fountain stands between two paths. He decides not to take either of the paths and climbs the fountain instead. Why? Later, as Unk, why might he be thinking of the fountain?

3. **The painting of Beatrice:** Analyze the painting of the young Beatrice.

   Early in the novel, Malachi sees a painting of a little girl dressed all in white, holding the reins of a pony. Consider the details of the painting. Rumfoord reveals that it is a painting of Beatrice as a child. An analysis of the painting, therefore, requires some analysis of Beatrice, with emphasis on the ways in which her character functions symbolically. Since the focus of your paper is determining what the painting represents, your essay needs to be more than a simple character evaluation of Beatrice. In other words, your paper should include an analysis of Beatrice, but it should also lead back to an exploration of the ideas and themes represented in the painting (and mirrored in Beatrice). Rumfoord proposes that the look on the young Beatrice's face is an outward expression of her fear of getting dirty. Do you believe this is correct? When readers encounter Beatrice as an adult, she is wearing a white dressing gown and appears on a white staircase. Why is the color of Bee's clothing in the painting significant? How does this tie in with Beatrice's refusal to participate in Rumfoord's roller coaster view of life? Consider what Beatrice experiences and how she changes throughout the story: She loses her wealth and her husband: She is raped, becomes a mother, crashes in the Amazon rainforest, loses her front teeth, and works with the Martian army. How does the painting help readers to take note of Beatrice's transformation?

Comparison and Contrast Essays

Since *The Sirens of Titan* and Vonnegut's first novel, *Player Piano,* share similar thematic concerns and both utilize elements of science fiction to create a dialogue about these themes, you might choose to compare the two texts, perhaps drawing some conclusions about Vonnegut's early work. Some scholars and critics maintain, however, that *The Sirens of Titan* marks a significant departure from Vonnegut's earlier work, showing signs of the formation of his signature style. If you are interested in this analysis of the work, you would write an essay that establishes the differences between *Sirens* and *Player Piano,* showing where in *Sirens* readers find characteristics of his later works. In other words, after comparing and contrasting *Sirens* and *Player Piano,* you could compare *Sirens* to works written later by Vonnegut, showing how the elements in *Sirens* set the tone for his future work. The novel also lends itself to comparison and contrast with other works of literature. Consider the journey and transformation of the characters in *Sirens,* its commentary on war, or its function as satire. While you may choose to compare *Sirens* to another work of literature (there are many allusions to Lewis Carroll's *Alice's Adventures in Wonderland,* for instance), you should show readers what makes Vonnegut's work unique. Consider, for instance, Vonnegut's ideas about postwar, post-Depression life. Try to illuminate for readers what makes Vonnegut's approach distinctive—and more (or less) effective.

Sample Topics:

1. ***The Sirens of Titan* and *Player Piano:*** Compare and contrast these two novels.

   Begin by noting how these works are similar. Consider similarities in genre, such as the function of the works as science fiction and satire; themes such as progress, purpose, and control; and patterns in characterization, such as the parallels between the husband-wife and father-son relationships in the two books. How does each create a sense of journey and transformation, and how do the settings and plots reflect this? If you choose to focus on similarities between the texts, you might conclude by explaining how these congruencies evidence some consistency in Vonnegut's early works. Alternatively, you might begin by demonstrating how the two works are alike but conclude that *Sirens* marks a clear departure from previous examples of Vonnegut's work, citing these remarkable differences.

2. ***The Sirens of Titan* and the works of George Orwell:** Compare and contrast these works.

   First, you would need to choose at least one of Orwell's texts for comparison. You could use *Animal Farm,* focusing on an exploration of nonhuman characters and satire, for example, or *1984,* considering how elements of fantasy and science fiction reveal a dialogue about social and philosophical issues. How did each author abandon realism in order to speak more directly about reality? How does each text generate a dialogue about timely cultural and social concerns? Explain what formal elements are the most significant in the case of each. You may wish to conclude by making a case for whichever text you feel is more effective.

3. **The accidental in *The Sirens of Titan* and *Slaughterhouse-Five:*** Evaluate the accidental in these two works.

Consider "If the accident will" of *Slaughterhouse-Five* and the mantra of Malachi at the end of *The Sirens of Titan:* "I was a victim of a series of accidents." Think about the idea of luck in *Sirens,* including Rumfoord's assertion that luck is not the hand of God but an accident and the analogy of the roller coaster. The bulk of your paper will probably center on Malachi Constant and Billy Pilgrim, but consider the supporting characters as well. Are the characters in these two books only victims of accidents, or can they exert control within their lives? How influential are these accidents truly?

4. **The deserter in *The Sirens of Titan* and Stephen Crane's *The Red Badge of Courage:*** Compare and contrast representations of the deserter in these two works.

Although *The Red Badge of Courage* was published in the nineteenth century, it shares much in common with *Sirens.* Notably, both works feature a soldier who becomes a deserter in a time of war—in *Sirens,* Unk and in *Red Badge,* the young soldier Henry Fleming. Chapter 6 of *Sirens,* titled "A Deserter in a Time of War," and the chapters that follow will be most useful. Consider each character's reaction to war, his motivation to desert his fellow soldiers, and the consequences of his desertion. Are the soldiers motivated by the same factors? What happens to them after they desert? How do they change, and what do they learn? How do their experiences affect their identity, and how does each author reflect this in the text? Does the knowledge of their desertion alter our perception of both characters in the same way? How do the characters function allegorically? You might compare the journey of the two characters while contrasting genre, form, and the means that each author adopts in depicting this journey.

Bibliography and Resources for *The Sirens of Titan*

Clancy, L. J. "If Accident Will: The Novels of Kurt Vonnegut." *Meanjin Quarterly* 30 (1971): 37–45.

Coker, Jeffrey W. *Franklin D. Roosevelt: A Biography.* Westport, CT: Greenwood, 2005.

Cowan, S. A. "Track of the Hound: Ancestors of Kazak in *The Sirens of Titan.*" *Extrapolation* 24 (1984): 280–87.

Crane, Stephen. *The Red Badge of Courage.* New York: Simon & Schuster, 2005.

Klinkowitz, Jerome. "Coming to Terms with Technique." *The Vonnegut Effect.* Columbia, SC: U of South Carolina P, 2004. 46–74.

Marvin, Thomas F. "*The Sirens of Titan* (1959)." *Kurt Vonnegut: A Critical Companion.* Westport, CT: Greenwood, 2002. 43–58.

Morse, Donald E. "No Survivors: The Early Novels." *Kurt Vonnegut.* Rockville, MD: Starmont House, 1992. 31–58.

Mustazza, Leonard. "*The Sirens of Titan* and the 'Paradise Within.'" *Forever Pursuing Genesis: The Myth of Eden in the Novels of Kurt Vonnegut.* Cranbury, NJ: Associated U Presses, 1990. 45–58.

Orwell, George. *Animal Farm* and *1984.* New York: Houghton Mifflin Harcourt, 2003.

Polenberg, Richard D. *The Era of Franklin D. Roosevelt, 1933–1945: A Brief History with Documents.* Boston: Bedford/St. Martin's, 2000.

Rose, Ellen Cronan. "It's All a Joke: Science Fiction in Kurt Vonnegut's *The Sirens of Titan.*" *Literature and Psychology* 29 (1979): 160–68.

Sigman, Joseph. "Science and Parody in Kurt Vonnegut's *The Sirens of Titan.*" *Mosaic* 19 (Winter 1986): 15–32.

Vonnegut, Kurt. *The Sirens of Titan.* New York: Dial, 2009.

Wolfe, G.K. "Vonnegut and the Metaphor of Science Fiction: *The Sirens of Titan.*" *Journal of Popular Culture* 5 (1972): 964–69.

MOTHER NIGHT

READING TO WRITE

Framed as the true confessions of Howard W. Campbell Jr. (an accused Nazi war criminal who claims to be an American agent), Vonnegut's third novel marked a significant departure from his earlier ones, exhibiting major changes in genre, form, and theme. With *Mother Night*, Vonnegut abandoned the science fiction-fantasy platform of previous works, employing structural elements that would allow the text to masquerade as memoir and historical testament. The story was set within a realistic time and space, with action taking place in Germany, the United States, and Israel in the years between World War I and 1961—the year of the book's initial publication. Narration shifted from a sweeping omniscient point of view to an intimate first-person perspective, with Campbell serving not only as narrator of the story but as the central character or protagonist. The book displayed other notable changes in characterization as well. Devoid of the aliens, robots, and other nonhuman "characters" that inhabited his first two novels, *Mother Night* mixed infamous historical figures like Rudolf Franz Hoess and Paul Joseph Goebbels with a cast of fictional characters made up of secret agents and Holocaust survivors. Instead of pitting "good" characters against "bad" characters, Vonnegut presented an assembly of characters who were strikingly—alarmingly—alike despite their varied ages, roles, and backgrounds. Using metafiction, Vonnegut even included himself as a character, posing as the editor of Campbell's confessions. The many adjustments in the formal composition of *Mother Night* allowed Vonnegut to change course thematically as well. While earlier novels focused on matters of progress and purpose,

Mother Night presented a dialogue about two complex issues frequented by psychologists and philosophers: identity and truth.

For those familiar with Vonnegut's earlier novels, a comparison and contrast essay (which begins with a comparison of like elements and segues into an exploration of the structural changes and thematic shift in *Mother Night*) may be an excellent choice. However, even without knowledge of Vonnegut's earlier works, the genre, form, and characterization of *Mother Night* stand out because they present an unexpected twist on traditional applications of these elements. *Mother Night* not only utilizes elements consistent with genres different from those to which his earlier novels belong, it subverts genre by posing as that which it is not (memoir, war novel, historical document, and work of humor). The narration does not only shift from omniscient to first person, it switches from presumably reliable narration to storytelling from a source described by Vonnegut himself as dishonest. The characters are not only more realistic than those presented in previous novels; they also resist the traditional hero-villain format commonly applied in literature. And, finally, the framework of metafiction that allows Vonnegut himself to become part of the work is not utilized traditionally—to remind readers of the fictional nature of the work—instead, it perpetuates the notion that *Mother Night* is memoir rather than fiction, raising weighty questions about identity, but also reliability, authenticity, and truth.

Close readings of the key passages that feature these elements will begin to expose important information about the major themes of the book. Exploring the relationship of these passages to the text as a whole will then lead you to uncover patterns of significant questions and ideas that can be used to generate a thesis. For example, the editor's note and introduction (amended in later editions) create a framework of metafiction that presents generous information about the major thematic concerns of *Mother Night.* Both passages suggest important questions and information that tell readers what to look for in the passages ahead. Consider the following excerpt from the editor's note:

> In preparing this, the American edition of the confessions of Howard
> W. Campbell Jr. I have had to deal with writings concerned with more
> than mere informing or deceiving, as the case may be. Campbell was
> a writer as well as a person accused of extremely serious crimes, a one-

time playwright of moderate reputation. To say that he was a writer is to say that the demands of art alone were enough to make him lie, and to lie without seeing any harm in it. To say that he was a playwright is to offer an even harsher warning to the reader, for no one is a better liar than a man who has warped lives and passions onto something as grotesquely artificial as a stage.

And now that I've said that about lying, I will risk the opinion that lies told for the sake of artistic effect—in the theater, for instance, and in Campbell's confessions, perhaps—can be, in a higher sense, the most beguiling forms of truth.

I don't care to argue the point. My duties as an editor are in no sense polemic. They are simply to pass on, in the most satisfactory style, the confessions of Campbell. (ix–x)

Posing as the editor of Campbell's confessions, Vonnegut expounds upon Campbell's nature, raising questions about his character. Those interested in writing about the theme of identity in *Mother Night* could, therefore, use the information in this passage as a starting place to discuss identity and authenticity in the novel, considering other places in the book where similar questions of identity and authenticity arise. Following this line of thinking, a careful reader will notice that while Vonnegut questions Campbell's reliability as a narrator, the passage also calls Vonnegut's own reliability into question. We know that Vonnegut is not really the editor of an accused war criminal's memoirs as he claims, but, rather, the author of a work of fiction. Furthermore, Vonnegut suggests that all writers lie for the sake of their art. What, then, does this say about Vonnegut himself? Moving beyond this passage, readers discover that not only are Vonnegut and Campbell unreliable narrators and writers, but some of the Nazis are also writers, and in the passages cited from *Faust*, it is the devil Mephistopheles who narrates. What good reader would accept his word as truth? The pervasiveness of the theme of truth in *Mother Night* should remind readers to approach the text with certain questions in mind: Which characters are speaking to us? What is their background? Do they seem to wish to impress a certain viewpoint on readers? Does their view seem neutral and unbiased? Is it well-supported? These questions can be used not only as a guide to effective reading but, in conjunction with the information found in the editor's note and beyond, as the basis for a paper about point of view, narration, reliability, and truth in literature.

The introduction to *Mother Night*, added in 1966, expanded the framework of metafiction with insightful, self-conscious reflection on the text, telling readers: "This is the only story of mine whose moral I know. I don't think it's a marvelous moral; I simply happen to know what it is: We are what we pretend to be, so we must be careful about what we pretend to be" (v). Like the editor's note, the passage would be helpful for those writing about identity. After examining the ideas and questions about identity in both the introduction and the editor's note, one could explore other representations of identity in the book, focusing on the treatment of Campbell, Helga's role as actress, Resi's adoption of her sister's identity, and the alternate identities of not only Campbell and Resi, but George Kraft, and Campbell's betrayed friend Heinz. The introduction also echoes some of the questions of truth and authenticity suggested in the editor's note, although it does so with greater subtlety. It is not often that an author presents a moral to readers in such an upfront and straightforward fashion. Readers usually rely on the text to reveal important information about key themes. So, in this instance, good readers will be suspicious. Careful readers will note that Vonnegut builds upon this sense of suspicion and unease throughout the text until, finally, it is Frank Wirtanen who proposes the folly of looking for a moral in all things:

> "I'm not used to things having form—or morals, either," he said. "If you'd died, I probably would have said something like, 'Goddamn, now what'll we do?' A moral? It's a big enough job burying the dead without trying to draw a moral from each death," he said. (185)

If, as the text seems to suggest, it is not common or advisable to seek a moral in all things, some important questions are raised. Why does Vonnegut profess a moral to his story in advance? Is it truly the moral of the story? How does the presentation of this moral work in combination with other elements to generate a skeptical reading of the text? Why would Vonnegut want readers to approach the text in this way? Is he, perhaps, making a statement about the way that we approach—or should approach—texts presented as truth, such as memoirs and historical works? This is just one example of how the analysis of a single element can be used to generate many different ideas for your paper.

TOPICS AND STRATEGIES

In the sections that follow, you will find a variety of suggested topics accompanied by questions and observations to assist you in the task of writing successfully about *Mother Night*. Remember that it is not a comprehensive list, and the statements and questions that appear after each suggested topic are merely a guide to help spark your own ideas about the work. A successful paper will present a strong thesis based upon your own original ideas and will be supported by relevant examples resulting from close readings of the text. A wide variety of interpretations will be possible as you consider each topic. Use the strategic questions and observations to stimulate your own thoughts about the text and to assist you in developing your thesis. Remember to read through the text more than once, making note of those elements that support your argument. It will be equally important to make note of those elements that contradict your thesis, as this will help you to refine your argument and present a stronger case.

Themes

As you approach any text, the major question that you should be seeking an answer to is: What is this book about? Essentially, in attempting to answer this question, you will be working to identify the themes of the book. A novel will typically center on one or two major topics that give the work its shape and provide direction, but, in the course of creating a dialogue about these major topics, a text will often touch on many other subjects as well. In *Mother Night*, for instance, identity and truth are easily, almost immediately, identifiable as key themes, but a close reading reveals countless other themes for exploration: allegiance, patriotism and nationality, prejudice and racism, love and friendship, deception and betrayal, mental illness, suffering and death, to name a few. While these themes become visible in the interaction between characters, the other elements of the work—imagery, symbolism, genre, and form—also provide important information about these topics. This means that an almost limitless number of approaches will be possible as you write about theme. Regardless of the theme you choose as your subject or which formal elements you choose to discuss in writing about this theme, your mission remains the same: to identify an important theme and tell readers what you believe the book says about that particular subject, to show readers how you have reached this conclusion by demonstrating how the text supports your claim, and to explain the significance of this information (i.e., Does the text lend support to a particular viewpoint or uphold a certain ideal or set of ideals? Or does it present an unexpected or unpopular view that suggests the need for change?).

Since the themes treated in *Mother Night* encompass broad subjects, writing about them requires that you narrow your topic and maintain focus in your paper, first, by identifying what you want to say about your subject and, second, by developing a specific strategy for revealing this point and building a case that supports it. For example, if you choose to write about identity, you might wish to assert that *Mother Night* presents a vision of the dual nature of man that highlights the role of choice and moral action in defining who we are. You might choose to make this point by performing a close analysis of the characters in *Mother Night*, showing how a balanced treatment of the characters lends credibility to this assertion. Alternatively, a close reading of the text may have left you wary of the veracity of the professed moral of the story: "We are what we pretend to be, so we must be careful what we pretend to be" (v). If so, you might construct a paper that disputes the validity of this statement by providing examples of instances where what a character pretends to be is not in line with his or her true character, concluding with an explanation of why Vonnegut might offer readers a moral that isn't absolutely true. A third option would be to consider a broader definition of identity, exploring how our allegiances shape our identity for better or worse. This could be accomplished by considering how the characters align themselves and what they are faithful to, positing the effect of these allegiances by identifying patterns and trends in the text. Likewise, if you choose to write about truth in *Mother Night*, there are an equally vast number of variations to contemplate. The text addresses the intersection of truth and identity (by asking if we are, indeed, who we pretend to be), truth in relationships (in the portrayal of love and friendship, deception and betrayal), truth as it pertains to art and literature (in the proposition that lies in art are acceptable because they illuminate a higher truth), and truth and authenticity in the representation of history (by raising questions about propaganda and point of view). Any of these topics can serve as the foundation for a successful paper, but remember to keep your thesis—the point that you are trying to make about your subject—in mind as you write. Develop a clear strategy for revealing and supporting this point, and be faithful to it. In other words, while it may be helpful initially to note all of the places where your theme is referenced in the text, not all of the information that you collect will be relevant to your specific argument. Therefore, the most persuasive arguments will be built on evidence that corresponds directly to your thesis and that shows, clearly, how the text supports your assertions.

Sample Topics:

1. **Identity:** In the introduction added to the novel in 1966, Vonnegut says that the moral of *Mother Night* is: "We are what we pretend to be, so we must be careful what we pretend to be" (v). What does this really mean? Does the text actually support this professed moral, or are there examples where the text contradicts this statement?

   Writing about identity requires that you focus primarily on the treatment of the characters. Begin by establishing where readers find examples of characters pretending. The most obvious example, of course, is Howard W. Campbell Jr., but consider the supporting characters as well. Helga is an actress. Resi poses as her missing sister and is a Russian agent. George Kraft is also an agent named Iona Potapov. Even Campbell's betrayed friend Heinz is revealed to be an Israeli agent. How do the guards and other characters also pretend, and for what purpose? You will need to identify how a character's alternate identity relates to his or her true nature. Are the two necessarily aligned or are they in opposition? Frank Wirtanen makes an interesting observation about George Kraft that "He can be many things at once—all sincerely" (197). What does this mean? How does this apply to the other characters? Can one's identity be separated from one's actions? In other words, does the text present examples of instances when it is acceptable or necessary to act in opposition to one's true identity?

2. **Truth:** Does the novel suggest that there is such a thing as absolute truth, or does it refute such a concept by proposing instead that "truth" is variable and dependent upon point of view?

   In addressing this question, it will be most important to consider narration, character, point of view, and the information afforded to readers via metafiction. Where do readers find examples of truth or, alternatively, lies, dishonesty, or a lack of authenticity in the novel? Is the narrator reliable? Is Vonnegut reliable? Are the characters honest with themselves and with each other? Does point of view change the "truth" or redefine it, or is there some undeniable truth presented in the text? If you believe that there is some message presented as truth regardless of point of view, you might conclude that the text supports the concept of absolute truth. On the other hand, does the text indicate that there are some instances when dishonesty is permissible—advisable even? In the interest of serving some higher good? For self-preservation? What about Vonnegut's assertion that lies in literature can expose a higher form of truth? Many philosophers have written about the nature of truth. Although it isn't strictly necessary, you might incorporate examples from philosophical texts to bolster your assertions, showing how Vonnegut aligns himself with a certain representation of truth or how *Mother Night* proposes a new view of the nature of truth. If you do choose to approach this subject from a philosophical vantage point, it will be particularly helpful to consider texts that elaborate on universality and relativism as well as ethics.

3. **Allegiance:** Evaluate representations of allegiance in the novel. Does the text seem to present a positive view of allegiance or a negative one? What, if anything, does the novel suggest one should show allegiance to?

In order to write successfully on this subject, you will need to study the characters, focusing on how they pair or group up and what they are dedicated to. Consider obvious pairs such as Campbell and his wife, Helga, and less obvious groupings such as Dr. Jones and his cronies. What draws these characters to one another and what are these characters bound by? Although allegiance is typically discussed in closest association with patriotism and fidelity to one's nation, consider broader definitions of the term. Think, for instance, of allegiance to ideas and beliefs, to one's own identity and one's convictions, and to other people. Why is Campbell's claim that he has no affinity for nationality significant? Once you have discussed examples of allegiance in the text, consider their effect. Is there a positive or negative effect of these variations of allegiance? How does the text suggest, for example, that strict allegiance to certain things—countries, religion, ideas— breeds racism and prejudice? And what does the novel suggest about allegiance in love and friendship suggested in the concept of the nation of two and the relationships among Campbell, Kraft, and Resi? Are there indications that allegiance to another single person is advisable? Or does the text suggest that this kind of allegiance leaves one vulnerable and, therefore, at a disadvantage—subject to pain, betrayal, and loss?

4. **Mental illness:** Explore mental illness as a theme of the text.

Begin by noting examples of—or suggestions of—mental illness in the text. How are the alter egos and alternate identities of the characters suggestive of schizophrenia? Evaluate Frank Wirtanen's assertions that espionage "offers each spy an opportunity to go crazy in a way he finds irresistible" (191) and that people "can be many things at once—all sincerely" (197). Think about Campbell's recollections of his mother. Revisit the chapter titled "Chemicals" and consider the patrolman's musings. Does the text seem to indicate that undiagnosed and untreated mental illness is at the root of many of the world's

problems? Or do you believe the text is suggesting the existence of a kind of pervasive cultural mental illness caused by
societal and cultural factors?

Character

While works of literature often contain characters that can be identified easily as either heroes or villains, the characters of *Mother Night*
resist such classification. In a work inhabited by Nazis, spies, and war
criminals, this point is of major significance. Vonnegut maintains a
shockingly balanced portrait of his characters—including the accused
Howard W. Campbell Jr. Therefore, focusing on the shocking or unexpected elements of a character's nature—the positive elements of a
character who would otherwise be classified as bad or evil, or the
negative qualities that readers find in an otherwise good or heroic
character—reveals many interesting topics for consideration. Think of
Resi's love for Campbell, which seems to trump even her devotion to
her country; the friendship of George Kraft and Campbell; Bernard
O'Hare's hatred for Campbell and obsession with killing him; the
strange, evenhanded treatment of the Nazis; Dr. Jones's response to
the death of his wife; and the bodyguards' excitement over the reunion
of "Helga" and Campbell. Furthermore, while it is typically good
advice to study characters in opposition, those writing about character in *Mother Night* will be better served by focusing on the similarity of the characters. Because they are of varied age, background, and
experience, their stunning likeness is hugely significant. Without clear
classification as good or evil, hero or villain, and without the typical contrast and variation found in characterization, the judgment of
the characters becomes a major point for consideration: how readers
perceive and judge the characters, how the characters perceive and
judge one another, and how Vonnegut assigns—or refuses to assign—
judgment. If Vonnegut refrains from assigning judgment to his own
characters, why does he refrain? Does the treatment of the characters
actually work to expose the dangers inherent in judging others? After
all, how does judgment lead to prejudice, racism, war, and persecu-
tion? These are only a few of the questions raised by the treatment of
the characters in *Mother Night.*

Sample Topics:

1. **Howard W. Campbell Jr.:** Analyze this character.

Because Campbell takes on so many roles throughout the story, this is a bountiful subject. The bulk of the work, therefore, lies in analyzing each element of his character while, ultimately, demonstrating the significance of his portrait as a whole. In other words, why has Vonnegut created a character like Campbell, and how does Vonnegut's treatment of Campbell give voice to key themes? Consider Campbell's self-description as "an American by birth, a Nazi by reputation, and a nationless person by inclination" (1). He is also a playwright and poet, a husband, friend, son, a propagandist, and an accused war criminal. Most notably, he is the narrator of the story. Is he reliable? What are readers to make of Vonnegut's assertion that he is a liar? At the close of the story, can we confirm that Vonnegut is correct? Does Vonnegut's treatment of Campbell evoke sympathy or contempt? How do the other characters respond to him? Does Campbell change throughout the story? Consider his relationships with the other characters and the motivations for his actions. Is Campbell a traditional protagonist and narrator? Why or why not? Finally, how does Campbell serve as a model for the other characters? Why is this important?

2. **Campbell's guards:** Early portions of *Mother Night* are devoted to an introduction of Campbell's guards, with a chapter assigned to each. Why?

Evaluate each of the chapters where the guards appear. How is each guard described? Note their ages, origins, backgrounds, and life experiences. What do they share in common? Do all of the guards seem to feel the same about Campbell? Do they have a traditional jailor-jailed relationship with Campbell? Why is this relationship significant? Consider the fact that some of the guards have also experienced incarceration. Why is this important? Does the text indicate that each of the guards feels the same about the war and the Holocaust, or do they maintain varied points of view? How do they present a vision of the complexity of moral choice and represent a variety, or a lack of variety, of point of view? What relevance do indications of the passage of time and the movement from light to dark have in these passages? How are the guards like or unlike the other characters in the book? Why are these similarities or differences notable?

3. **Historical figures:** Vonnegut incorporates real historical figures in *Mother Night,* mixing them with fictional characters. Why? Evaluate the effect of this.

Look for passages where these historical "characters" appear. Who does Vonnegut include? Are they recognizable figures or more obscure figures? How are they portrayed in the novel? For instance, are they depicted in the act of committing a crime or an act of violence? Is their dialogue expected? Can readers identify them easily as "good" or "bad"—evil even? Does Vonnegut present a realistic portrayal of them or an absurd one? Are they like or unlike the other characters? How does their incorporation in the novel lend the story authenticity? Or does it destroy authenticity? Why is this important? Consider, also, that Vonnegut mixes well-known figures from history with references to an obscure historical figure: Tilgath-pileser the Third. What might be the purpose of this contrast?

4. **Doctor Abraham Epstein and his mother:** Evaluate the significance of this pair.

How do these characters respond to Campbell, and what are their reactions to the Holocaust and the events of World War II? Do they share the same point of view? Do you believe they represent a generational response to these events? Or would you contend, rather, that they represent a varied response to a shared experience? If you contend the latter, you might elaborate on how the pair represents a variety of points of view in the interpretation of historical events and/or moral decision-making. Finally, instead of focusing solely on an analysis of the two characters, you might choose to write about Campbell's intersection with these characters. How do they meet? Consider the mother's translation of *auf wiedersehen*. Does their repeated meeting suggest something about fate, karma, destiny, or retribution? If so, are there suggestions of this elsewhere in the text?

History and Context

One of the most interesting revelations about *Mother Night* is that it is not really about war. While much of the story is set in Germany during the World War II, with characters consisting primarily of war criminals and Holocaust survivors, accounts of the war are limited and are not the primary focus of the story. For this reason, while representations of the effects of the war raise important ethical and philosophical questions, those interested in writing about *Mother Night* from a historical perspective will find more profitable topics to write about. However, it will still be helpful to do some background reading and research to familiarize yourself with the events of the war in order to enhance your overall comprehension of the story. Likewise, some background reading on the other historical and cultural events referenced in the text will be necessary. From a historical and cultural perspective, *Mother Night* covers a lot of territory, broaching the time period after World War I through the early 1960s, with action taking place in Germany, the United States, and Israel. The presence of George Kraft and Resi Noth as Russian agents suggests the tensions of the cold war, while their role as spies (and Campbell's role as an American agent) make patriotism and espionage interesting subjects to reflect on. The inclusion of propagandists and the Nazi interpretation of the Gettysburg address open up a dialogue not only about propaganda but also about American nationalism and idealism. It is, however, the oscillation between past and present, represented in the order and structure of the story and in symbolic references in the text, that is most notable. While Campbell draws readers back in time, Vonnegut uses metafiction—an original editor's note and an introduction added in 1966—to bring readers back to the present. Likewise, the notorious figures in the text draw readers back in time, while characters such as Arnold Marx and Doctor Abraham Epstein represent a current generation with its own point of view. Finally, the book suggests a notion of history repeating and forgotten, but what does it suggest about the malleability of history and the effect of the individual in shaping it?

Sample Topics:

1. **Patriotism and espionage:** Analyze the portrayal of patriotism and espionage in *Mother Night*. Does the novel confirm that there is virtue or some greater good in acts of espionage undertaken in the name of patriotism, or does it present an alternative point of view? How does this viewpoint hold up against the proof of history?

   Mother Night is written in the style of a popular spy novel. Therefore, it will be important to consider genre, form, and character, but, specifically, it will be important to think about whether the text functions traditionally within this genre or whether it diverges in some way from the traditional format of the spy novel. For instance, is the protagonist typical? The plot? How does the story conclude? Who is Campbell hunted by? Consider the other agents in the book—Resi Noth, George Kraft, and the spies described by Frank Wirtanen. What are they dedicated to? What are the consequences of their actions as spies? Consider both cultural impact and personal effect. What is Campbell's fate and what are the fates of the other spies depicted in the novel? After enumerating on representations of espionage in the novel, it will be necessary to cite and discuss relevant historical examples of espionage. Of course, Campbell dedicates his confessions to Mata Hari, but look beyond the text for other representatives that suit your specific argument. Consider how they served their country or betrayed their country to serve another. If you decide that the book demonstrates the merits of espionage, you will wish to focus on spies who had a positive impact. If you decide the opposite, you may wish to choose to write about spies like Julius and Ethel Rosenberg. If you choose the latter course, it may be interesting to consider whether betrayal is an inherent part of espionage and, if so, how does this tie in with depictions of betrayal in *Mother Night*?

2. **Propaganda:** Analyze the treatment of propaganda in the text.

Consider examples of propaganda in the text, such as Campbell's speeches, the play commissioned by the Nazi Party, the photo of Campbell and the photo and article on Werner Noth, and Dr. Jones's paper. How can something be clearly identified as propaganda? What defines it as such? Revisit the passage in which the Nazis discuss the Gettysburg Address. Does the dialogue reveal some subtext about the relationship between propaganda and point of view? Does this notion of propaganda also reveal some subtext about the notion of American supremacy? Does it shape or change our understanding of international relations? How do these ideas relate to George Orwell's idea that all art is propaganda? Is the novel itself an example of propaganda? Why or why not?

3. **History repeating and forgotten:** Evaluate the vision of history presented in *Mother Night*. Does the text suggest that we are doomed to repeat ourselves, or does it propose that history can be effectively shaped by the individual citizen?

Consider Campbell's reflections on history at the start of the story—his feeling that war crimes are "as ancient as Solomon's old gray stones" (3), his sense of the passage of time, and his interaction with Arnold Marx. What are readers to make of Marx's ignorance about World War II? Why is it significant that he works as an archaeologist? How does the reference to the ruins of Hazor create a vision of history repeating? Consider Goebbel's sentiments about the past. How are complicity and cultural forgetfulness presented as dangers in perpetuating a repetitive course of history? Think, for example, of the briquettes, of Campbell's role in the Nazi Party, of Marx's ignorance and Dr. Epstein's desire to move on and forget. Finally, look for indications that the individual has the power to shape history for better or worse. What does Campbell's steamroller poem seem to suggest?

Philosophy and Ideas

Mother Night presents a rather extensive and complex dialogue on philosophical subjects such as identity, truth, freedom, and ethics. Contained
within Campbell's story, and constructed around the lingering question
of his innocence or guilt, *Mother Night* hinges on gray areas, questions,
uncertainty, and ambiguity. Therefore, no matter which philosophical
topic you choose to write about, it will be helpful to anchor your paper
by asking if one point of view on your subject dominates the text. Is there
repetition of certain imagery, language, or ideology that leads you to this
conclusion? If the answer is yes, this provides some certainty about what
Vonnegut is trying to say and the viewpoint he wishes to promote. If the
answer is no—if no single point of view dominates the text—Vonnegut
may be creating a dialogue meant to provoke the reader to consider,
reconsider, or question certain ideologies or points of view. Therefore, if
it seems that a question is posed but not conclusively answered in *Mother
Night,* it may be productive to devote your paper to an explanation of
why these questions are left unanswered. Finally, as you consider philosophical issues in the text, remember to consider how they are framed.
Who is revealing the information about these subjects? Is he or she a reliable source? (If an absurd or evil character speaks about a certain issue,
it may be safe to assume that the author wants us to disregard, question,
or see the folly in his or her viewpoint.) Look beyond character. Be sure
to consider, also, how the author uses specific imagery, symbolism, and
language to release information on these subjects.

Sample Topics:

1. **Morality and ethics:** Analyze morality and ethics in the novel.
   Does the text suggest that there is some fixed moral or ethical
   code that one should live by? Or does it suggest a more flexible
   ethical system wherein motive, circumstance, and point of view
   become defining factors?

   Begin by evaluating the moral dilemmas experienced by
   Campbell, Resi Noth, George Kraft, the guards, and the other
   characters. Are there similarities in the situations they are
   faced with and the choices they make? Consider issues like
   ambiguity, motivation, responsibility, and complicity. Are

there instances where the seemingly immoral is acceptable or permissible? Survival, for instance? Patriotism? How are inaction, ignorance, and complicity depicted as immoral or unethical? Finally, does the text suggest what one's greatest ethical responsibility should be to? One's self? Others? One's nation?

2. **The dual nature of man:** Evaluate the concept of the dual nature of man in the text. What does the pervasiveness of this concept in *Mother Night* imply about identity, control, and moral choice?

The dual nature of man is a philosophical theme. Accordingly, your paper will rely on an analysis of the characters but should lead into a discussion of choice, morality, and ethics. First you will need to establish where this concept is represented in the text. Start by showing how Vonnegut has created a balanced representation of the characters. This means demonstrating not only how seemingly bad characters exhibit positive qualities, but how seemingly good characters exhibit negative or destructive qualities. Focus on the congruencies in the treatment of the characters. How do we feel about the characters? Do they seem to be defined by some fixed nature, or are the characters in control of themselves and their identity? Can the characters be identified as good or evil? Look beyond characterization. Where else is the view of the dual nature of man referenced in the text? Consider the title, the references to *Faust,* and other symbolism. If the characters are neither wholly good nor evil, does this indicate that we are relieved of some responsibility? Or does it place greater weight on our actions and choices?

3. **Art and literature:** Evaluate depictions of art and literature in *Mother Night.*

Many of the characters in *Mother Night* are artists and writers or wish to be. There is Campbell as playwright and poet, Helga as actress, and George Kraft as a painter. Even the Nazis want to write. Does this expose some universal desire or motivation? What does George Kraft mean when he asserts that future civilizations will judge men by the "extent to which they've been artists" (56)? How do art and literature shape society and influence history? Where do we find examples of this in the text? Consider also how the introduction and editor's note and the discussion of propaganda raise issues of censorship, truth, and authenticity in art. What conclusions can one come to, then, about the form, function, and purpose of art and literature?

Form and Genre

Mother Night is a memoir that is not true, a historical work that is not really about war, a spy novel that incriminates its protagonist, and a book about grave issues that incorporates humor and the absurd. For these reasons, genre—often, one of the more unassuming elements of a work—becomes a very hot topic. You might explore Vonnegut's varied uses of genre, examining how this hybrid of subverted genres works as a vehicle to speak about key themes, or you might adopt a more refined approach, choosing to analyze a particularly notable element of form like narration, metafiction, or point of view. How do these elements inform us about the major concerns of the work and shape our reception and understanding of the text? A simple way to answer this question is to consider how our response would be different without these elements. Finally, the work masquerades within certain genres, raising another important question for consideration: How should *Mother Night* truly be classified?

Sample Topics:

1. **Genre:** Evaluate the classification of *Mother Night*. What genres does it masquerade as? But does it truly belong to these genres? If not, how should it be properly classified?

   Consider *Mother Night* as historical document, spy novel, confessions and memoir, or a hybrid of all of these. What elements of the text allow readers to identify it as such? How does it diverge from traditional concepts of these genres? How does Vonnegut twist or subvert genre to speak about major themes?

Why is this important? What genre does *Mother Night* really belong to? Answering this question means identifying key characteristics of the book and determining their purpose. Do they, for instance, work together to present a portrait of some tragedy? Do they allow the text to document the historical? Do they expose a satire of cultural issues? Is the text realistic or fantastical?

2. **Form:** How does Vonnegut use form to shape reader response and guide interpretation of the text?

   The form is the overall structure and composition of the book. Therefore, you should examine setting; the order of events; and framing devices such as metafiction, narration, and shifting point of view. What is the collective effect of these elements? Do not overlook small details such as the dedication and the title. It may be helpful to consider how our reception of the text would be different if Vonnegut had taken a different approach to form.

3. **Point of view:** Analyze point of view in the text.

   Consider the various points of view represented in the novel. Think about narration. How does metafiction reveal an alternate and unexpected point of view? Think about the information revealed through plot and dialogue, including the information presented by the supporting characters. Does one view contradict another, or do they reinforce each other? Analyze Mengel's assertion that everyone thought he was right during the war. What are we to make of the fact that Campbell receives both fan mail from people who think he told the truth in the war and hate mail and death threats? Consider Campbell's bio in *The White Christian Minuteman* and Vonnegut's assertion that if he were born in Germany he might have been a Nazi. How does point of view contribute to a sense of the complexity of moral choice and ambiguity? Finally, does one point of view ultimately dominate the text? If so, what does this point of view suggest? If not, how do the shifting points of view collectively make a statement?

4. **Black humor and the absurd:** Analyze Vonnegut's use of black humor and the absurd in the novel. What purpose does it serve, and is it an effective device? Explain.

Look for examples of humor and the absurd in the text. Evaluate the dentist Dr. Jones and his associates, Robert Sterling Wilson's ideas about race, the death of Krapptauer, Resi's view of the majorettes, and the Nazis' preoccupation with writing their memoirs. Consider that the use of humor and the absurd is a distinguishing element of satire: What issues do these devices draw attention to in *Mother Night*? How do these elements create a sense of the absurdity of some of the things that divide us, such as prejudice, racism, and extreme nationalism?

Language, Symbols, and Imagery

Since *Mother Night* functions as a parody of realistic genres like memoir and historical document, symbolism is used sparingly. The major symbolism lies in the title reference to mother night and the imagery of mingling light and darkness (commonly used symbols in literature). In *Mother Night,* these carry heavy significance and multiple meanings, speaking about the dual nature of man, good and evil, tension, ambiguity, the old and the new, the unknown and undiscovered, the passage of time, and more. The concept of mother night is not only cited literally, either, but is presented figuratively throughout the novel. Another symbol common to Vonnegut's works surfaces in *Mother Night*—the game—specifically, a game of hide and seek with the haunting call of Olly-olly-ox-in-free. Finally, a symbolic element that can be easily overlooked is the epigraph—here, a passage from Sir Walter Scott's narrative poem "The Lay of the Last Minstrel." Whether you choose to write about symbolic imagery, a motif or pattern of symbolism in the text, or the symbolic value of a particular passage, you should attempt to uncover the relationship between symbol and theme by identifying patterns and recurring ideas in the text.

Sample Topics:

1. **Mother Night:** Why do you think that Vonnegut chose to name this novel *Mother Night*? How does the title symbol reflect the key concerns of the novel?

   Determining the motive behind the naming of Vonnegut's novel requires an analysis of the term "Mother Night." Taken from Goethe's *Faust,* the concept of Mother Night and mingling light and dark appears in many places throughout the novel—literally, but also figuratively by way of symbols and metaphors. Because of the origin of this phrase, you might begin by approaching this subject as if you are comparing and contrasting *Faust* and *Mother Night.* If you are not already familiar with *Faust,* this will require a bit of preliminary research. When was it written? What is the story about? Next, revisit *Mother Night* and identify where the same concepts are represented in the text. Consider the title, the passage cited from *Faust,* and other literal representations. What does the imagery cited in the passage seem to represent? Where are these concepts mirrored in other elements of the text? Consider the characters, plot, and, ultimately, theme.

2. **Hide and seek:** Analyze the game of hide and seek as symbol in *Mother Night.*

   Return to passages where the game of hide and seek is referenced. You will need to move past obvious associations and consider other concepts that the game brings to mind. How does the game conjure topics such as innocence, freedom, discovery, and the desire for redemption? How might it serve as a metaphor for that which we hide from ourselves and others? Why is the call of Olly-olly-ox-in-free so haunting to Campbell? How is it like the call of the Sonderkommando? Frank Wirtanen says that no one will ever call out to Campbell. What does he mean? Think about the relationship of the game to the chapter in which it appears. Consider the contrast of the game with the setting and themes of *Mother Night*. How does the game also work in tandem with the portrayal of the child character in the novel—little Resi Noth?

3. **Epigraph:** Analyze the epigraph.

The epigraph of *Mother Night* is a passage from Sir Walter Scott's narrative poem "The Lay of the Last Minstrel." Therefore, some background on Scott, as well as his poem, will be necessary. Consider his role as poet and playwright. Scott is also known as the creator of the modern historical novel and had a strong international reputation throughout his life. Why are these details significant? What does the passage mean? Consider imagery, symbolism, language, and theme. How does Scott's passage relate to *Mother Night*? Look for shared elements—theme, symbolism, and language, for example.

Comparison and Contrast Essays

While many of the differences between *Mother Night* and Vonnegut's earlier novels were illuminated in earlier sections of this chapter, it is also useful to consider those elements that remain consistent among the novels and the significance of these unchanged elements. Likewise, while contrast is often a useful revelatory device, in the case of *Mother Night*, the similarities between characters gain significance and, therefore, a comparison of the characters in *Mother Night* and the characters of Vonnegut's other novels is an excellent option. What do these similarities expose? Remember, however, that you do not need to limit yourself to a consideration of Vonnegut's novels only. *Mother Night* lends itself easily to comparison with works by other authors. Also, while it may seem obvious to compare it to other novels set during World War II, consider other commonalities. If you are interested in working from a historical or cultural point of view, think about topics such as the cold war or espionage and consider the correlation to other works that adopt this subject. For instance, those interested in representations of the cold war and espionage could compare *Mother Night* to works by Ian Fleming or Graham Greene. Another idea is to compare and contrast *Mother Night* with another work that merges fact and fiction, weaving the historical and the fantastic. In either of these cases, a comparison to certain works by Norman Mailer will work well; however, there are countless other options, and the comparison does not need to be restricted to works of the same period. The relationship between *Mother Night* and Goethe's *Faust* shows how the work relates to older works as well. Since *Mother Night* addresses universal and timeless issues such as identity, truth, and ethics, there are few restrictions.

Sample Topics:

1. **Howard W. Campbell and the Reverend Doctor Lionel Jason David Jones, DDS, DD:** Campbell insists that he is nothing like Dr. Jones. Is he correct? What is the significance of the relationship between these two characters?

Consider the biography of Jones and the autobiographical information provided by Campbell. Although the biography of Jones is more compact, Campbell's is spread throughout the novel. Both characters, however, have chapters devoted to their respective backgrounds. What are Campbell's feelings about Jones? How do the other characters respond to Campbell and to Jones? Campbell says Jones is ignorant and insane, but how are the two characters similar? Consider their relationships and motivations, their experiences, their friendships and ability to love, their reaction to the deaths of their wives, and their professions. What do these similarities ultimately signify?

2. **Campbell in *Mother Night* and in *Slaughterhouse-Five*:** Howard W. Campbell Jr. makes an appearance in Vonnegut's *Slaughterhouse-Five*. Compare and contrast his character in these two texts. Is his character consistent between the texts?

Consider Campbell's character in *Mother Night* and in *Slaughterhouse-Five*. Are they very similar depictions? How do the characters respond to him in *Slaughterhouse-Five* as opposed to in *Mother Night*? Does the presentation of Campbell in *Slaughterhouse-Five* change our perception of him in *Mother*

Night or vice versa? What is his purpose in each of the texts? What might be the purpose of recycling this character?

3. ***Mother Night* and Norman Mailer's *Barbary Shore:* Compare and contrast these two works.**

Think about how the works are similar and how are they different. Look not only at plot and characters but also at genre, form, and theme. Consider representations of espionage in the texts, the relationships between characters, the atmosphere of uncertainty, and questions of truth in each. Think about the time period in which the books were written. How do both texts reflect cold war tensions of the period in which they were written? Do the authors use the same methods to treat this subject? If not, does one method seem to be more effective than the other?

4. ***Mother Night* and Norman Mailer's *Armies of the Night:*** Compare and contrast these two works.

The subtitle of Mailer's *Armies of the Night* is "History as a Novel, The Novel as History." Compare and contrast the works as such. Consider form, themes, and characterization. Look for references to truth and authenticity. How do the works merge the realistic with the fictional? Does one present a more realistic historical framework than the other? How do the texts make use of real-life personalities and metafiction? Both books were published in the 1960s. One idea is to discuss these works within the context of other works written during the same period, showing how the texts present evidence of some particularly pervasive cultural concerns. Do the texts reveal something about shifts in form and genre in American literature during this time?

Bibliography and Resources for *Mother Night*

Goethe, Johann Wolfgang Von. *Faust.* Trans. Peter Salm. New York: Bantam, 1988.

Jamosky, Edward and Jerome Klinkowitz. "Kurt Vonnegut's Three Mother Nights." *Modern Fiction Studies* 34.2 (Summer 1988): 216–20.

Lessing, Doris. "Vonnegut's Responsibility." *New York Times Book Review* 4 February 1973: 35.

Mailer, Norman. *Armies of the Night: History as a Novel, The Novel as History.* New York: Plume-Penguin, 1994.

———. *Barbary Shore.* New York: Vintage-Random House, 1997.

Marvin, Thomas F. "Mother Night (1961)." *Kurt Vonnegut: A Critical Companion.* Westport, CT: Greenwood, 2002. 59–76.

Mustazza, Leonard. "Das Reich der Zwei: Art and Love as Miscreations in *Mother Night*." *Forever Pursuing Genesis: The Myth of Eden in the Novels of Kurt Vonnegut.* Cranbury, NJ: Associated U Presses, 1990. 59–75.

Orwell, George. *All Art is Propaganda: Critical Essays.* New York: Houghton Mifflin Harcourt, 2008.

Scholes, Robert. "Vonnegut's *Cat's Cradle* and *Mother Night*." *Fabulation and Metafiction.* Urbana, IL: U of Illinois P, 1979: 156–62.

Tew, Philip. "Kurt Vonnegut's *Mother Night* (1961): Howard W. Campbell Jr., and the Banalities of Evil." *New Critical Essays on Kurt Vonnegut.* Ed. David Simmons. New York: Palgrave Macmillan, 2009. 11–26.

Vonnegut, Kurt. *Mother Night.* New York: Dial, 2009.

The Walter Scott Digital Archive. Edinburgh University Library. Retrieved 18 March 2011. <http://www.walterscott.lib.ed.ac.uk/home.html>.

CAT'S CRADLE

READING TO WRITE

After you have completed an initial pass of the text, performing a close reading of key passages can help to solidify your comprehension of the work while allowing you to identify topics that can serve as the subject of your paper. Look for important imagery, symbolism, and language; analyze characterization, dialogue, and action; and note key ideas or questions presented by the author. Once you have settled on a topic of interest, continue on to identify where these same notable elements or topics are represented elsewhere in the text. As you engage in this process, you should begin to see a thread running throughout the text that illuminates important information about your subject topic and begins to reveal the author's intent. This material will help you to write the thesis statement that will give your paper form and purpose. It will also provide you with the evidence you need to support your claim. While close reading can be performed on any work of literature, the episodic form of *Cat's Cradle* makes it particularly well-suited for this method. The organization of the story into more than 100 compact chapters—digestible sections with titles that suggest the primary subject matter addressed in each—cuts out much of the preliminary work of sifting through peripheral material. A close reading of any chapter can be used as an effective starting place for generating ideas for exposition, but one of the most interesting and informative passages in *Cat's Cradle* comes early in the text in the form of a letter written by Newton Hoenikker, a failing medical student and the son of one of the (fictional) creators of the atom bomb. The narrator—an author who is writing a book about the day that the atomic bomb was dropped on Hiroshima—inquires as to what Newt's father was doing on "The Day the World Ended." Newt's answer spans three chapters. Consider the following excerpt:

> I was playing on the carpet outside his study on the day of the bomb . . . and Father was in his study, playing with a loop of string.
>
> It so happens I know where the string he was playing with came from . . . Father took the string from around the manuscript of a novel that a man in prison had sent him. The novel was about the end of the world in the year 2000, and the name of the book was 2000 A.D. It told about how mad scientists made a terrific bomb that wiped out the whole world . . . We had it for years, and then my sister Angela found it. . . . She burned it up, and the string with it. She was a mother to Frank and me, because our real mother died when I was born. . . .
>
> Anyway, Father looked at that loop of string for a while, and then his fingers started playing with it. His fingers made the string figure called a "cat's cradle." . . . Making the cat's cradle was the closest I ever saw my father come to playing what anybody else would call a game. . . . He must have surprised himself when he made a cat's cradle out of the string, and maybe it reminded him of his own childhood. He all of a sudden came out of his study and did something he'd never done before. He tried to play with me. Not only had he never played with me before; he had hardly ever spoken to me. . . . Cigar smoke made him smell like the mouth of Hell. So close up, my father was the ugliest thing I had ever seen. I dream about it all the time. . . . I burst into tears. I jumped up and I ran out of the house as fast as I could go. . . . Maybe I did hurt him, but I don't think I could have hurt him much. . . . People couldn't get at him because he just wasn't interested in people. I remember one time, about a year before he died, I tried to get him to tell me something about my mother. He couldn't remember anything about her. (17–19)

The letter provides information about Newt, his sister Angela, his mother and father, and the relationships between them. Through Newt's account of what happened in his household the day that Hiroshima was bombed and his mention of the prisoner's novel, it provides the first glimpse of the motif of apocalypse that pervades the book. And the passage also introduces the primary symbol of the novel: the cat's cradle. Therefore, one idea would be to use the passage as a starting place for a paper that explores Newt's relationship with his father. In his letter, Newt reveals that his father never played with him and hardly ever spoke to him. From here, we must ask some questions about Dr. Hoenikker. What does the passage suggest about his character or nature? Does he treat his other children the same way? Does their relationship reveal something about the American family in modern society? Once you have gathered enough evidence to characterize the relationship between Newt and his father and have determined what this information tells readers, you would be ready to write your thesis statement. Newt's letter could also be used as a starting place for an analysis of Dr. Hoenikker's character. Again, you will need to break down the passage and make note of what Newt's letter tells us about his character and then move on to other passages that relate information about his nature. Ask questions: What seems to be important to Dr. Hoenikker? Is he a typical scientist? What do we know about his inventions and their impact on society? Finally, how does his character reveal Vonnegut's preoccupation with the theme of the effects of scientific progress, and what message is the author sending about this theme through this character? In other words, how does Dr. Hoenikker serve as an allegorical or symbolic figure? Finally, since this passage also yields the story's major symbol—the cat's cradle—you might use the information to begin exploring the cat's cradle as symbol and revelatory device. Consider what the cat's cradle stands for and how it relates to the major themes of the novel. We know that cat's cradle is a game and, therefore, it conjures the notions of innocence and childhood, but what else does it represent? You will need to go beyond the references to the cat's cradle in Newt's correspondence, considering where else it is found in the text and how it is used. Look first for literal references, but remember that you are writing about symbolism; therefore, you need to consider the ideas that the game represents and search for these concepts in the text. How does the cat's cradle call to mind some Bokononist concepts, such as the sinookas, the tendrils of life; or how does it suggest the interconnectedness of people reflected in karasses and duprasses? How does the cat's cradle relate to themes of truth and illusion? The symbol reappears later in the text:

"Hello," I said. "I like your painting.
"You see what it is?"

"I suppose it means something different to everyone who sees it."

"It's a cat's cradle. . . . For maybe a hundred thousand years or more, grownups have been waving tangles of string in their children's faces. . . . No wonder kids grow up crazy. A cat's cradle is nothing but a bunch of X's between somebody's hands, and little kids look and look and look at all those X's . . ."

"And?"

"No damn cat. And no damn cradle." (113–14)

In several other places in the text, Newt uses the phrase to expose illusions such as with Angela's marriage and in reference to religion. You might consider what the repetition of this phrase underscores, or an analysis of the symbolism of the game of cat's cradle could be used as a starting place to discuss Vonnegut's treatment of religion, postwar living, the search for knowledge, truth and illusion, or the complex drive for scientific advancement and progress.

Since many other sections of *Cat's Cradle* function similarly to Newt's letter—as biographical entries that reveal information about character and expand into a dialogue about theme—identifying and analyzing these passages can be a good place to start. *Cat's Cradle* opens with one such biographical passage—an autobiographical monologue delivered by the narrator:

Call me Jonah. My parents did, or nearly did. They called me John.

Jonah—John—if I had been a Sam, I would have been a Jonah still—not because I have been unlucky for others, but because somebody or something has compelled me to be certain places at certain times, without fail. . . .

Listen:

When I was a younger man—two wives ago, 250,000 cigarettes ago, 3,000 quarts of booze ago. . . .

When I was a much younger man, I began to collect material for a book to be called The Day the World Ended.

The book was to be factual.

The book was to be an account of what important Americans had done on the day when the first atomic bomb was dropped on Hiroshima, Japan.

> It was to be a Christian book. I was a Christian then.
>
> I am a Bokononist now. (11)

This particular passage introduces many ideas that could be explored profitably. The passage discusses the apocalyptic, begins to suggest some of the dangers inherent in modern society, and references religion. Collectively, the information presented by John could be used as a starting place to analyze his character, with particular attention paid to the symbolic relevance of his names. Since John speaks in first person, the passage could also lead you to conduct to an analysis of the narration of *Cat's Cradle*. Just as Newt reveals important information about Dr. Hoenikker in his letter and John divulges information about himself through monologue, information about Mona Aamons is also presented in an unusual form—as an index entry:

> 'Aamons, Mona:' the index said, 'adopted by Monzano in order to boost Monzano's popularity, 194–199, 216 n.; childhood in compound of House of Hope and Mercy, 63–81; childhood romance with P. Castle, 72f; death of father, 89ff; death of mother, 92f; embarrassed by role as national erotic symbol, 80, 95f, 166n., 209, 247n., 400–406, 566n., 678; engaged to P. Castle, 193; essential naïveté, 67–71, 80, 95f, 116n., 209, 274n., 400–406, 566n., 678; lives with Bokonon, 92–98, 196–197; poems about, 2n., 26, 114, 119, 311, 316, 477n., 501, 507, 555n., 689, 718ff, 799ff, 800n., 841, 846ff, 908n., 971, 974; poems by, 89, 92, 193; returns to Monzano, 199; returns to Bokonon, 197; runs away from Bokonon, 199; runs away from Monzano, 197; tries to make self ugly in order to stop being erotic symbol to islanders, 80, 95f, 116n., 209, 247n., 400–406, 566n., 678; tutored by Bokonon, 63–80; writes letter to United Nations, 200; xylophone virtuoso, 71. (85–86)

The entry provides brief, but revelatory information about her childhood, her character, and her relationships. Again, the information presented could be used as a starting place to perform a character analysis that speaks to readers about how the treatment of her character gives voice to key themes. If you believe that Mona is representative of some trend in Vonnegut's treatment of the female character, you might use this passage as a starting place to write about the depiction of women in *Cat's Cradle* or the treatment of female characters throughout Vonnegut's oeuvre. The entry called "essential naïveté" is certainly curious and worthy of deeper exploration.

Close readings do not need to be limited to biographical passages, however, and passages can and should be used in combination. The passages about Bokonon and San Lorenzo that John finds in Philip Castle's book *San Lorenzo: The Land, the History, the People* demonstrate how information about one topic can inform us and shape our understanding of other subjects:

> Bokonon, I learned from Castle's book, was born in 1891. He was a Negro, born an Episcopalian and a British subject on the island of Tobago.
>
> He was christened Lionel Boyd Johnson . . .
>
> Young Lionel Boyd Johnson was educated in Episcopal schools, did well as a student, and was more interested in ritual than most. As a youth, for all his interest in the outward trappings of organized religion, he seems to have been a carouser. (74–75)

The passage begins with a brief biography of Bokonon, "a Negro, born an Episcopalian and a British subject on the island of Tobago" who "seems to have been a carouser" (74–75) and introduces his intersection with an army deserter named McCabe and their landing at San Lorenzo, described below:

> When Lionel Boyd Johnson and Corporal Earl McCabe were washed up naked onto the shore of San Lorenzo, I read, they were greeted by persons far worse off than they. The people of San Lorenzo had nothing but diseases, which they were at a loss to treat or even name. By contrast, Johnson and McCabe had the glittering treasures of literacy, ambition, curiosity, gall, irreverence, health, humor, and considerable information about the outside world. (87)

In presenting a biography of Bokonon, Vonnegut also begins to reveal a portrait of San Lorenzo. The passage continues on to describe the repeated exploitation of the inhabitants, including their exploitation by Castle Sugar, and to suggest Johnson and McCabe's desire to invent a new religion that would raise the people up. Chapter 60, titled

"An Underprivileged Nation," reveals the outcome: that "Johnson and McCabe had failed to raise the people from misery and muck" (93). In combination, the information about Bokonon and San Lorenzo could be used to write a paper about imperialism, focusing on passages that discuss the settlement and changing leadership of San Lorenzo and the intent and effect of this leadership. Such a paper would also need to consider the outsiders' perspective of San Lorenzo and the symbolism of the site as a metaphor for that which is foreign. The same passages could be used to initiate an examination of the treatment of religion in the novel.

No matter which passages you focus on, remember to read not only for plot but with an eye for imagery, symbolism, characterization, language, and form. In other words, observe not only what is presented but how the information is presented. By approaching these elements with an eye for detail, you will begin to see the threads that hold the text together—patterns of elements and ideas that expose the relationship of one passage to the next and reveal information about the author's intent and the purpose and meaning of the work.

TOPICS AND STRATEGIES

In the sections that follow, you will find a variety of suggested topics accompanied by questions and observations to assist you in the task of writing successfully about *Cat's Cradle.* Remember that it is not a comprehensive list, and the statements and questions that appear after each suggested topic are merely a guide to help spark your own ideas about the work. A successful paper will present a strong thesis based upon your own original ideas and will be supported by relevant examples resulting from close readings of the text. A wide variety of interpretations will be possible as you consider each topic. Use the strategic questions and observations to stimulate your own thoughts about the text and to assist you in developing your thesis. Remember to read through the text more than once, making note of those elements that support your argument. It will be equally important to make note of those elements that contradict your thesis, as this will help you to refine your argument and present a stronger case.

Themes

Cat's Cradle functions as a cultural commentary and work of satire. Therefore, looking for the issues the text satirizes by identifying where Vonnegut uses elements of humor, parody, sarcasm, and wit will lead you to the key subjects of the text. For example, the fictional religion of Bokononism with its absurd calypsos and strange rituals forms a parody of religion. The ridiculous pairings of Newt and his dwarf lover, Zinka, and Angela and her husband act as an odd reminder of the international arms race. And San Lorenzo with its exaggerated history and unique customs exposes a host of issues ranging from prejudice to imperialism. Any of these topics can make an excellent subject for your paper, but a word of caution: Read carefully and avoid sweeping generalities. You will need to read with an eye for detail, considering the subtleties of the dialogue Vonnegut creates around these topics. While the absurd portrayal of religion might make it appear that Vonnegut is attempting to point out the folly of religion itself, consider how he might be creating a more refined dialogue about the usefulness of religion and the folly of failing to recognize the limits of human knowledge and understanding. Furthermore, does the novel indicate that Vonnegut is critical of science and progress, or, rather, is he wary of the consequences of the misappropriation of scientific innovations? While, for the purposes of this book, many of these parent subjects appear under their corresponding sections (religion under Philosophy and Ideas, imperialism and the arms race under Historical and Cultural Context, for example), the section below considers how Vonnegut's treatment of these general topics leads to the exposure of other themes: the quest for knowledge and the dangers in modern society.

Sample Topics:

1. **The most valuable commodity on Earth:** Dr. Asa Breed contends that knowledge is the most valuable commodity on Earth. Does the text actually support this view?

   Writing about this topic calls for an evaluation of the quest for knowledge and truth in the text, and you will need to determine whether the results of this quest are ultimately positive or negative. Of course, Dr. Asa Breed, Dr. Hoenikker, and the scientists come to mind with their "pure research," but remember to consider how the other characters are also caught up in a search for knowledge and truth. How does their quest become complicated? Consider the Episcopalian woman's assertions and John's observation that one cannot understand God's intentions. Think about Miss Faust's question: How can truth be enough in and of itself? Think about the reference to fata morgana and representations of illusion in the text, symbols such as the cat's cradle, and Newt's slogan "no damn cat, no damn cradle." How does the existence of foma affect this quest? Remember to consider illusion and the application of new knowledge. What problems does the quest for knowledge cause? Alternatively, what benefits result from this quest? If you believe that the text reveals that the quest for knowledge is ultimately positive, or at least necessary, you will need to conclude by focusing on the insights of the characters, explaining how knowledge or truth shapes their lives or impacts their culture in a positive way. If you determine that it is negative, you may wish to write about the intersection of the quest for knowledge and prejudice, false ideas, illusion, and ignorance, providing corresponding evidence from the text.

2. **The dangers in modern society:** Evaluate the text's presentation of the dangers in modern society. What are they? Does the text seem to indicate whether or not they can be avoided or surmounted?

In order to identify the dangers presented in the text, you will need to look for examples of negative consequence and effect in the story. Think about the problems the characters face and what threatens them. The characters provide their own input as to what is dangerous and threatening: Asa Breed proposes that superstition is a danger, and Marvin Breed believes that there are "too many people in high places who are stone-cold dead" (53), but what other problems are evidenced in the text? Is there evidence of evil in the story? If not, why is its absence noteworthy? Consider how the text treats issues such as complacency, indifference, lack of self-awareness, prejudice and racism, extremism and false superiority, apathy, the folly of pretending to understand, the consequences of a movement away from a relationship with nature, the destruction of family, and the absence of love. Finally, remember not to focus only on plot. In addition to writing about how the characters and the action evidence these dangers, you should spend some time writing about genre and form. Again, considering the work as a work of satire will be helpful. How does the apocalyptic and dystopic nature of the book help to make these dangers apparent, create a sense of unease, and call out a warning? Finally, you will need to determine whether there is evidence that these dangers can be avoided or overcome. Are the characters able to overcome the obstacles they are faced with? If so, how do they accomplish this?

Character

As noted in the Reading to Write section, *Cat's Cradle* contains many passages that function as biographical entries about the characters. Think of John's autobiographical monologues, Newt's letter about his father, the index entry for Mona Aamons, and the story of Bokonon that is woven throughout the text. The characters also act as informers, providing information about one another through dialogue—often in the absence of the character they are speaking about. Because of this detail, it is imperative that you evaluate point of view. This means considering who is presenting the information and whether or not the information provided is reliable. If the source and the information are reliable, you might ask what we learn about the character being spoken about. If the source or the information is not reliable, what does the information reveal about the character speaking? By using the information presented through dialogue, plot, and narration in combination, you will be well equipped to perform an analysis of a notable individual character like John, Dr. Felix Hoenikker, or Dr. Asa Breed. Another alternative is to write an essay that conducts a study of the characters in groups or pairs. Consider karasses, duprasses, granfalloons, families, relationships, and the organization of characters by nation, religion, and gender. Since the development of the characters is not a major concern of the text, it will be helpful to focus instead on the various concepts and ideas they represent, keeping in mind that the goal of your essay should be to illuminate the link between character and theme.

Sample Topics:

1. **"Call me Jonah"**: Analyze the narrator based upon an evaluation of his names. Why does he wish to be called Jonah? What significance do the names John and Jonah have?

At the opening of the story, John introduces himself to readers. He reveals that John is his birth name but says that he might as well have been named Jonah. Consider the meaning of both names. Explore John as a Christian and biblical name, but also as a common name. How does he relate to biblical figures by this name? And how does he serve as an everyman? In other words, how is John representative of something universal? Jonah is referenced not only in the Bible, but there are also figures named Jonah found in the religions of Islam and Judaism. Consider the relationship between John and these figures. How do these relationships correspond to the major themes of the book? John's instruction to call him Jonah is also an obvious reference to Herman Melville's *Moby-Dick* and the well-known phrase "Call me Ishmael." This should lead to a refined and focused comparison and contrast of *Cat's Cradle* and *Moby-Dick*, showing how parallels in characterization (including narration) reveal similarities in theme.

2. **Dr. Felix Hoenikker**: Analyze this character. Should Dr. Hoenikker be considered an allegorical figure? Why or why not?

Addressing this topic calls for a thorough evaluation of Dr. Hoenikker's character and a final determination of whether or not his character functions symbolically. Keep in mind that Dr. Hoenikker is deceased, so everything in the story is recollection and remembrance of him. Also, there are many points of view presented in text. Is there some commonality among the points of view presented? Consider Newt's letter to John, Dr. Asa Breed's point of view, Miss Faust's comments, and Angela's point of view. How is Dr. Hoenikker perceived by these characters? How is he perceived by John as an outsider? Does the text suggest that history will record another view? Is Dr. Hoenikker presented as a typical scientist or a typical father and husband? It may also be helpful to research the real-life inspiration for his character: the Nobel Prize–winning chemist Irwin Langmuir. Once you have evaluated his character, consider what this portrait reveals about love and family, the pursuit of knowledge and the drive for progress, self-awareness, and innocence. Of course this is a limited list, and your analysis may suggest a dialogue about other topics, but your primary endpoint should explain whether or not his character acts as a vehicle for the revelation of some message or moral.

3. **Women:** Evaluate the portrayal of women in *Cat's Cradle*.

In addressing this topic you will be determining whether the female characters are treated as individuals or whether, collectively, they perpetuate—or counter—some stereotype. Look at Angela Hoenikker, Emily, Miss Pefko, Sandra, Miss Faust, the secretaries, Mona, Mom Crosby, and Claire Minton. It will be helpful to consider their roles as mothers or motherly characters, as sexual beings, and as workers. Consider how they are described by other characters and how they are portrayed by Vonnegut. Are they presented as intellectual, talented, ignorant, or naïve? Are they presented in an exaggerated or realistic manner? If you conclude that they do seem to represent some unified vision of women, you may wish to discuss how this ties in with shifts in the cultural perceptions of women around the time the book was written. Is the portrait of women in *Cat's Cradle* expected or challenging?

History and Context

Although *Cat's Cradle* is not a story about the bombing of Hiroshima, the reference to "the day the world ended" at the start of the story is a very important one. By referencing an actual horror—the decimation of the Japanese city of Hiroshima by an atomic bomb dropped by the United States in World War II—Vonnegut reminds readers that *Cat's Cradle* is focused on very real and significant cultural issues. This is a deeply significant reminder in a work that incorporates humor and the absurd. Remember, also, that *Cat's Cradle* was written during the cold war, a period of intense political and military tension between the United States and the Soviet Union, culminating with an international arms race that threatened humanity. Your paper might evaluate the significance of the appearance of either of these historical events in the text, or it might consider how, together, the inclusion of these topics allows Vonnegut to generate a dialogue about issues such as the consequences of the misplaced application of technological and scientific inventions, foreign relations, nationalism, imperialism, the international arms race, and more. In any case, your paper should conclude by indicating the relevance of these topics for readers today.

Cat's Cradle is also very much about identity—not only personal identity (reflected in the many biographical passages that make up the novel) but cultural identity as well. Through the relationship between the Americans and the inhabitants of San Lorenzo, Vonnegut creates a layered dialogue about national identity, supremacy, international relations, imperialism, and that which is foreign to us. Through the relationships among the characters, Vonnegut also explores major postwar cultural shifts, including changes in religious beliefs, gender roles, and the construct of the American family—topics common to literature of this time. Either of these could become the subject of your paper. Focusing on Vonnegut's distinctive technical and aesthetic approach will ensure that your paper does more than state the obvious.

Sample Topics:

1. **The cold war, communism, and the international arms race:**
   How does the novel address cold war tensions and the international arms race? Does the text suggest some lesson or moral through its discourse on these subjects?

   Begin with some historical background, setting up context for your readers, and then spend some time revealing where these historical subjects are represented in the text. Does the text reveal some popular American sentiments about communism at the time the book was written or does it provide a different point of view? How do the genre, plot, and structure of the work create a mood that corresponds to the national and international mood of that time? It will be helpful to focus on ice-nine, the relationship of Newt and Zinka, and the relationship of Angela and her husband. Consider, also, Claire Minton's letter, Crosby's sentiments about Horlick Minton, and Papa Monzano's comments about the absence of communism on San Lorenzo. You should also consider, more generally, the relationship of the characters to that which is foreign to them. Finally, do the references to these subjects present some message or moral? Is there any indication of the evil or negative impact of communism found in the text, for example? Are the characters right to be afraid or intimidated by the inhabitants of San Lorenzo, or is their reaction unfounded? Does this reveal anything about the way that Vonnegut feels Americans react to that which is different or foreign?

2. **Imperialism:** How does *Cat's Cradle* reveal a critical commentary of imperialism?

Focus on passages pertaining to San Lorenzo, its settlement, leadership, and history, and the relationship of outsiders to this culture. You will need to revisit the passages that explain how Bokonon and McCabe came to San Lorenzo and their intentions as leaders. Consider, also, the Americans' perceptions of San Lorenzo and their response to the religion and language. Other notable passages pertain to the Castle sugar industry and the hospitality industry. You will need to address the issue of exploitation, and, here, it will be necessary to focus on the Crosbys' bicycle industry as well as John's desire to industrialize and reform. Are the ideas presented by foreigners necessarily better? Do the attempts to industrialize and convert the inhabitants of San Lorenzo promote peace and create a better nation? Do Bokonon and McCabe succeed in their attempts?

Does Monzano? Or John? Consider the symbolism of the castle and the crumbling of the castle tower. What is the significance of the hotel being empty? Finally, how does the dialogue created via fictional elements in the text correspond to examples of the effects of imperialism throughout history?

3. **Portrait of Americans:** Does *Cat's Cradle* generate a critical portrait of Americans? Explain.

This will require a focused analysis of the American characters: John, Philip Castle, the Hoenikkers, the scientists, the Mintons, and the Crosbys. How do these characters relate to one another? More importantly, consider their relationship to San Lorenzo and that which is foreign to them. How do they perceive this other culture? Alternatively, do they seem to possess any awareness of how they are perceived by others? You might conclude by explaining how this fictional portrait relates to American culture at the time the text was written. How does the portrait presented compare to our own cultural identity today? Consider Claire Minton's opinions that Americans are hated elsewhere, that the worst thing is for Americans to imagine they are not loved everywhere, and that Americans are always looking for love where there is none. You should also think about her observations about "the vanished frontier." The chapter called "The Happiness of an American" will be useful. Finally, how does Bokononism, with its granfalloons, contribute to a dialogue about nationalism?

Philosophy and Ideas

The most prominent philosophical themes of the book have to do with religion (revealed in the tension between Christianity and Bokononism) and the quest for knowledge (represented most obviously by the scientists). Within the treatment of these two major topics, other overlapping philosophical themes emerge: truth, fate and free will, ethics and responsibility, to name a few. While philosophical concerns can sometimes be difficult to recognize, Vonnegut makes philosophy visible through his use of the Bokononist language. Consider how the concept of foma allows him to discuss truth and the usefulness of religion, or how zah-mah-ki-bo allows him to address fate and free will. And how does the granfalloon allow him to discuss prejudice and boundaries? If you choose to write about philosophy by discussing its presentation via the Bokononist doctrine, there is one major question you should consider: Does the presentation of these concepts—as philosophical notions posited by a fictional calypso singer-turned-religious icon—negate the validity of these ideas and render them absurd? If so, what might Vonnegut be trying to tell readers about faith, truth, the quest for knowledge, and the limits of human understanding?

Sample Topics:

1. **Religion:** Analyze the treatment of religion in the *Cat's Cradle*. Does the text suggest that religion is valuable or useless?

   Consider all references to religion in the text. Does the novel suggest that truth in religion is a necessity? Does the absence of truth render religion valueless? Consider the descriptions of the roots of Bokononism, its rituals, and its doctrine. Think about Julian Castle's notion of religion as an "instrument of hope" (118). How is the attractiveness of that which is unknown and forbidden tied in with religion? At the start of the story, John claims that it is foolish to try to understand God's workings. Does the text present a completely absurd view of religion, or does there seem to be some purpose or usefulness in it? How do those characters who practice religion seem to benefit from it (or not)?

2. **Zah-mah-ki-bo:** In the Bokononist language, *zah-mah-ki-bo* is translated as "irreversible destiny." Analyze this concept in the text.

   Look for examples of fate and the unalterable in the book. Consider John's confrontation with the stone angel bearing his name. At the opening of the novel, John also says he was always where he was supposed to be. Does the text seem to indicate that this is accurate, or does John ever appear to be in control of his actions and his fate? Frank lands on San Lorenzo, as do Bokonon and McCabe. Do these seem to be events resulting from some irreversible destiny, or do they seem to be arbitrary events? Think about other, more indirect examples of destiny in Bokononism—the way that people are drawn together into duprasses or karasses, the forces of vin-dits, wampeters, and kan-kans. Does the absurdity of the religion of Bokononism invalidate the concept of irreversible destiny? Does the text suggest, rather, that the characters use the idea of destiny to fulfill some desire for understanding that which is mysterious and foreign to them? Finally, is any contrary view presented? Is there anything in the text that suggests that the characters have control over their own fate?

3. **Granfalloons:** Analyze the Bokononist concept of the *granfalloon.*

You will need to begin by defining the granfalloon and explaining the term's origin. Next, consider where this idea is represented in the text. Look for examples cited literally but also examples presented in characterization. How does the granfalloon expose various prejudices or ignorance? How does Vonnegut use a sense of folly, humor, and the absurd to underscore these points? Finally, while the granfalloon exposes those who are unified falsely or foolishly, does the text suggest what should unify people?

4. **Wrang-wrang:** In Bokononism a *wrang-wrang* is defined as a person who steers people away from a line of speculation by reducing it to an absurdity. How does this relate to Vonnegut's own work as author of *Cat's Cradle*?

Begin by identifying where this concept is identified in the text. John tells us that the poet Krebbs steered him away from nihilism, but are there other more subtle examples of this in the text? How does *Cat's Cradle* itself function as an example of this concept? What does the book render absurd? How does it accomplish this? What might Vonnegut be steering his own readers away from? Answering this means performing an analysis of elements of genre—specifically the use of the absurd in the text and the satirical nature of the work.

Form and Genre

After Vonnegut's previous novel, which masqueraded as historical novel and memoir, *Cat's Cradle* marked a return to Vonnegut's signature use of science fiction and fantasy. However, the book is primarily identifiable as a work of satire that addresses major cultural and philosophical subjects. Though dependent on humor and the absurd, the book has also been recognized as an anthropological work. *Cat's Cradle* was accepted as Vonnegut's thesis in anthropology—the study of humans, their behavior, and their organization in societies—by the University of Chicago in 1971 after the school failed to pass him years earlier. Considering the text from this vantage point presents many possibilities for exposition. No matter which genre or element of form you choose to write about, it will be helpful to consider the relationship between fantasy and reality: How do the fantastic elements of the work expose important truths about reality and what are these truths?

Sample Topics:

1. ***Cat's Cradle* as satire:** Analyze *Cat's Cradle* as a work of satire.

   Consider the use of irony, wit, sarcasm, parody, humor, and the absurd to illuminate follies and provide criticism. How does the book challenge convention in its treatment of religion, science and progress, family, love, and national identity? Evaluate characterization, symbolism, language, and form. Is the book successful as a work of satire? What message does it ultimately seem to impart about the subjects it satirizes?

2. ***Cat's Cradle* as anthropological text:** Evaluate *Cat's Cradle* as an anthropological text.

   You will need to begin by explaining how and why *Cat's Cradle* can be classified as an anthropological work. How is the novel a study of humans—how they behave, how they group up, and how they function in societies? While satire focuses on specific cultural or political issues, anthropology focuses on people. Therefore, this topic calls for a consideration of the treatment of characters as individuals and in groups in the book. What does the text reveal about humans and about societies and families? Look for patterns in the text. What trends in behavior, motivations, and experiences are evident in the text?

3. **Form:** Analyze the form of *Cat's Cradle*. How does the form correspond to the major themes of the text?

Consider the structure and organization of the book. Is the structure of the book typical of works belonging to this genre? What other kinds of texts share this same structure and form? Think about narration and point of view. Is the conclusion of the story typical? How does the order of the text relate to genre, creating a feeling of disease and disorder? The text is interrupted by quotes from Bokonon and calypsos. It is also broken into passages that function as biographical entries. How do all of these details and elements relate to the genre (or genres) of the work and, ultimately, to theme?

4. *Cat's Cradle* **as apocalyptic tale:** Analyze the novel as an apocalyptic tale.

Begin by identifying the characteristics of the text that allow us to identify it as an apocalyptic text, but consider how the text strays from typical apocalyptic texts. Consider plot, structure, resolution, and characterization. Does the novel address themes common to the apocalyptic subgenre? What causes disaster in typical apocalyptic books? And in *Cat's Cradle*? How do the characters respond to disaster? Who survives? Does *Cat's Cradle* present a typical conclusion? Accordingly, does the novel seem to promote a fatalistic or nihilistic outlook or to resist it?

Language, Symbols, and Imagery

The title symbol—the game of cat's cradle—holds many meanings and could, therefore, serve as the basis for a variety of papers. Consider its association to Bokononism and the interconnectedness of humans and the sinookas or tendrils of life; its association with innocence and childhood; its philosophical implications and relationship to the theme of illusion; its link to the apocalyptic and the dangers associated with modern living. Many of the remaining symbols in *Cat's Cradle* correspond to issues of the foreign—not only what is geographically foreign, but philosophically and emotionally foreign—the unexplored and the misunderstood. The places where the action of the novel takes place also function symbolically. Hiroshima—the Japanese city devastated by the atom bomb dropped by the United States in World War II—becomes representative of the dangers of the misplaced application of scientific innovation and bad international relations, while San Lorenzo acts as a metaphor for that which is foreign to us. The symbolic function of the various components of its culture—its history as evidence of the effects of imperialism; the Bokononist religion as representative of the absurdities, but also the usefulness, of religion; its language as a metaphor for communication and understanding (or misunderstanding, as the case may be)—can all be explored individually in greater depth.

Sample Topics:

1. **The cat's cradle:** Why do you think that Vonnegut chose to name his novel *Cat's Cradle*? Analyze representations of the cat's cradle in the text and explain the significance of this symbol.

   Consider both literal references to the game in the text and more figurative applications. Think about the game's association with childhood and innocence, but, also, how does the game of cat's cradle come to represent something more complicated? How does it correspond to the concepts found in Bokononism such as the notion of sinookas or the interconnectedness of people in a karass or duprass? How does Newt use the game as a metaphor for illusion, and what does he use it in reference to? Finally, how does the game of cat's cradle relate to the genre of the book and the novel's major thematic concerns?

2. **San Lorenzo:** How does San Lorenzo function not only as setting but as symbol?

Refer to all representations of San Lorenzo in the text. Consider its history and its customs, including religion and language. How does the site come to represent the foreign and
raise issues of understanding, communication, and miscom-
munication? It will be important to consider the relationship
of outsiders to this culture. How does the setting help to reveal
the major themes of the text? How does it act as a vehicle to
enable the work to function as satire?

Comparison and Contrast Essays

Cat's Cradle revisits many of the elements found in Vonnegut's earlier
novels and, therefore, it lends itself to comparison with *Player Piano,
The Sirens of Titan,* and *Mother Night.* One idea would be to compare
Cat's Cradle generally with another text, such as *Player Piano,* showing
how the texts evidence one of Vonnegut's thematic preoccupations. You
might choose instead to consider how a specific element such as character, theme, symbolism, or genre is treated in *Cat's Cradle* and another
text, exposing some trend or notable difference between the texts. A
comparison of *Cat's Cradle* to works by other authors will also work
well. You might compare *Cat's Cradle* to other dystopic works, evaluating the use of science fiction in multiple texts; consider the relationship
between Vonnegut's novel and the social commentary of an author like
H.G. Wells or George Orwell; or compare the book to another work of
fiction, such as John Hersey's *Hiroshima.* These are just a few of the possible topics. There are limitless options.

Sample Topics:
1. *Cat's Cradle* and *Player Piano:* Compare and contrast these
two texts.

There are many similarities between *Cat's Cradle* and Vonnegut's first novel, *Player Piano.* While you will want to explain
these similarities, ultimately, you need to either explain why
these similarities are significant or show how, despite all of

these similarities, the works evidence some major, notable difference or development in Vonnegut's work. Consider genre, including the application of elements of science fiction and fantasy and the use of black humor and the absurd. Look for similarities in plot, setting, and character. Most importantly, do the books treat the same key themes? How do both texts address the concept of dystopia? Consider the treatment of class division, questions of nationalism and boundaries, and the exploration of religion in each text. How are the conclusions of each story alike or different?

2. **Mountain as symbol in *Cat's Cradle* and Norman Mailer's *The Naked and the Dead:*** Compare and contrast the use of the mountain as symbol in these two texts.

Both texts reference a mountain that one or more characters are preoccupied with conquering. Consider the description of these mountains and the relationship of the characters to the mountains. It will also be important to consider the general relationship of the humans to nature in these texts. Is nature presented as a positive force, a nurturing force, or a dominating force in each? Consider the philosophical concept of naturalism. Should both of these texts be considered naturalist works? How does the mountain suggest issues of control, choice, and desire? Are the mountains ultimately conquered? What significance does this have?

3. **Good and evil in *Cat's Cradle* and *Mother Night:*** Consider the treatment of good and evil in the texts. Do the texts present a similar vision of good and evil?

Conduct a comparison of theme by analyzing character, but consider other formal elements as well. Are there good and evil characters in each text—heroes and villains? In *Cat's Cradle,* does evil cause the problems that threaten the characters? In *Mother Night*? Evaluate the notion of dynamic tension mentioned in *Cat's Cradle*—the idea that it benefits society when good and bad are pitted against each other. Does this extend to the effect of good and evil pitted against each other within the individual? Besides in characterization, how is this notion represented in the texts? Are good and evil presented as viable philosophical concepts or as outdated concepts?

4. ***Cat's Cradle* and Vonnegut's nonfiction:** Explore the relationship between *Cat's Cradle* and Vonnegut's nonfiction.

Although you may wish to include other works, Vonnegut's *A Man Without a Country* and *Armageddon in Retrospect* will work well. Consider how each of the works treats similar themes. What literary devices does Vonnegut use in each text to speak about these themes? Does one genre seem to be more effective than the other, or do they complement one another? Do the texts provide some evidence that Vonnegut's ideas and preoccupations evolved or changed over the course of his career, or do they reveal a clear and cohesive picture of his ideas on politics and culture?

5. ***Cat's Cradle* and John Hersey's *Hiroshima:*** Compare and contrast the two books.

Consider how both works treat the subjects of nuclear war, the personal and cultural impact of war, and the application of technological innovation for military purposes. How do the authors' approaches differ? Evaluate genre and form, exploring the realism of *Hiroshima* versus the elements of science fiction, fantasy, and the absurd in *Cat's Cradle*. Does one form seem to be more effective than the other?

Bibliography and Resources for *Cat's Cradle*

Allen, Claire. "Wampeters and Foma? Misreading Religion in *Cat's Cradle* and *The Book of Dave.*" *New Critical Essays on Kurt Vonnegut.* Ed. David Simmons. New York: Palgrave Macmillan, 2009. 213–26.

Doxey, William S. "Vonnegut's *Cat's Cradle.*" *The Explicator* 37.4 (1979): 6.

Hersey, John. *Hiroshima.* New York: Knopf Doubleday, 1989.

Leff, Leonard. "Science and Destruction in Vonnegut's *Cat's Cradle*." *Rectangle* 46 (Spring 1971): 28–32.

Leverence, W. John. "*Cat's Cradle* and Traditional American Humor." *Journal of Popular Culture* 5.4 (Spring 1972): 955–63.

Mailer, Norman. *The Naked and the Dead*. New York: Picador-Macmillan, 2000.

Marvin, Thomas F. "*Cat's Cradle* (1963)." *Kurt Vonnegut: A Critical Companion*. Westport, CT: Greenwood, 2002. 77–96.

McGinnis, Wayne. "The Source and Implications of Ice-Nine in Vonnegut's *Cat's Cradle*." *American Notes and Queries* 13 (1974): 40–41.

Melville, Herman. *Moby-Dick*. New York: Random House, 1981.

Orwell, George. "You and the Atomic Bomb." Originally pub. in *The Tribune*. 19 October 1945. Reprinted online. Nuclear Age Peace Foundation. Retrieved 4 April 2011. <http://www.wagingpeace.org/articles/0000/1945_orwell_you-and-the-bomb.htm>.

Scholes, Robert. "Vonnegut's *Cat's Cradle* and *Mother Night*." *Fabulation and Metafiction*. Urbana, IL: U of Illinois P, 1979: 156–62.

Thomas, Paul L. "'No Damn Cat, and No Damn Cradle': The Fundamental Flaws in Fundamentalism According to Vonnegut." *New Critical Essays on Kurt Vonnegut*. Ed. David Simmons. New York: Palgrave Macmillan, 2009. 27–46.

Vonnegut, Kurt. *Cat's Cradle*. New York: Laurel, 1988.

Zins, Daniel L. "Rescuing Science from Technocracy: *Cat's Cradle* and the Play of Apocalypse." *Science-Fiction Studies* 13 (July 1986): 170–81.

SLAUGHTERHOUSE-FIVE, OR THE CHILDREN'S CRUSADE: A DUTY-DANCE WITH DEATH

READING TO WRITE

In 1943, Kurt Vonnegut enlisted in the U.S. Army. On December 19, 1944, at the age of 22, he was captured by the Germans during the Battle of the Bulge, the last major German offensive of World War II. As a prisoner of war, he was taken to Dresden, where he witnessed the firebombing of the city by the Allies in February of 1945, an event that resulted in the deaths of more than 100,000 Germans, including many civilians, and decimated the city of Dresden. Vonnegut struggled to write about this subject for almost a quarter of a century before presenting the cumulative result of his efforts in 1969 with the publication of *Slaughterhouse-Five*—the story of Billy Pilgrim, an optometrist and former chaplain's assistant in the U.S. Army who claims to have become "unstuck in time," experiencing the events of his life before, during, and after his capture by the Germans in World War II and his survival of the bombing of Dresden in no certain order.

As you prepare to write, drafting a brief overview or summary of the work can be a helpful first step. In answering the question *What is this book about?* you will be summarizing the major points of the plot, identifying the protagonist or central characters, making note of the most important and memorable elements of the text, and uncovering key themes. The overview of *Slaughterhouse-Five* presented above—though limited to a single sentence—points the way toward several topics that could be explored more fully. The element of time travel could be used as a starting place for the examination of the form of the story or the theme of mental illness. Considering the significance of Billy Pilgrim's roles as soldier, prisoner of war, chaplain's assistant, or optometrist would enable you to write an essay that exposes the crucial link between character and theme. Focusing on the framing subjects of World War II and the bombing of Dresden would allow you to write about *Slaughterhouse-Five* from a historical or cultural perspective, examining the relationship between reality and fiction or issues of truth and authenticity. An analysis of the combination of history and science fiction could lead to an intriguing essay about genre, while, for those knowledgeable about Vonnegut's own background, the basic plotline reveals the semiautobiographical nature of the text. The summary above also suggests several of the primary themes of the text—time, religion, ways of seeing, and war—which all might be explored in greater depth. After choosing a topic of interest, you would identify where the topic is represented in the text and analyze related passages to determine what the elements therein reveal about your subject. This is one simple method that you might use to begin generating ideas for a topic and gathering information that will allow you to shape your thesis and supporting argument.

Because the subject of war pervades the text, a consideration of this particular subject can also be an excellent starting place to generate ideas for your paper. You might begin by asking some questions: What is Vonnegut ultimately saying about war? What kind of portrait of war does the book present? What particular elements of war does the story focus on? How is the soldier characterized? How is *Slaughterhouse-Five* similar to or different from other novels that take war as their subject? How does the book's treatment of war fulfill or challenge our expectations? From a historical perspective, is the book accurate? How does the treatment of war in *Slaughterhouse-Five* correspond to historical and cultural events taking place around the time of the book's initial publication? Finally, what message does the book's treatment of war hold for readers today? With these questions in mind, you would return to the text and perform a close reading of notable passages, evaluating formal elements to uncover the answers to these questions.

A close reading of the very first chapter of the book, for instance—a self-conscious reflection on the long, frustrating process of writing *Slaughterhouse-Five*—confirms that the book is not only about the effects of war but also about the way that we remember, talk about, and depict war in media. In this chapter, Vonnegut visits fellow veteran Bernard O'Hare to gather ideas for his book about Dresden, and in a memorable exchange with O'Hare's wife, Mary, he promises not to perpetuate a romanticized view of war:

> Mary admired the two little girls I'd brought, mixed them in with her own children, sent them all upstairs to play games and watch television. It was only after the children were gone that I sensed that Mary didn't like me or didn't like *something* about the night. She was polite but chilly.
>
> . . . .
>
> O'Hare was embarrassed, but he wouldn't tell me what was wrong. I couldn't imagine what it was about me that could burn up Mary so. . . . She fixed herself a Coca-Cola, made a lot of noise banging the ice-cube tray in the stainless steel sink. Then she went into another part of the house. But she wouldn't sit still. She was moving all over the house, opening and shutting doors, even moving furniture around to work off her anger.
>
> . . . .
>
> So we tried to ignore Mary and remember the war. . . . We would chuckle or grin sometimes, as though war stories were coming back, but neither one of us could remember anything good. . . . She finally came out in the kitchen again for another Coke. She took another tray of ice cubes from the refrigerator, banged it in the sink, even though there was already plenty of ice out.
>
> Then she turned to me, let me see how angry she was, and that the anger was for me. She had been talking to herself, so what she said was a fragment of a much larger conversation. "You were just *babies* then!" she said.
>
> "What?" I said.
>
> "You were just babies in the war—like the ones upstairs!"
>
> I nodded that this was true. We *had* been foolish virgins in the war, right at the end of childhood.

"But you're not going to write it that way, are you." This wasn't a question. It was an accusation.

"I—I don't know," I said.

"Well, I know," she said. "You'll pretend you were men instead of babies, and you'll be played in the movies by Frank Sinatra and John Wayne or some of those other glamorous, war-loving, dirty old men. And war will look just wonderful, so we'll have a lot more of them. And they'll be fought by babies like the babies upstairs."

So then I understood. It was war that made her so angry. She didn't want her babies or anybody else's babies killed in wars. And she thought wars were partly encouraged by book and movies.

So I held up my right hand and I made her a promise: "Mary," I said. "I don't think this book of mine is ever going to be finished. I must have written five thousand pages by now, and thrown them all away. If I ever do finish it, though, I give you my word of honor: there won't be a part for Frank Sinatra or John Wayne.

"I tell you what," I said. "I'll call it 'The Children's Crusade.'"

She was my friend after that. (15–19)

Notice how each element of this passage works to undermine romantic representations of war, contributing to a dialogue about the way that war is—and should be—presented in the media. Vonnegut and O'Hare struggle to remember anything of note about the war; there are no triumphs or victories to recall. Through dialogue Vonnegut presents the idea that soldiers are someone's children rather than invincible heroes, introducing the motif of the Children's Crusade. He pairs this with the imagery of the two little girls in white dresses, who are sent off to play. Without close reading and analysis, this passage might seem peripheral to the text. It has the characteristics of a preface: Vonnegut refers to himself in the first person and reflects on the process of writing the book. However, even the placement of the passage is deliberate. Vonnegut incorporates this section as a chapter rather than annexing it as a preface, thereby declaring its significance and inseparability from the rest of the story. By employing metafiction, he is able to generate credibility, building a sense of intimacy and authenticity. The exchange takes place between two real people rather than fictional characters. More specifically, it takes place between a veteran and a woman who is a mother and veteran's wife—individuals representative of those most directly affected by the horrors of war. From here you could consider how this passage works in conjunction with the rest of the text to break down romantic representations of war and to call attention to the way that war is remembered and depicted in the media.

Slaughterhouse-Five remains Vonnegut's best-known and most challenged work, commonly appearing on lists of the top novels of all time and lists of the top censored or banned books of all time. And so, a third option is to begin by identifying those elements that make the book memorable and relevant or challenging and provocative. Certainly, the places where fantasy meets reality are striking—the genre (a strange combination of science fiction and history) and form (a postmodern construction of metafiction, nonlinear narrative, and curious repetition). The characterization is also memorable. Vonnegut makes use of unconventional characters, such as the pathetic Billy Pilgrim, portrayed as a fumbling, failing clown throughout; aliens; and the author himself. As for what makes the book challenging and provocative, its brash language and imagery (think of the latrine scene and references to the pornographic) commanded the attention of censors, but, more important, is the matter of the critical nature of the work. *Slaughterhouse-Five* presented a provocative, penetrating criticism of war, religion, the American family, and more. An analysis of any of these elements could lead to an interesting and engaging paper.

No matter which method you adopt, there is some advice that will be helpful: As you are gathering information, observe not only what is present in the book but also what is omitted. For example, readers will find numerous representations of death, suffering, and mental illness in the story, but representations of romantic love, faith, and triumph are notably absent. These absences contribute indispensably to the dialogue created around the book's key themes. Also, keep in mind that while the subject of war pervades the text, your essay does not need to be limited to this subject. *Slaughterhouse-Five* also addresses a wide range of philosophical issues, challenging our most basic preconceptions about time, faith, death, memory, love, and free will. Finally, one of the most striking lines in the novel—Vonnegut's statement that his book "is so short and jumbled and jangled because there is nothing intelligent to

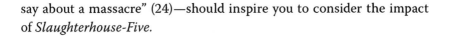

say about a massacre" (24)—should inspire you to consider the impact of *Slaughterhouse-Five.*

TOPICS AND STRATEGIES

In the sections that follow, you will find a variety of suggested topics accompanied by questions and observations to assist you in the task of writing successfully about *Slaughterhouse-Five.* Remember that it is not a comprehensive list, and the statements and questions that appear after each suggested topic are merely a guide to help spark your own ideas about the work. A successful paper will present a strong thesis based upon your own original ideas and will be supported by relevant examples resulting from close readings of the text. A wide variety of interpretations will be possible as you consider each topic. Use the strategic questions and observations to stimulate your own thoughts about the text and to assist you in developing your thesis. Remember to read through the text more than once, making note of those elements that support your argument. It will be equally important to make note of those elements that contradict your thesis, as this will help you to refine your argument and present a stronger case.

Themes

References to historical events in fiction act as a vehicle for the treatment of complex themes. The tangible, devastating effects of these events often become one of the primary themes of such texts, but the exploration of wars and other great tragedies also allows the author to enter into a dialogue about any number of philosophical concerns: death and suffering, fate and free will, and the way in which we "see" or experience the world. In *Slaughterhouse-Five,* Vonnegut uses the backdrop of World War II and the firebombing of Dresden to create a dialogue about each of these topics and related subjects such as mental illness, love, time, and memory. Since many of these themes are common to literature, your essay should consider how Vonnegut's choice of characters, imagery and symbolism, form, and plot allow for a unique presentation and treatment of these themes. Your paper should explore how Vonnegut's message—and the means by which he delivers this message—contributes something new to an ongoing dialogue about these topics.

Sample Topics:

1. **Death:** Evaluate the treatment of death in *Slaughterhouse-Five*. Does the text suggest how one should think of death and respond to the death of others?

    There are an overwhelming number of examples of death in the book, and many are unrelated to the war. Begin by considering all examples of death in the novel. What causes these deaths? Were they preventable? What do the persistent repetition and volume of deaths in the novel suggest? Is there any glory or redemption associated with death in the novel? How do the characters react to these deaths? Are grieving and mourning represented, for instance? How does the portrayal of death in the book compare to the portrayal of death in other works of literature? Consider the Tralfamadorian view of death. Does the book indicate whether adopting their view would be beneficial?

2. **The devastating effects of war:** What are the effects of war, and does the text present any evidence that there is some redeeming factor that makes this devastation necessary or worthwhile?

    As you write about this subject, consider not only the most obvious effects of war, such as injury, death, and destruction, but the less tangible and lingering effects. While the effect on the soldiers is important, how do the other characters seem to be impacted? Remember that you will need to explore not only the personal effect on specific characters but the cultural effect as well. As stated in the Reading to Write section above, it will be important not only to note what is observable in the text but what is absent. How, for instance, does the war seem to shape the characters' views of love and faith? Are the effects of war presented in *Slaughterhouse-Five* in line with the effects typically represented in literature and the media? Alternatively, does the text suggest any positive effects of war that counter this devastation? In order to answer this question, you will need to consider whether there are any examples of redemption, victory, or some greater good represented in the text. What does the conclusion of the novel suggest? Is there a happy ending or some clear resolution?

3. **Vision and ways of seeing:** *Slaughterhouse-Five* contains many literal and figurative references to sight. Explore vision and ways of seeing as major themes of the text.

Begin by thinking broadly about the word *sight*. How does the text treat sight extending beyond physical sight with one's eyes? How does vision become a metaphor for ways of understanding? It may be helpful to start by considering the most obvious symbolic representation of sight in the novel: Billy's profession as optometrist. Next, you might consider the relationship between Billy's profession and related issues such as memory, perspective, insight, introspection, understanding, point of view, and truth—all variations of ways of seeing. How does the form of the story correspond to this theme? For example, think about how narration and metafiction create a sense of introspection or how the nonlinear narrative, which oscillates between past and present, creates a metaphor for remembering the past and anticipating the future. Consider the application of elements of science fiction in the story. How do Kilgore Trout's ideas and the views of the aliens from Tralfamadore suggest alternative or foreign ways of seeing and understanding? How does Billy try to change the way that people "see," philosophically speaking? Is he successful? Ultimately, your essay should explain what message the book ultimately presents about sight or ways of seeing. Does it propose some correct way of seeing? Are there any characters, for instance, who seem to possess a correct or dominant point of view, or does the book indicate that there is no single, correct way of seeing? How does the novel itself change the way that we "see" or view specific subjects such as war, religion, time, and death?

Character

Slaughterhouse-Five contains a very interesting and diverse cast of characters, from the science fiction writer Kilgore Trout to the pathetic and clownish Billy Pilgrim and the motley assortment of soldiers. Vonnegut even incorporates himself as a character in the story. It may be helpful, initially, to think about these characters collectively. Are the characters very similar, or is there great variety among them? Do they represent contrasting points of view? What do they share in common? Once you have familiarized yourself with the general characterization, you might choose to focus on a refined element such as the symbolism of one of the professions of Billy Pilgrim or a more general feature of characterization such as the depiction of the soldier in the novel or the use of the tragicomic figure in *Slaughterhouse-Five*. No matter which character or characters you choose to write about, you will need to carefully consider how they are described, make note of their dialogue and actions, and observe how they relate to and respond to the other characters. Think, also, about the feelings they evoke from you as a reader and consider why the author may have been trying to elicit this response.

Sample Topics:

1. **Billy Pilgrim:** Analyze this character.

   Most of the text is devoted to Billy Pilgrim and his experiences before, during, and after the war, although not in that order. Note descriptions of Billy, including his clothing, appearance, and attitude. What language does Vonnegut use to describe him? Consider the many roles of this character: soldier, veteran, optometrist, chaplain's assistant, husband, and father. Is his treatment as a soldier and as a protagonist traditional or unexpected? Is there anything heroic about Billy? How is he treated by the other characters? Can we determine whether or not Billy is mentally ill? What is the significance of Billy's name? Why would Vonnegut have chosen the surname "Pilgrim"? How does Billy function as a pilgrim, and how does he represent some cultural sentiment or reference some philosophical or existential quest or pilgrimage?

2. **The soldier:** Analyze representations of the soldier in the novel. How does the portrait of the soldiers in *Slaughterhouse-Five* shape our understanding of two key themes: the effects of war and the recollection and representation of war?

Consider all representations of soldiers in the story, including Billy and the U. S. soldiers, the German soldiers, and the British soldiers. Observe details such as their age, clothing, and character. How does Vonnegut describe them? What do they have in common? Are they well trained and prepared for war? How do they treat one another? Do they triumph over their adversaries? What kind of view of war do they embody— glorified, tragic, absurd, realistic? Most importantly, you will need to explain why Vonnegut would have wished to create such a view of the soldier by showing how the characterization of the soldier corresponds to his overall treatment of war. How does the presentation of the soldiers relate to Vonnegut's pledge to Mary O'Hare in chapter 1?

3. **Valencia and Lily:** Two minor characters of note are Billy Pilgrim's wife, Valencia, and Rumfoord's companion, Lily. How are these two characters alike, and why are they significant?

Because Valencia and Lily appear minimally in the novel, you will be evaluating the symbolic relevance of these characters. How are they described? What do they have to say? What do they represent, and what response do they evoke from readers? The hospital scenes and the honeymoon flashbacks will be the most important scenes for exploration. Are these characters allegorical figures, representing some pervasive cultural sentiment? Do they suggest anything about what is significant and of value in postwar, modern living? Consider their views on love and war. Do they necessarily represent a "female" view of love and war? How, for instance, do they compare to other female characters in the story such as Bernard O'Hare's wife, Mary?

History and Context

Despite the stunning magnitude of its destruction (akin to the devastation caused by the bombings of Hiroshima and Nagasaki), the firebombing of Dresden was a relatively unknown event at the time of the initial publication of *Slaughterhouse-Five*. An interesting topic for exposition, then, is the treatment of this subject in the book, considering how it is portrayed and what role the novel played in increasing awareness and shaping public perception of this event. Tackling this subject means evaluating the complex relationships between fact and fiction, literature and historical testament. If you choose to write about this subject, your paper should consider accuracy, but it should also thoroughly explore point of view.

Another idea is to consider the book from a broad, cultural perspective, analyzing *Slaughterhouse-Five* as a portrait of the postwar modern condition. In other words, you will be determining whether the text reflects some pervasive changes in living caused by the war. This could be accomplished through an evaluation of character, symbolism, and form and will require a look at representations of love, family, faith, and physical and mental health in the book.

Finally, keep in mind that when an author addresses a historical event, he or she does so because of a belief that it will have some resonance with contemporary readers and allow them to create a dialogue about timely themes. Accordingly, one of the most interesting elements of *Slaughterhouse-Five* is the link between past and present. The book opens with a passage that takes place within a contemporary time frame. It reflects on the past but suggests concern for how we will talk about and respond to war and major cultural or political events in the future. Vonnegut also employs a nonlinear format that whisks Billy—and readers—back and forth between past and present and incorporates references to more recent cultural and political events such as the race riots, the assassinations of Martin Luther King Jr. and Robert Kennedy, and the Vietnam War. This last subject in particular could make an excellent essay topic. The timing of the book's creation and publication suggests that Vonnegut did not write about the bombing of Dresden only to purge himself of the memories of a tragedy. At the time of the book's initial publication, the United States was enmeshed in the Vietnam War, one of the most highly contested conflicts in the nation's history, and Vonnegut includes many references to this conflict in the text. Therefore, you might consider what message the text bears about this subject in particular. Continuing along this line of thought, no matter which historical subject you choose to write about, your essay should demonstrate what message the book has for readers today, revealing how the text speaks about our own political and cultural landscape.

Sample Topics:

1. **The firebombing of Dresden:** Evaluate the treatment of the firebombing of Dresden in the text.

Begin by exploring how this event is represented in the text. How would you characterize Vonnegut's portrayal of this event? Is it realistic, tragic, or absurd? How do you feel after reading the text, and how does Vonnegut elicit this response? Consider how elements such as form, genre, and characterization contribute to this portrait. What is the effect of a fictionalized representation of a lesser-known historical event? Does the knowledge that the text is semiautobiographical change your perception of the text? Consider issues of accuracy and authenticity. Does the book provide an accurate representation of the bombing of Dresden? How significant or insignificant do you believe this is in light of the fictional nature of the book?

2. **The Vietnam War:** Is *Slaughterhouse-Five* best characterized as a World War II novel, or is it better characterized as a novel about the Vietnam War?

Because the book focuses on the bombing of Dresden during World War II, you will need to establish how the Vietnam War becomes a key subject of the text. Discuss the timing of the book's publication, and explore the correlation between representations of World War II in the text and the Vietnam War. You should consider all literal references to the Vietnam War in the text, as well as the general treatment of war and related subjects. For instance, what does the book tell readers about the effects of war? How does it depict the soldier? Does Vonnegut seem to think that war is necessary? What elements of the text reveal this to us? Your paper should explain whether or not the book was representative of popular sentiment about the Vietnam War. Consider, for example, the passages where Vonnegut refers to his book as an antiwar novel and his assertion that he might as well have written an antiglacier novel. How do these sentiments reflect public frustrations with policy surrounding the Vietnam War? Is *Slaughterhouse-Five* successful as a work of protest or an antiwar novel? You might answer this question by exploring how the novel compares to some other examples of protest or antiwar literature of the period. Do you believe that Vonnegut's book is more successful or memorable than other antiwar novels or other means of protest? If so, what elements make it effective and memorable?

3. **The postwar, modern condition in the United States:** Analyze the book as a portrait of the postwar, modern condition.

The cultural impact of war and the effect of this war on postwar living were popular subjects in literature following World War II. Begin by explaining what characterizes the postwar, modern condition. How did life change for Americans following World War II? Consider topics such as love and romance, family, faith, and mental and physical health. This calls for a consideration of the effects of war, but you should also explore the symbolic nature of the work. The primary focus will probably be on characterization, considering how the characters become representatives of this new mode of living. How do the characters live? How do they relate to one another, and what do they seem to value? Think about other symbols and metaphors in the book. How do the imagery, language, and form contribute to a portrait of postwar living? Explain how these elements not only present a picture of postwar living but how they provoke a particular emotional response from readers. Why would Vonnegut be trying to elicit this response?

Philosophy and Ideas

In *Slaughterhouse-Five,* Vonnegut uses representations of a large-scale historical event and a fictionalized account of his own personal experiences to initiate a dialogue about perception and the human experience, challenging our most basic presumptions about life—the way that we think about our own mortality and react to the death of others, our sense of time, and our most fundamental ways of seeing and understanding. The work also addresses topics such as fate, free will, futility, and fatalism through the weary chaplain's assistant Billy Pilgrim and a cast of supporting characters. Meanwhile, the book's references to Christianity raise interesting questions about faith, ritual, and the usefulness of religion in modern times. In order to write about these topics, you will need to first identify how these intangible ideas become "visible" in the text, considering elements such as dialogue, symbolism and imagery, characterization, and form. For instance, think about Vonnegut's employment of elements of science fiction to present an "alien" point of view with respect to these topics. Keep in mind that the tone of the book, shaped by black humor, irony, and elements of fantasy, demands a careful, close reading of the text. The ultimate message of the book has been disputed by scholars and critics, and this dispute might even be adopted as the subject of your paper as long as your argument is grounded in evidence from the text itself.

Sample Topics:

1. **Futility:** Explore the relationship between *Slaughterhouse-Five* and the philosophy of futility. Is the book essentially a defeatist text that promulgates this philosophy?

   Begin by exploring futility, both as a general concept and as a philosophy surfacing during a period of postwar American industrialism. It will be helpful to consult Paul Nystrom's *Economics of Fashion.* What are the origins of this philosophy, and how is it characterized? Next, note where readers find this philosophy represented in *Slaughterhouse-Five.* How does the text suggest that the philosophy of futility is still applicable, even so many decades after Nystrom coined the term? What characters seem to embody this philosophy? Many scholars have suggested that the repetition of the phrase "So it goes" and the bird call are symbolic of futility, while others have interpreted them as symbols of the cyclical nature of things. What does the text ultimately indicate? If you believe that the book does promulgate the philosophy of futility, be sure to consider whether the book employs any other literary devices that would undermine such a reading. For example, does the story possess any moral or message, or does it suggest that resignation is our only option? While Vonnegut says that the book is jumbled and jangled because there's nothing intelligent to say about war, he has written the book. Does the action of writing the book counter the notion of futility, or not necessarily?

2. **Fatalism:** Is *Slaughterhouse-Five* a fatalistic text, or does the story indicate that we have control over our own fate?

This will be a consideration of fate and free will in the text, which will call, primarily, for a study of character and plot but which should also lead into a consideration of elements of genre and form. Are the fates of the characters decided for them, or are they able to maintain some control over their respective fates? Consider the alien notion that only on Earth is there talk of free will and the taxi cab driver's notion of the accidental. Why might Vonnegut choose to employ, in particular, elements of science fiction to create a dialogue on this subject? If the characters are not in control of their own fates, are they able to control anything else? For instance, how does Vonnegut create a dialogue about resolve, memory, understanding, and point of view?

3. **Faith and religion:** Analyze the treatment of religion and faith in the text.

Begin by considering all representations of religion in the novel, including all references to Christianity. Does the book seem to promote a definitive view of religion or Christianity in particular? For example, does religion seem to be useful or a source of hope, or is it depicted as defunct in light of modern conditions? Think about Billy's role as chaplain's assistant and the fate of the chaplain's assistant before him. Do readers find any representations of faith and hope in the novel? How does the treatment of religion in the story correspond to Friedrich Nietzsche's idea that "God is dead" and other trends in philosophy around the time of the book's publication? Collectively, what view of religion does the story promote? Does the book indicate what the role of faith and religion is in the modern world? Does the text suggest anything that might effectively replace traditional religion? How, for instance, do the ideas in the book tie in with Vonnegut's interest in humanism?

Form and Genre

Considering that the most visible subject of the book is war, the distinctive genre of *Slaughterhouse-Five*—an unconventional hybrid of history and science fiction—begs a closer look. While works of science fiction and fantasy typically depict interplanetary or fictitious wars, in *Slaughterhouse-Five*, Vonnegut uses elements of science fiction to treat a wide range of themes and present a foreign or "alien" point of view on these subjects. Alternatively, you might evaluate the text as historical testament, as antiwar novel or protest literature, or as a semiautobiographical work. Considering the work as an example of modern tragedy or tragicomedy can also work well. The form of *Slaughterhouse-Five* is also a subject with great potential for exploration. You might write about the purpose and impact of certain elements of form such as metafiction, nonlinear narrative, and repetition, or you might evaluate those elements of the story that call to mind children's literature, illuminating the relationship of these elements to the book's major themes. Yet another interesting topic for consideration is the architecture of the story—not only the organization and order of the story, but whether or not the story adopts a classic rising action/falling action/resolution format. In the first chapter, Vonnegut tells O'Hare that the execution of Edgar Derby will serve as the climax of the novel, but is this event the true climax of the story?

If not, your paper might explore the true climax of the story or explain the significance of the absence of a traditional climax, if you believe that Vonnegut deliberately omitted one.

Sample Topics:

1. **Science fiction in *Slaughterhouse-Five:*** Evaluate the use of elements of science fiction in the novel. Why has Vonnegut injected elements of fantasy into a book about a real historical event?

   Given that the major subject of the story is the firebombing of Dresden during World War II, the use of elements of science fiction in the novel is shocking. What elements allow us to characterize a work as science fiction, and where do readers find these elements in *Slaughterhouse-Five*? Consider elements of form such as order, narration, and metafiction, including their relationship to the treatment of topics such as time, death, and free will. What does the science fiction writer Kilgore Trout represent? Why does Vonnegut include Kilgore Trout in close proximity to the scenes about mental illness and recovery? Consider the views of the aliens from Tralfamadore. How do they serve as a symbol of that which is "alien" or foreign to us? How might our reading of the text be different if these elements were absent and Vonnegut presented a purely realistic story?

2. **The form of *Slaughterhouse-Five:*** Analyze the form of the book. How does the form of the book expose the key themes of the text?

   You will need to consider the overall form of the book as well as the individual components of the work's form. Think about the order—or disorder—of the story. Look at the details of the construction of the story, such as metafiction, narration, and the architecture of each chapter. Why has Vonnegut chosen to employ short sentence structure and repetition? How do these elements correspond to the major themes of the work?

Is there one major story line or more than one? How does the subject of the bombing of Dresden act as an anchor or lend organization to the form of the book? Think about the opening of the novel and the conclusion. Does the story have an identifiable rising and falling action and resolution? Why is this significant?

3 **Metafiction:** How does Vonnegut's use of metafiction shape reader response to the story?

Consider the scenes where Vonnegut creates a self-conscious reflection on the text and the places where he inserts himself as a character in the story. What effect do these passages have? Does the use of metafiction foster or destroy any sense of suspense? How does metafiction create a link between past and present rather than allowing the text to loom in the past? Consider the relationship of metafiction to theme. How does metafiction reflect autobiographical concerns and create a sense of introspection, intimacy, and self-conscious reflection that mirrors the major concerns of the work? Finally, it may be helpful to consider how your interpretation of the text would be different if Vonnegut did not utilize metafiction.

Language, Symbols, and Imagery

The language of *Slaughterhouse-Five* is simple and direct, but it is also deliberate and powerful. Therefore, an evaluation of the language in *Slaughterhouse-Five* can easily serve as the basis of an engaging paper. Consider word choice and meaning and even order and arrangement. The simplicity and repetition of the language, for instance, evokes a childlike quality that corresponds to the motif of the Children's Crusade and the major themes of the text, while the use of profanity and vulgarity creates a greater sense of realism as Vonnegut treats gruesome topics such as war and death. The imagery in the book is equally striking, and so you might also discuss the role that imagery plays in shaping reader response, explaining how it contributes to our understanding of the book's primary themes. Whether you choose to write about language or imagery, you should be trying to determine why Vonnegut made the choices he did. Your paper should illuminate what the words and images evoke and, ultimately, explain how this corresponds to the major themes of the text. Another option is to consider the symbols found in the story. The title points the way to two of the major symbols of the text—the slaughterhouse and the Children's Crusade. Because these seem to be simple—even factual—historical references, their symbolic application might be overlooked, but these two symbols are central to the text. You will need to do more than look for direct references to these symbols in the story. Although this will be a good way to begin, you should consider not only what these symbols represent but also how they introduce certain motifs or dominant patterns of symbolism and metaphor in the text. Ultimately, your paper should explain how these symbols shape and influence our response to the story and what the key symbols and motifs reveal about the major themes of the text.

Sample Topics:

1. **The slaughterhouse:** Evaluate the slaughterhouse as symbol.

   As a prisoner of war, Kurt Vonnegut really was incarcerated in a slaughterhouse, and in the novel, Billy Pilgrim and his fellow soldiers are also incarcerated in one, but how does the slaughterhouse also function symbolically within the novel? For example, what do we associate with a slaughterhouse? How does it create a sense of doom, serve as a reminder of death, and recall animals? Where else do these ideas appear in the text? For instance, consider how Vonnegut uses language and symbolism to liken the characters to animals. How does this direct a reader to think about what makes us human? What role do the British soldiers play in relation to this subject?

2. **The Children's Crusade:** Analyze the motif of the Children's Crusade in the text.

   In chapter 1, Vonnegut introduces the idea of the Children's Crusade, explaining to readers how he came to choose the subtitle of the book. Consider all of the places where Vonnegut references the Children's Crusade in the text. Vonnegut incorporates quotations about this subject from certain reference works in the first chapter. What do these passages reveal about this motif and, more specifically, the subject of war? Consider other representations of children or that which is childlike in the book. Think about Billy's flashbacks to childhood, the outlining of the novel in crayon, the language and construction of sentences that make the book resemble a children's book, and the inclusion of songs and jokes. How does Billy's daughter contribute to the dialogue about this subject? Finally, your essay should explain how this motif shapes our understanding of the personal and cultural impact of war.

Comparison and Contrast Essays

Because Vonnegut struggled to write about the bombing of Dresden and his experiences as a prisoner of war for so many years, *Slaughterhouse-Five* has an innate connection to the works that preceded it, and this relationship can be a topic that you explore in greater depth. Specifically, you might compare representations of war and the soldier in *Slaughterhouse-Five, The Sirens of Titan,* and *Mother Night* or evaluate the fictional representation of history in *Slaughterhouse-Five* and *Mother Night,* explaining whether there is consistency among the texts or whether *Slaughterhouse-Five* evidences some development or shift. You might also isolate a particular feature or element of *Slaughterhouse-Five* and discuss it in relation to the work of another author. For example, you could compare language in *Slaughterhouse-Five* and the works of Ernest Hemingway or metafiction and genre in Vonnegut's novel and certain works by Norman Mailer. You could also compare *Slaughterhouse-Five* to older works, illuminating similarities that reveal some consistency or trend in literature. Vonnegut references the French writer Céline in *Slaughterhouse-Five.* An analysis of the connection between Céline and *Slaughterhouse-Five* could serve as the basis of an insightful essay.

As stated in the Reading to Write section, you do not need to limit your essay to an exploration of war. Thinking about characterization and genre, you could compare *Slaughterhouse-Five* to a work such as Arthur Miller's *Death of a Salesman,* writing about modern American tragedy. Observing another interesting element—the use of humor and the absurd—would allow you to compare *Slaughterhouse-Five* to some works by Shakespeare. Alternatively, you might choose to focus on one of the more challenging aspects of the book—its language, which comprises the vulgar and the profane—considering how Vonnegut's use of language compares to the use of provocative language in other notable works of literature such as Mark Twain's *The Adventures of Huckleberry Finn* or Norman Mailer's *The Naked and the Dead*.

Finally, because the form and genre of *Slaughterhouse-Five* are so unusual, a good approach would be to analyze the text as a postmodern work, discussing whether it reveals the necessity of an evolution of form in literature. Explore the link between developments in literary style and technique and historical and cultural context. You might consider how other authors have responded in similar fashion, considering various periods or movements in fiction and their characteristics. Rather than simply listing similarities or noting important differences between texts, your essay should illuminate what makes *Slaughterhouse-Five* groundbreaking, symbolic, or important.

Sample Topics:

1. **Depictions of postwar living:** Compare and contrast *Slaughterhouse-Five* with other works that address postwar life in the United States.

   Choose a few other texts that seem to create a dialogue about postwar living. The works of Ernest Hemingway and F. Scott Fitzgerald would work well, but there are many other options. How do these authors create a portrait of postwar life through characterization, symbolism, and imagery? Do they present a consistent view of postwar living? Do the works share similarities in form, and do they work within the same genres to accomplish this? How do the works evidence truths about love, relationships, family, faith, health, and mental illness in a postwar period? Finally, what makes Vonnegut's treatment of this subject stand out?

2. ***Slaughterhouse-Five* and postmodernism:** How does the postmodern form of *Slaughterhouse-Five* and other novels suggest the necessity of an evolution of form in literature?

Although there are many texts that you could write about, Joseph Heller's *Catch-22* and Thomas Pynchon's *Gravity's Rainbow* would work quite well. You might try to analyze no more than three or four texts so you are not overwhelmed and do not overwhelm your reader, although more texts might be generally referenced within your essay. Begin by introducing postmodernism, including its defining characteristics. Your essay should be an analysis of the relationship between the postmodern form of Vonnegut's book and its major themes. Therefore, you will need to analyze the structure of the text, including chapters and other divisions, order of events, metafiction, narration, and point of view. Also, look for examples of the use of black humor and irony, intertextuality, and pastiche of past styles. Finally, you will need to explain why previous literary forms would not have been as effective in the discussion of the contemporary themes these authors are treating. Provide examples of how this new, postmodern form is more effective.

3. **Céline and *Slaughterhouse-Five*:** Vonnegut references the French writer Céline directly in the novel. Explore the connection between Céline and *Slaughterhouse-Five*.

This will require some research that concentrates not only on the works that Céline authored, such as *Journey to the End of the Night,* but also on the author himself. Consider similarities in *Slaughterhouse-Five* and the texts of Céline, such as the portrayal of the soldier and the antihero and thematic concerns like death, suffering, time, and mental illness. What similarities do we find between Céline and Billy Pilgrim, and how are Céline and Vonnegut alike? Céline's works were characterized by a new slang and speech that readers of the period were not accustomed to. How does this compare to the reception of Vonnegut's language in *Slaughterhouse-Five*? Finally, research indicates that Céline produced anti-Semitic materials, so Vonnegut's motivation for including him in a book about World War II might also be addressed.

Bibliography and Resources for *Slaughterhouse-Five, or the Children's Crusade: A Duty-Dance with Death*

Addison, Paul and Jeremy A. Crang, eds. *Firestorm: The Bombing of Dresden, 1945.* Chicago: Ivan R. Dee, 2006.

Battle of the Bulge. American Experience. PBS. Retrieved 28 June 2011. <http://www.pbs.org/wgbh/amex/bulge/>.

Bloom, Harold, ed. *Bloom's Guides: Slaughterhouse-Five.* New York: Chelsea House-Infobase, 2007.

———. *Kurt Vonnegut's Slaughterhouse-Five.* Bloom's Modern Critical Interpretations. New York: Chelsea House-Infobase, 2009.

Boon, Kevin Alexander. "The Problem with Pilgrim in Kurt Vonnegut's *Slaughterhouse- Five.*" *Notes on Contemporary Literature* 56.2 (1996): 8–10.

Céline, Louis-Ferdinand. *Journey to the End of the Night.* New York: New Directions, 2006.

Chabot, C. Barry. "*Slaughterhouse-Five* and the Comforts of Indifference." *Essays in Literature* 8.1 (1981): 45–51.

Crichton, Michael. "*Slaughterhouse-Five.*" *The Critic as Artist: Essays on Books, 1920–1970.* New York: Liveright, 1972: 100–07.

Edelstein, Arnold. "*Slaughterhouse-Five:* Time Out of Joint." *College Literature* 1 (1974): 128–39.

Greiner, Donald J. "Vonnegut's *Slaughterhouse-Five* and the Fiction of Atrocity." *Critique* 14.3 (1973): 38–51.

Gros-Louis, Doloros K. "The Ironic Christ Figure in *Slaughterhouse-Five.*" *Biblical Images in Literature.* Nashville, TN: Abingdon, 1975: 161–75.

Heller, Joseph. *Catch-22.* New York: Simon & Schuster, 1999.

Isaacs, Neil D. "Unstuck in Time: *Clockwork Orange* and *Slaughterhouse-Five.*" *Literature/Film Quarterly* 1 (1973): 122–31.

Jarvis, Christina. "The Vietnamization of World War II in *Slaughterhouse-Five* and *Gravity's Rainbow.*" *War, Literature, and the Arts* 15.1–2 (2003): 95–117.

Kazin, Alfred. "The War Novel from Mailer to Vonnegut." *Saturday Review.* 6 February 1971: 13–15, 36.

Klinkowitz, Jerome. *Slaughterhouse-Five: Reforming the Novel and the World.* Twayne's Masterwork Studies. Boston: G. K. Hall, 1990.

Matheson, T.J. "This Lousy Little Book: The Genesis and Development of *Slaughterhouse-Five* as Revealed in Chapter One." *Studies in the Novel* 16.2 (Summer 1984): 228–40.

McGinnis, Wayne. "The Arbitrary Cycle of *Slaughterhouse-Five:* A Relation of Form to Theme." *Critique* 17.1 (1975): 55–68.

Merrill, Robert and Peter A. Scholl. "Vonnegut's *Slaughterhouse-Five:* The Requirements of Chaos." *Studies in American Fiction* 6 (1978): 65–76.

Mustazza, Leonard. "Tralfamadore and Milton's Eden." *Essays in Literature* 13.2 (1986): 299–312.

Nystrom, Paul. *Economics of Fashion.* New York: Ronald Press Co., 1928.

Pynchon, Thomas. *Gravity's Rainbow.* New York: Penguin, 1995.

Siebert, Detlef. "British Bombing Strategy in World War II." BBC History. Last updated 17 Feb 2011. Retrieved 1 May 2011. <http://www.bbc.co.uk/history/worldwars/wwtwo/area_bombing_01.shtml>.

Taylor, Frederick. *Dresden: Tuesday, February 13, 1945.* New York: Harper Perennial, 2005.

"Vietnam Online." PBS American Experience. Retrieved 1 May 2011. <http://www.pbs.org/wgbh/amex/vietnam/>.

Vonnegut, Kurt. *Slaughterhouse-Five or The Children's Crusade: A Duty Dance with Death.* New York: Dial, 2005.

BREAKFAST OF CHAMPIONS, OR GOODBYE BLUE MONDAY

READING TO WRITE

By eschewing traditional suspense-building tactics in the preface and initial chapters of *Breakfast of Champions,* Vonnegut constructs an opening to his story that functions as a veritable cheat sheet for readers, predicting the major themes of the text and disclosing key points of plot that reveal precisely what can be expected in the pages that follow. The opening line of the first chapter, for instance—"This is a tale of a meeting of two lonesome, skinny, fairly old white men on a planet which was dying fast" (7)—tells readers that *Breakfast* will be a tale about the convergence of Dwayne Hoover and Kilgore Trout as well as the fragile state of the planet they inhabit. While not fully comprehensive (the story is as much about Vonnegut himself and the state of American culture as it is about the two men and the physical condition of the planet), it offers three subjects that might be utilized as starting points for analysis: the men, their meeting, and the state of the planet. Accordingly, these subjects should inspire at least three initial questions that can be used to generate ideas for a paper topic and, more specifically, to begin constructing a thesis: Who are the two men? What happens when they meet? Why is the planet "dying fast"? A writer who was struck by the narrator's characterization of the state of the planet and who wished to adopt this as the subject of his or her paper would look for all information about the condition of the planet in the text, including possible causes, the impact of this problem, and whether or not the book suggests any solutions or remedies. This would call for an evaluation, first, of the visual language employed in the text—imagery, symbolism, and illustrations—and, second, of the characters, who provide evidence of the effects of this problem on humankind. A writer who chooses instead to focus on the two men and their meeting could conduct an analysis of character and plot, beginning by making note of all passages in the text that relate to these two characters and their intersection. For instance, immediately following the opening line cited above, Vonnegut begins to describe the two men and to reveal details of the circumstances surrounding their meeting:

> One of [the men] was a science-fiction writer named Kilgore Trout. He was a nobody at the time, and he supposed his life was over. He was mistaken . . . He became one of the most beloved and respected human beings in history.
>
> The man he met was an automobile dealer . . . named Dwayne Hoover. Dwayne Hoover was on the brink of going insane. (7)
>
> Dwayne Hoover was fabulously well-to-do when he met Kilgore Trout. . . .
>
> And here's how much of the planet Kilgore Trout owned in those days: doodley-squat.
>
> And Kilgore Trout and Dwayne Hoover met in Midland City, which was Dwayne's home town, during an Arts Festival there in autumn of 1972.
>
> As has already been said: Dwayne was a Pontiac dealer who was going insane.
>
> Dwayne's incipient insanity was mainly a matter of chemicals, of course. Dwayne Hoover's body was manufacturing certain chemicals which unbalanced his mind. But Dwayne, like all novice lunatics, needed some bad ideas, too, so that his craziness could have shape and direction. . . .
>
> The bad ideas were delivered to Dwayne by Kilgore Trout.
> . . . .
> Here was the core of the bad ideas which Trout gave to Dwayne: Everybody on Earth was a robot, with one exception—Dwayne Hoover.

> Of all the creatures in the Universe, only Dwayne was thinking and
> feeling and worrying and planning and so on. . . .
> Only Dwayne Hoover had free will. . . .
> Trout did not expect to be believed. . . .
>
> . . . .
>
> But it was mind poison to Dwayne. (13–15)

At the conclusion of this passage, readers have been informed that Trout
is a poor, unknown science fiction writer who was later highly regarded,
while Hoover is a rich car salesman on the brink of insanity. Readers
have also been informed that Hoover will be tragically affected by Trout's
idea that everyone is a machine except Hoover. With this information in
mind, the next task would be to identify the significance of these details
by uncovering the link among character, plot, and theme. This could be
accomplished by looking for related patterns of words, symbols, imagery, and ideas in other passages of the book. Kilgore Trout, for instance,
is one of several writers in the story, while Dwayne Hoover is one of
many characters who exhibit symptoms of mental illness. Together the
repeated examples of writers and the mentally ill in the text form a pattern or motif that tells readers to take note. While either of these motifs
might effectively serve as the topic of a paper, when they are considered
in combination with the details of plot revealed in this passage—the two
characters converge at an arts festival and Hoover has a strange reaction
to the ideas in one of Trout's books—they reveal a key theme of the novel:
the powerful influence of art and ideas. The relationship among the three
subjects could, therefore, serve as the basis for a dynamic and engaging paper that expounds upon the effect of art and literature on both its
creator (through an analysis of Trout and Vonnegut) and its audience
(citing Trout's effect on Hoover; Rabo Karabekian's effect on Vonnegut;
and, finally, the effect of *Breakfast of Champions* on its readership). Of
course, these are only a few ideas resulting from a preliminary analysis of
the early passages of the opening chapter; an analysis of any passage will
typically yield many different ideas for exposition. For example, an evaluation of character and plot in the same passages cited above could lead
to a paper that explores what the book has to say about wealth, science
fiction, what it means to be human, or control and free will. Remember:
As the examples herein demonstrate, an analysis of characterization and

plot can serve as an excellent starting place, but a consideration of elements such as symbolism, imagery, language, and form can offer equal insight into the meaning of the story. Keep in mind that a paper that closely aligns itself with the text, evaluating Vonnegut's choices—his methods for disseminating information—will be much more successful than a paper that simply tells readers what the author is saying about a particular subject without showing them how he has accomplished this.

Just as the form of *Breakfast of Champions* provides a significant benefit to readers and writers, it also presents a major challenge: namely, processing the immense jumble of parts that make up the story. At the time of its initial publication, Vonnegut's novel met with a mixed critical reception due in large part to the disorderly, congested form of the book. *Breakfast of Champions* claimed not one, but three major characters (Kilgore Trout, Dwayne Hoover, and Vonnegut himself). It incorporated a diverse cast of supporting characters, many of whom were recycled from Vonnegut's previous works. The overlapping plotlines pertaining to Hoover and Trout were interrupted frequently, not only by accounts of Trout's strange science fiction tales but also by Vonnegut's own appearances as character. The story was translated to readers through a dense visual language composed of a dizzying array of images and symbols, including basic line illustrations of anatomy, animals, flags, and other symbols of American culture and life on Earth. Furthermore, Vonnegut packed the tale with a stunning number of historical references (addressing the settlement of the United States, slavery, industrialism, the auto age, communism, and the Great Depression, to name a few) and treated a staggering range of thematic topics including violence, prejudice, hypocrisy, mental illness, the effects of consumerism, dehumanization, sexuality, pornography, culture, pollution, the powerful influence of ideas, free will, liberation, and more. After completing an initial pass of the text, one idea would be to perform a second reading that evaluates one of the elements that contributes to this form. For example, a writer might prepare a paper that answers one of the following questions: Why are there three main characters rather than one? What is the purpose and effect of recycling characters? What does an analysis of the visual language of the book—including its imagery, symbolism, and language—reveal? What kind of portrait of the United States is exposed via the numerous historical references in the text? What insights does the book offer into philosophical subjects such as chaos and order and how does Vonnegut accomplish this? Alternatively, a writer might perform a reading and create an essay that considers how these elements function collectively—for example, how they allow the novel to function as a critical commentary about the state of American culture and living. In this case, a writer would begin by looking for any information in the text that tells readers what Vonnegut thinks about American culture and living, focusing on examples of imagery, symbolism, and language or details of characterization and plot that evidence a critical stance on these subjects. In the preface, for example, readers find an important initial confession from Vonnegut: "I have no culture, no humane harmony in my brains. I can't live without a culture anymore" (5). The author goes on to use his recollections of the deceased widow Phoebe Hurty to introduce his concern that something has been lost, has died, or has become defunct in the contemporary United States:

> The person to whom this book is dedicated, Phoebe Hurty, is no longer among the living, as they say. She was an Indianapolis widow when I met her late in the Great Depression. I was sixteen or so. She was about forty.
>
> She was rich, but had gone to work every weekday of her adult life, so she went on doing that. She wrote a sane and funny advice-to-the-lovelorn column for the Indianapolis *Times,* a good paper which is now defunct.
>
> Defunct.
>
> . . . .
>
> She would talk bawdily to me and her sons, and to our girlfriends when we brought them around. She was funny. She was liberating. She taught us to be impolite in conversations not only about sexual matters, but about American history and famous heroes, about the distribution of wealth, about school, about everything.
>
> I now make my living by being impolite. I am clumsy at it. I keep trying to imitate the politeness which was so graceful in Phoebe Hurty. . . . She believed what so many Americans believed then: that the nation would be happy and just and rational when prosperity came.

> I never hear that word anymore: *Prosperity.* It used to be a synonym
> for *Paradise.* And Phoebe Hurty was able to believe that the impoliteness
> she recommended would give shape to an American paradise.
>
> Now her sort of impoliteness is fashionable. But nobody believes any-
> more in a new American paradise. I sure miss Phoebe Hurty. (1–2)

Vonnegut also uses his remembrance of Hurty's "impoliteness" to
introduce the idea of critical commentary. In the chapters that follow,
Vonnegut begins to establish his own critical commentary, presenting
an unapologetic look at basic elements of American culture, including
famous symbols and national history:

> Trout and Hoover were citizens of the United States of America, a coun-
> try which was called America for short.
>
> . . . .
>
> The undippable flag was a beauty, and the anthem and the vacant
> motto might not have mattered much, if it weren't for this: a lot of citi-
> zens were so ignored and cheated and insulted that they thought they
> might be in the wrong country, or even on the wrong planet, that some
> terrible mistake had been made. . . .
>
> If they studied their paper money for clues as to what their country
> was all about, they found, among a lot of other baroque trash, a picture
> of a truncated pyramid with a radiant eye on top of it. . . .
>
> A lot of the nonsense was the innocent result of playfulness on the
> part of the founding fathers of the nation of Dwayne Hoover and Kilgore
> Trout. . . .
>
> But some of the nonsense was evil, since it concealed great crimes.
> For example, teachers of children in the United States of America wrote
> [1492] on blackboards again and again, and asked children to memorize
> it with pride and joy. . . .
>
> The teachers told the children that this was when their continent was
> discovered by human beings. Actually, millions of human beings were
> already living full and imaginative lives on the continent in 1492. That was
> simply the year in which sea pirates began to cheat and rob and kill them.
> (7–10)

From here, a writer could perform a close reading of other passages, looking for additional places where Vonnegut expounds upon American culture and living. The imagery in the book, for instance—which includes a landscape decimated by industrialism, dominated by trucks and tourist traps, and littered with advertising—creates a visual portrait of a polluted and cultureless place, while the treatment of topics such as slavery, violence and crime, prostitution and pornography, adultery, violence, and hypocrisy generate a portrait of a country that is being destroyed not only physically but culturally. Such a paper should also consider how elements such as narration and form contribute to this dialogue, while characterization and plot could be analyzed for information about the causes and effects of living in an endangered, cultureless state. At this point a writer would have sufficient evidence to make a claim about what Vonnegut is saying about American culture and living. This claim would be the thesis, while the evidence gathered would be used to construct an argument that supports this claim and lends power to the thesis.

Finally, when a book can be identified as a work of satire or a critical cultural commentary, it is imperative to consider context. A consideration of context will enhance your comprehension of the story and can also uncover ideas for a paper that reveals fresh insights about a text. This could mean evaluating the historical or cultural context of the book by researching what was happening politically or culturally at the time the book was written and published, or it can mean considering the book within its literary context, exploring how the book evidences some development, evolution, or progress in the author's work; how it relates to or stands out from other works of the same genre or period; or how it influenced writers of a later generation. In interviews, Vonnegut revealed that *Breakfast of Champions* had its genesis in one of his earlier and most popular novels, *Slaughterhouse-Five,* and so, an analysis of the relationship between these two works could serve as the basis for an engaging paper. *Breakfast* could also effectively be compared more broadly to all of Vonnegut's previous works. While a comparison with previous works is a good option for any text that comes later in an author's career, *Breakfast* provides a particularly unique vantage point: Vonnegut incorporates himself as a character and his struggle with the writing process, including his evolution as a writer, becomes a primary story line in the text. A writer comparing *Breakfast* to Vonnegut's previous works would, therefore, consider patterns in characterization, recurring themes, and similar applications of elements of genre and form, but he or she would also explore the significance of Vonnegut as a character in *Breakfast* and evaluate the meaning of some of the stranger elements of the book, such as the author's decision to set his characters free at the story's conclusion. If you do choose to write about literary context, your paper should not simply list likenesses between *Breakfast* and the other texts. It should ultimately reveal how *Breakfast* marks some important change or development in Vonnegut's work, or—if you are considering how *Breakfast* compares to texts written by other authors—how it evidences an important pattern or shift in literary trends.

TOPICS AND STRATEGIES

In the sections that follow, you will find a variety of suggested topics accompanied by questions and observations to assist you in the task of writing successfully about *Breakfast of Champions.* Remember that it is not a comprehensive list, and the statements and questions that appear after each suggested topic are merely a guide to help spark your own ideas about the work. A successful paper will present a strong thesis based upon your own original ideas and will be supported by relevant examples resulting from close readings of the text. A wide variety of interpretations will be possible as you consider each topic. Use the strategic questions and observations to stimulate your own thoughts about the text and to assist you in developing your thesis. Remember to read through the text more than once, making note of those elements that support your argument. It will be equally important to make note of those elements that contradict your thesis, as this will help you to refine your argument and present a stronger case.

Themes

The formal elements of *Breakfast of Champions* create a sense of disorder and chaos rather than order, but key themes function like anchors, providing central ideas that each piece of the text corresponds to. Although there are many subjects that help to unify the text, a few major themes stand out, namely, mental illness, the powerful influence of ideas, the defunct notion of prosperity, and pollution. While the narrator often presents direct information about these topics, you should consider how these themes are revealed in characterization and plot and how imagery, symbolism, and form also contribute to a dialogue about these subjects. A strong paper should tell readers what Vonnegut has to say about a particular topic, but it should also investigate the methods that the author uses to relay this message, explaining the significance of both the message and the means by which this message is revealed.

Sample Topics:

1. **The defunct notion of prosperity:** What message does the book present about the defunct notion of prosperity in the United States?

   Vonnegut introduces the idea of the defunct notion of prosperity in the preface through his recollections of Phoebe Hurty (a character who receives the book's dedication but who does not appear in the story). Therefore, your paper should explore Vonnegut's motivations for opening the book with these recollections and illuminate the relationship of these passages to the rest of the book. You may wish to begin by defining prosperity, giving consideration to historical context. Think about the relationship, for instance, between prosperity and postwar, post-Depression living, including the industrialism and consumerism in the United States. Where is an absence of prosperity represented in the text? How is the defunct notion of prosperity related to Vonnegut's observations about an absence of culture? Remember to consider not only where this concept appears literally in the text but how it is presented metaphorically through symbolism, imagery, characterization, and details of plot. What does the defunct nature of prosperity suggest about cultural changes in the United States? How are the characters affected? Dwayne Hoover is prosperous and runs a successful business; is this enough to make him happy?

2. **Mental illness:** What does the book have to say about mental illness? Are its causes revealed, and does the story suggest any remedy?

Analyze characters such as Dwayne Hoover and Vonnegut himself, and evaluate references to other characters who suffer from mental illness, such as Hoover's wife and Vonnegut's mother. Are there other characters who are also portrayed as suffering with mental health issues? Does the book indicate what is causing this? What does the prevalence of mental illness in the story suggest? Vonnegut explores mental illness from a biological standpoint in the text, but it may also be helpful to consider this topic from another perspective: Is Vonnegut also using mental illness metaphorically to represent a kind of widespread cultural illness? If so, what cultural factors are causing this? Does the novel suggest any remedy? For instance, do any of the characters recover? What do the ideas of Kilgore Trout add to a dialogue on this subject? As a character in his own work, what does Vonnegut contribute to this dialogue?

3. **Pollution:** What kind of commentary does the novel present about pollution?

It may be most helpful to start with an analysis of the imagery presented in the text, including the descriptions of the American landscape, Midland City, and the places that Trout experiences on his way to the arts festival. Look for other references to the destruction of the natural such as the extinction of the Bermuda erns and the damage to Sacred Miracle Cave. How do the stories of Kilgore Trout tie in with this subject? Explore the link between consumerism, industrialism, and pollution. You might also think about how Vonnegut uses pollution as a metaphor for the corruption of the human experience. Consider pollution in the form of bad ideas, pornography, hypocrisy, prejudice, and false pursuits. No matter which approach you take, it will be necessary to consider cause and effect. What causes either kind of pollution and where do readers find evidence of its effects in the story? It may be interesting to explore whether these two kinds of pollution are related.

Is there any indication that either form of pollution can be avoided or reversed?

4. **The powerful influence of ideas:** What message does *Breakfast of Champions* present about the powerful influence of ideas?

A writer might choose to focus on either the positive effect or the negative effect of ideas or to construct a paper that explores both. What examples of the influence of ideas do readers find in the text? Explore the relationships between the characters and note how they influence one another. Consider the artists and writers represented in the text and their effect on other characters in the story. It will also be helpful to focus on Kilgore Trout—not only his influence on Dwayne Hoover, but his own notions about the power of ideas to influence and to heal. If you wish to focus your paper on the positive impact of ideas, you might consider representations in the book of the power of ideas to educate, to heal, and to improve humans' treatment of one another. If you choose to focus on the negative impact of ideas, you might explore the book's treatment of subjects such as obscenity, pornography, vulgarity, and racism.

Character

Any of the main characters of *Breakfast* can serve as the subject of an engaging paper, but the relationships between the characters also provide an interesting avenue for exposition. Consider not only the literal intersection of the characters in the text via dialogue and plot but also the way that the characters influence one another and the relationships between the ideas that each character embodies. Kilgore Trout and Dwayne Hoover, for instance, can be studied individually, but in the text their stories are ultimately intertwined and, therefore, it is quite profitable to study them as a pair. Another idea would be to write about the relationship between Kilgore, Dwayne, and Vonnegut, exploring how the two fictional characters represent different parts of Vonnegut himself. *Breakfast of Champions* also presents an interesting cast of minor characters for consideration. Again, you would need to establish how these supporting characters correspond to the major characters and explore the ideas they represent. For example, Vonnegut dedicates his story to Phoebe Hurty and writes about her in the preface, but she does not actually appear in the story. Therefore, you might write a paper that explores Vonnegut's reasons for including her and the relationship of this character to the story that follows. Several of the characters in *Breakfast* first appeared in Vonnegut's earlier stories, so another option is to write an essay that explores the significance of this recycling, culminating with an analysis of the conclusion of *Breakfast of Champions* that exposes the relevance of Vonnegut's act of setting his characters free. Finally, you might write a paper that identifies and evaluates a particular motif in characterization, showing how this motif creates a dialogue about a particular theme. For instance, you could explore man as machine, the mentally ill, tragic characters, writers and artists, or the characterization of African American characters, so long as your focus remains on illuminating the link between character and theme.

Sample Topics:

1. **Kilgore Trout and Dwayne Hoover:** What message is imparted through the pairing of these two characters?

   Vonnegut establishes a relationship between these two characters through the form of the text—individual story lines that alternate until they collide. Why is this pairing significant? You will need to consider details of characterization for each character separately first and then determine what the relationship is between the two. What do they share in common? Alternatively, what do their differences reveal? What themes does their pairing illuminate? Think of issues of wealth, health and mental illness, and perspective. Your paper should focus on the relationship of character to theme and should expose how the pairing of the characters reveals some message about a particular theme.

2. **Vonnegut as character:** Evaluate Vonnegut's role as a character in his own book.

At the start of the story, the narrator says that the book is about two men on a planet that was dying fast, but is this accurate? Consider all of the passages in which Vonnegut appears as a character, including the preface. How does his presence as a character alter your understanding of the text? How does Vonnegut relate to the other characters in his story? How is he like or unlike them? Are the characters representative of some elements of Vonnegut's character or nature? How, for instance, do Kilgore Trout and Dwayne Hoover correspond with Vonnegut? How does the inclusion of Vonnegut as a character create a self-conscious reflection on the writing process? Does this aspect of the text change the book's genre and, ultimately, inspire us to reconsider the way that we classify the book? How would the book be different if Vonnegut did not include himself as a character?

3. **Phoebe Hurty:** Explain the significance of this character.

Although Phoebe Hurty is not incorporated as a character in the body of the story, she is a key figure of the text. Analyze characterizations of her. How is she described or portrayed? Where else are these ideas represented in the text? Are the other characters like her? What does she represent? Why are details such as her status as a deceased person and as a former widow significant? You might spend some time writing about her role in establishing the critical tone of the book and instigating a dialogue about American culture, consumerism, and the defunct notion of prosperity.

4. **Man as machine:** Analyze the motif of man as machine in the text. What does Vonnegut ultimately conclude about the idea of man as machine?

This is a study of character but also of symbolism in the text. Consider Dwayne Hoover's reaction to Kilgore Trout's story and all other representations of man as machine in the text.

For instance, how does Vonnegut present the idea of man as machine in the preface? How does Vonnegut's discussion of the chemical nature of man contribute to this dialogue? Think about how this motif initiates a dialogue about dehumanization and what it means to be human. Does the story indicate what makes us human and separates us from machines? Does it suggest what may be the cause of dehumanization? How do the characters evidence the effects of treating man as machine? What does the story conclude? Can humans truly be likened to machines?

History and Context

The form of *Breakfast of Champions,* including its peculiar narrative style, establishes the text as a primer for an audience unfamiliar with the planet Earth and, more specifically, the United States we know. Accordingly, the book presents a survey of historical happenings and issues including wars and the Great Depression, consumer culture and industrialism, the auto industry, communism, and slavery. One idea is to write an essay that reveals what these references say about the world we inhabit when considered collectively. Refining further, another idea (as introduced in the Reading to Write section above) is to consider how these references present a critical portrait of the United States. Refining further still, a paper might explore the text's interpretation and representation of a particular period, event, or development in American history. This could be accomplished by choosing a specific topic such as consumerism and industrialism or slavery and prejudice and analyzing representations of it in the text. Even a seemingly minor detail, such as Vonnegut's reference in the preface to the change of Armistice Day to Veteran's Day, could become the starting place for an engaging paper. Since this change is referenced in more than one of Vonnegut's works, a writer could explore this detail as a piece of a more extensive commentary about tradition, changes in American culture, or the way that we remember and respond to war. As you write about these topics, consider not only what is said but what is shown. Look for emerging patterns in imagery, symbolism, and characterization. It will also be helpful to consider language, point of view, and tone. An analysis of Vonnegut's use of exaggeration, sarcasm, and the absurd, for example, speaks volumes about the author's thoughts on topics of historical and cultural significance.

Sample Topics:

1. **Portrait of the United States:** Explore *Breakfast of Champions* as a portrait of the United States. What kind of nation does this portrait reveal?

   This paper should start with a consideration of genre, which means that it will be necessary to identify the elements that allow readers to identify the work as a satire or cultural commentary. Therefore, you would be looking not only for the topics that the book treats in relation to the portrait of the United States but the tone Vonnegut uses in discussing these subjects. The story addresses a postwar, post-Depression period of industrialism and consumerism in the United States but also reaches further into the past to expose the hypocrisy and failings that have been prevalent since the initial founding of the country. The first chapter of the book will be particularly useful, as will the preface and dedication, although subsequent chapters also contribute greatly to this portrait. Consider the imagery and symbolism that Vonnegut employs and evaluate the characters, paying attention to their relationships and any indications about the quality of their lives. How are the characters, including Vonnegut himself, affected by the changes in American culture?

2. **Slavery and prejudice:** Evaluate the treatment of slavery and prejudice in the book. What statement does the text present on this subject?

   Consider all references to slavery and prejudice in the text. There are many literal references to these subjects, but you will also need to evaluate the overall treatment of African American characters throughout the book. What tone does Vonnegut use in the treatment of this subject and its corresponding characters? Does he present a realistic portrait or an absurd portrait? Is his treatment literal or tongue-in-cheek?

3. **Consumerism:** What message does the book seem to impart about consumerism and its effects?

Consider, first, how the text creates a portrait of an age of consumerism by evaluating symbolism, imagery, and language. Think about setting: not only Midland City, but the places that Kilgore Trout encounters as he travels to Midland City. What is the significance of Dwayne Hoover's profession? How do the characters seem to be affected or influenced by consumerism? Consider the overall representation of their lives, their relationships, their professions, their ambitions, and their emotional health. How does the information presented in the preface tie in with this subject? How does this dialogue about consumerism tie in with Vonnegut's concerns about a lack of, or death of, culture? Finally, what significance does this topic have for readers today?

Philosophy and Ideas

Breakfast of Champions finds its characters—including Vonnegut—struggling with issues of control, fate and free will, purpose, fulfillment, and meaning. The story also presents characters faced with or responding to death, illness, mental illness, tragedy, and poverty. Therefore, an effective way to begin would be to identify an issue that a particular character is struggling with and analyze corresponding passages, considering what is causing this struggle and evaluating the character's response. Next, you might look for other characters who are struggling with this same issue, looking for patterns that indicate whether Vonnegut is making some definitive statement on a particular subject. Remember, however, that while a study of characterization is a good place to begin and might even be adopted as the central approach of your paper, you will need to explore how other elements of the text contribute to a dialogue about these philosophical subjects.

Sample Topics:

1. **Fate and free will:** Does the story suggest that humans determine their own fate, or does it indicate that humans are ultimately bound by forces beyond their control?

Consider the characters' impact on one another, including prominent examples of influence such as how Kilgore Trout affects Dwayne Hoover and how Vonnegut affects Trout and his characters. What other external factors, if any, seem to impact the characters? Do readers find examples of willful choices determining outcomes? What does Vonnegut's act of setting his characters free at the conclusion of the story indicate?

2. **Humanism:** How does *Breakfast* create a dialogue about humanism?

Although the term *humanism* is not literally found in the text, look for the places where this concept seems to be referenced or represented in the story. You will need to begin by establishing context, providing some definition of humanism. A good place to start is with the website for the American Humanist Association (http://www.americanhumanist.org/Who_We_Are/About_Humanism). The historical and philosophical roots of humanism, including Thomas Paine's idea of "the religion of humanity," should be explored. Consider the relationships among the characters. Is there any evidence of religion being a helpful or comforting factor in their lives, or do they turn to one another for support and compassion? Think about Kilgore Trout's gravestone and his notions about the importance of humane ideas. How does the portrayal of the United States in the opening chapter create a commentary about humanism? Finally, your paper should consider Vonnegut's own interest in humanism and his role in promulgating it during the course of his life.

3. **Purpose, meaning, and fulfillment:** What does the book say about purpose, meaning, and fulfillment in the human experience?

Begin by looking for examples of the characters seeking meaning in their lives. Do any of the characters seem to be filled with a sense of purpose? What seems to be lacking in their life? Consider the narrator's thoughts on lust and the desire for wealth and look for related language and dialogue. What does Kilgore Trout say is the purpose of man? What does the book indicate is the purpose of life? In the book, what hinders the search for purpose and meaning, and what seems to fill humans with a sense of purpose? Are the characters ultimately fulfilled? If so, how does fulfillment seem to be defined?

Form and Genre

The unique form of *Breakfast* has left some readers and critics struggling to effectively categorize the book. If you find yourself in this position, one way to orient yourself is to consider how *Breakfast* compares to the literature that came before it and how it has influenced the literature produced after it. The book has been characterized as a postmodern text, and this can certainly be an interesting topic for a paper, but an essay on genre might also explore the relationship between *Breakfast* and other, perhaps more unexpected, genres. For example, a writer might consider how the text evidences characteristics of romanticism or elements of Victorian literature. A writer might even choose to write about the problems inherent in categorizing the book, looking for distinctive applications or combinations of elements not previously seen in literature that reveal how the book evidences a new form or new genre. However, a paper on this topic needs to be more than a list of these elements and combinations—it should also illuminate their function and purpose. In other words, you will be writing about the relationship between form and function. Similarly, the function of particular elements of form—such as the use of illustrations, the oscillation of the story between the two characters or the interruptions of Vonnegut, the use and effect of metafiction, and the significance of the strange conclusion of the story—all offer excellent avenues for exploration. Ultimately, your job is to explain how these elements of form create a dialogue about a key theme such as mental illness, chaos and order, or the effects of industrialism and consumerism, to name just a few.

Sample Topics:

1. **Postmodern form:** How does the postmodern form of the text complement the major themes of the text?

A writer would need to begin by identifying the postmodern-ist elements of the text. There are many reference entries on postmodernism available online, but a good place to start may be with a text such as *The Cambridge Introduction to Post-modern Fiction* edited by Bran Nicol. How do the postmodern elements help to reveal and reinforce the major themes of the text? Do they create a sense of order, unity, chaos, or disor-der? Ultimately, you will be explaining how the text would be different, better, or more or less successful without this form. You might go so far as to suggest that this development in form is necessary in effectively treating the major themes of the text. This would call for some explanation of why other forms would not have been successful.

2. **Romanticism and *Breakfast of Champions:*** How does the novel evidence elements of romanticism?

Begin by establishing a definition of romanticism and provid-ing some explanation of the ideas and characteristics associ-ated with it. You might begin by consulting a work such as *Romanticism: An Oxford Guide* by Nicholas Roe. Next, tell your readers where these elements are found in the text. This essay should be more than a simple list of romantic elements in the text, however. It should demonstrate how the applica-tion of elements of romanticism allows Vonnegut to treat key themes effectively. You might conclude, however, with some discussion of how and why the text strays from being a wholly romantic text.

3. **Metafiction:** How does Vonnegut's use of metafiction shape readers' understanding and perception of the text?

This essay should evaluate Vonnegut's use of metafiction and reveal its role in the treatment of major themes. Although Vonnegut used metafiction in previous works, in *Breakfast* he takes it to an extreme. An evaluation of the progression or evolution of the use of metafiction in Vonnegut's works could become central to your paper. Consider the link between the use of metafiction and the work as a semiautobiographical text. What themes does this allow Vonnegut to treat in the book? How would readers' interpretations of the text be different without the use of metafiction?

Language, Symbols, and Imagery

Vonnegut employs a deliberate, carefully crafted visual language in *Breakfast of Champions,* meaning that much is shown rather than stated. A paper might evaluate this visual language as a whole or analyze a particular component of it, such as the imagery or the use of line illustrations in the text. A writer might also explore the role of language in establishing a visual language. In other words, in addition to bold images such as the trucks and polluted landscape, think about how word choice and the pervasiveness of slogans and mottos in the text, such as the title slogan, also contributes to this visual language. The text also presents many interesting symbols that could become the focus of your paper. Look for the places where these symbols appear literally, but consider the ideas they represent and the feelings they evoke. Next, look for other places in the book where these ideas are evident or where a similar feeling is evoked. You should also consider whether the symbol has a singular meaning or whether it has a variety of meanings. A successful paper will present a thorough analysis of its subject element while exposing the relationship of imagery, symbolism, or language to theme.

Sample Topics:

1. **Visual language:** Evaluate the visual language of the text, including its effectiveness. Is Vonnegut's choice to show rather than tell helpful in disseminating the major message of the text?

   Writing a paper on this topic calls for an analysis of all of the elements that make up the visual language of the story. This means evaluating the basic imagery but also the illustrations, mottos, and slogans. What does this visual language convey? Where do readers find examples of Vonnegut showing rather than telling? How, for instance, do the characters become part of the visual language? Is Vonnegut's method an effective means for creating a dialogue about the major themes of the text, or do we rely more on language and dialogue?

2. **Heliogabalus:** What is the significance of the reference to the Roman emperor Heliogabalus in the text?

This will be an exploration of symbolism that leads into a consideration of the text's historical and cultural concerns. Accordingly, some historical research will be necessary. Heliogabalus was a real Roman emperor. How is he represented or portrayed in the text? How do the details of his life and the time period in which he reigned correspond to the major themes of *Breakfast*? Consider the relationship between this figure and the notion of false quest or false pursuits that entrap humans in their desire for meaning and purpose. Why is the status of this Roman emperor meaningful in light of Vonnegut's dialogue about America?

3. **Birds:** Evaluate Vonnegut's use of birds as symbols.

Begin by considering all references to birds in the book. Are there many other examples of animals or the natural in the text? Are the birds in the text living? Are they caged or free? You will need to establish the purpose of their inclusion in the text by exploring their relationships to major themes. What is the significance of the extinction of the Bermuda erns? How does Kilgore's pet bird serve as a metaphor for the desire for freedom, purpose, and meaning? It may be helpful to consider what birds have represented in other works of literature. Do they seem to represent the same things in *Breakfast,* or does Vonnegut utilize birds in a new and different way?

Comparison and Contrast Essays

Comparing and contrasting two or more works illuminates important similarities between the texts, but it also exposes the original aspects of each work. Since the form of *Breakfast* is one of its standout features, you might choose this as the focus of your paper, comparing *Breakfast* to other postmodern texts, showing how the texts evidence a necessary or valuable shift in form. Alternatively, you might choose to compare a particular motif or theme of *Breakfast* to the same motif or theme in Vonnegut's other works. No matter what subject you choose to write about, the focus should remain on illuminating those elements that make *Breakfast* unique and important.

Sample Topics:

1. **Breakfast of Champions and postmodern works:** Compare *Breakfast* to other postmodern texts. Why do Vonnegut and the other authors adopt this form? Does the form of the work effectively capture particular cultural concerns?

   Begin by identifying the elements that allow readers to identify *Breakfast* as a postmodern work. Consider elements of form including order or disorder, structure, and metafiction. How do these elements correspond to the themes of the text? What do the works share in common? How do the texts show the demand for a change in form from realism or other previously applied methods in literature? Is *Breakfast* groundbreaking or is it indicative of some trend in literature at that time? You do not need to limit your study to a consideration of works that preceded the texts. Consider, also, the influence of *Breakfast* going forward.

2. **The theme of dehumanization in Breakfast of Champions and Vonnegut's other works:** Analyze the treatment of dehumanization as a recurring theme within Vonnegut's oeuvre. What message do the works present on this topic, and what makes the treatment of this theme in *Breakfast* different?

   You will need to begin by establishing how readers can identify dehumanization as a major theme of *Breakfast* and the other texts you have chosen. It will, of course, be helpful to focus on the characters in looking for examples of how they appear to be dehumanized, but consider genre, plot, imagery, and language as well. What seems to be the cause of this dehumanization?

Consider the impact of scientific advancement and war. Do postwar, post-Depression cultural factors play a part in this dehumanization? Does the text indicate whether such dehumanization is avoidable or reversible? Finally, why is the treatment of this subject in *Breakfast* more (or less) successful or powerful than the treatment of this subject in other texts?

3. **Showing versus telling in *Breakfast of Champions*:** Compare and contrast Vonnegut's method of showing and his method of telling in the novel. The author creates a strong visual language through imagery, illustrations, and symbolism, but he also utilizes dialogue and a strong narrative voice. Does one method seem to be more effective than the other, or are the two necessarily paired?

This will be a consideration of the visual language of the text, such as imagery and symbolism, versus the information revealed by the narrator and disseminated through dialogue. Consider the effect of each method. Does one method seem to have a greater impact in shaping your view of the text and helping to reveal the key themes, or does each method seem to support and enhance the effectiveness of the other?

4. ***Breakfast of Champions* and *Slaughterhouse-Five*:** In interviews, Vonnegut revealed that *Breakfast of Champions* began as part of an earlier novel, *Slaughterhouse-Five*, but then spun off into its own story. Explore the relationship between the texts by comparing and contrasting the two.

Start by considering any commonalities between the texts. It will be helpful to explore characterization, the use of metafiction, and theme. How does each text function as a cultural portrait and critique and as a philosophical text? What vision of postwar American life does each present? Consider semi-autobiographical elements of both texts. Do the books incorporate like symbols? Ultimately, you should be establishing all similarities while illuminating what distinguishes the works. This requires some focus on *Breakfast*'s most notable elements. Your essay should demonstrate how *Breakfast* evidences some breakthrough or development in Vonnegut's work. Do you believe that Vonnegut's decision to separate the two stories was a good one? Explain why or why not. What does a comparison illuminate about each text that might not be immediately visible without such a comparison?

Bibliography and Resources for *Breakfast of Champions, or Goodbye Blue Monday*

Alsen, Eberhard. "*Breakfast of Champions:* Kurt Vonnegut on the Nature of Man and God." *Romantic Postmodernism in American Fiction.* Amsterdam; Atlanta, GA: Editions Rodpopi B.V., 1996. 110–32.

American Humanist Association. "About Humanism." Retrieved 27 June 2011. <http://www.americanhumanist.org/Who_We_Are/About_Humanism>.

Glickman, Lawrence B., ed. *Consumer Society in American History: A Reader.* Ithaca, NY; London: Cornell UP, 1999.

Lehmann-Haupt, Christopher. "Is Kurt Vonnegut Kidding Us?" Review of *Breakfast of Champions, or Goodbye Blue Monday. New York Times.* 2 May 1973. Retrieved 31 May 2011. <http://www.nytimes.com/1973/05/03/books/vonnegut-breakfast.html>.

McGinnis, Wayne. "Vonnegut's *Breakfast of Champions:* A Reductive Success." *Notes on Contemporary Literature* 5 (1975): 6–9.

Merrill, Robert. "Vonnegut's *Breakfast of Champions:* The Conversion of Heliogabalus." *Critique* 18.3 (1977): 99–109.

Messent, Peter B. "*Breakfast of Champions:* The Direction of Kurt Vonnegut's Fiction." *Journal of American Studies* 8.1 (1974): 101–14.

Nicol, Bran. *The Cambridge Introduction to Postmodern Fiction.* New York: Cambridge UP, 2009.

Paine, Thomas. *Collected Writings.* New York: Library of America, 1995.

Roe, Nicholas, ed. *Romanticism: An Oxford Guide.* Oxford; New York: Oxford UP, 2005.

Vonnegut, Kurt. *Breakfast of Champions, or Goodbye Blue Monday.* New York: Dial, 2006.

INDEX

absurdism and black humor, 72, 86–87, 88, 168, 190–191

American Humanist Association, 238

Armageddon in Retrospect, 196

Beatrice (*Sirens of the Titan*), 144–145

Billy Pilgrim (*Slaughterhouse-Five*)
  analysis of, 206
  as chaplain's assistant, 213
  schizophrenia of, vii
  and *seeing*, 205
  "unstuck in time," 198–199

black humor and absurdism, 72, 86–87, 88, 168, 190–191

Bloom, Harold, vi–viii

Bokonism, vii–viii, 85, 177–178, 179, 189–190

brainstorming, defined, 10

Breakfast of Champions
  American culture presented by Vonnegut, 227–228
  American history portrayed in, 84
  birds as symbols, 242
  categorization of, 239
  confession from Vonnegut, 226
  consumerism and, 83
  critical reception on publication, 225
  dedication to Phoebe Hurty, 226–227, 230
  dehumanization of characters in, 76
  man as machine, 234–235

mental illness, 230–231
message revealed in, 230–231
opening details plot of two men, 222–224
pollution forms, 231–232
positive power of ideas, 232
postmodernism and novel, 239–240, 243
preface to, 83, 222, 226, 235, 237
prosperity' and postwar living, 230
questions to answer, 225–226
second reading required, 225
sense of disorder in, 72, 84
setting characters free, 233
Vonnegut as character, 225, 228–229, 231, 233–234
word choice and, 241–242

Breakfast of Champions, or Goodbye Blue Monday. See Breakfast of Champions

Breakfast of Champions, sample topics
  birds, 242
  comparison to *Slaughterhouse*, 244–245
  consumerism, 237
  dehumanization, 243–244
  fate and free will, 237–238
  Heliogabalus, 242
  humanism, 238
  ideas as powerful influence, 232–233
  man as machine, 234–235

mental illness, 230–231
as metafiction, 239, 240–241
Phoebe Hurty's significance, 234
pollution, 231–232
postmodernism, 239–240
postmodernism compared, 243
prosperity as defunct notion, 230
purpose, meaning, fulfillment,
  238–239
romanticism, 240
showing vs. telling, 244
slavery and prejudice, 236
Trout-Hoover relationship, 232, 233
U.S portrait, 235, 236
visual language, 241–242
Vonnegut as character, 233–234

Cat's Cradle
anthropological thesis by Vonnegut,
  191–192
as apocalyptic tale, 192–193
autobiographical monologue by
  narrator, 177–178, 183
Bloom on, vi, vii–viii
Bokonism and, 85
Bokonon biography, 179
Castle sugar industry, 179, 187
critical portrait of Americans,
  188–189
cultural identity and, 186
dangers of modern society, 182–183
episodic form of, 174
Hiroshima and, 185–186, 193, 196
illusion and, 182–183
Melville referenced by "Call me
  Jonah," 184
Newton Hoenikker's letter, 174–176
satirical cultural commentary, 181,
  190–191
symbolism in cat's cradle, 176–177
women and, 185
writing of, 71
Cat's Cradle, sample topics
American portrait, 188
as anthropological text, 191–192

as apocalyptic tale, 192
cold war and arms race, 186–187
comparison of good and evil with
  Mother Night, 195–196
comparison with Hersey's
  Hiroshima, 196
comparison with *Player Piano*,
  194–195
comparison with Vonnegut's
  nonfiction, 196
dangers of modern society, 182–183
Dr. Felix Hoenikker, 184–185
granfalloons, 190
imperialism, 180, 187–188
knowledge as most valuable
  commodity on Earth, 181–182
mountains as symbols, 195
religion, 189
San Lorenzo as setting and symbol,
  187–188, 193, 194
as satire, 191
title analysis, 193–194
women in novel, 185
wrang-wrang, 190–191
zah-mah-ki-bo, 189–190
Céline (*Slaughterhouse-Five*), vi, 217, 219
character
  Breakfast of Champions, 232–235
  Cat's Cradle, 183–185
  Mother Night, 158–161
  Player Piano, 109–112
  Sirens of the Titan, The, 132–136
  Slaughterhouse-Five, 206–207
  writing about, 2–4
  writing about Vonnegut, 77–81
citations and formatting
  parenthetical citations, 55–56
  plagiarism, 59–61
  primary sources, 50–56
  quotations, 50–54
  sample essay, 61–68
  secondary sources, 56–57
  works cited pages, 56, 58–59
clustering, or *mapping,* defined, 10
Coker, Jeffrey W., 137–138

comparison and contrast essays
   Breakfast of Champions, 242–245
   Cat's Cradle, 194–196
   Mother Night, 170–-172
   Player Piano, 121–123
   Sirens of the Titan, The, 145–148
   Slaughterhouse-Five, 217–219
   writing about, 8–9
   writing about Vonnegut, 92–94
conclusions, 48–50
Cox, Jane Marie. *See* Vonnegut, Jane
  Marie Cox (wife)

dehumanization of characters
   Breakfast of Champions, 76, 243–244
   Player Piano, 76, 104, 107
   Sirens of the Titan, The, 76
Dolan, Brian, 103
Dr. Felix Hoenikker (*Cat's Cradle*),
  character of, 184–185
Dwayne Hoover (*Breakfast of
  Champions*), 222–223

Economics of Fashion (Nystrom),
  211–212
essay, sample, 61–68
essays, how to write
   attentive reading of material, 1–2
   body paragraphs, 40–48
   character, 2–4
   citations and formatting, 50–61
   comparison and contrast essays,
    8–9
   conclusions, 48–50
   cultural content explored, 1–2
   form and genre, 4–5
   history and context, 6–8
   introductions, 46–48
   language, symbols, and imagery,
    5–6
   objective of essay, 1
   outlines, 15–40
   philosophy and ideas, 8
   preparation, 9–10

sample essay, 61–68
themes, 2
thesis statements, 10–13

fate and free will as theme, 75, 140,
  237–238
FDR (Roosevelt., Franklin D.), 137–138
figures of speech, 5–6
"Fog" (Sandburg), 5–6
form and genre
   Breakfast of Champions, 239–242
   Cat's Cradle, 191–192
   Mother Night, 166–168
   Player Piano, 118–119
   Sirens of the Titan, The, 141–143
   Slaughterhouse-Five, 213–215
   writing about, 4–5
   writing about Vonnegut, 86–90
formatting. *See* citations and formatting
Franklin D. Roosevelt: A Biography
  (Coker), 138
freewriting, defined, 10

genre, defined, 4
George Kraft (*Mother Night*), 155–156
granfalloons, 190

Heliogabalus, 242
history and context
   Breakfast of Champions, 235–237
   Cat's Cradle, 185–188
   Mother Night, 161
   Player Piano, 112–116
   Sirens of the Titan, The, 136–139
   Slaughterhouse-Five, 208–213
   writing about, 6–8
   writing about Vonnegut, 81–84
Howard W. Campbell Jr. (*Mother Night*)
   analysis of, 11, 16, 18, 159
   fan mail and death threats for,
    167–168
   fate of, 162
   Hide and Seek and, 169–170
   identity of, 155
   mother and, 157

reflections on history, 163
thesis statement for, 13
humanism, 238

imagery. *See* language, symbols, and
imagery
introductions, 46–48
Inventing Entertainment (Dolan), 103

John (*Cat's Cradle*)
autobiographical monologue by,
177–178, 183, 184
control of actions by, 189–190
index entry on Mona Aamons,
178–179
Journey to the End of Night (Céline), vi,
217, 219–220

karass, vii
Kilgore Trout (*Breakfast of Champions*),
79, 88, 222–224, 231
Kilgore Trout (*Slaughterhouse-Five*), 88,
205, 214
Klinkowitz, Jerome, 59
Kroner (*Player Piano*), character
analysis of, 112

language, symbols, and imagery
Breakfast of Champions, 241–242
Cat's Cradle, 193–194
Mother Night, 168–170
Player Piano, 119–121
Sirens of the Titan, The, 143
Slaughterhouse-Five, 215–219
writing about, 5–6
writing about Vonnegut, 90–92
"Lay of the Last Minstrel, The" (Scott),
168, 170

Malachi Constant (*Sirens of the Titan*),
133, 147
Man Without a Country, A, 196
Mary O'Hare (*Slaughterhouse-Five*),
200–201
mental illness, 76–77, 157–158, 230–231

metafiction
Breakfast of Champions as, 239,
240–241
Mother Night as, 59, 150, 152,
161–162
Slaughterhouse-Five as, 201–202,
215–216
writing about Vonnegut, 89–90
metaphors, 5–6
Mill, John Stuart, 116–117
Miller, Arthur, 217
*MLA Handbook for Writers of Research
Papers*, 55, 56, 57, 58
Mona Aamons (*Cat's Cradle*), 178–179
Mother Night
approaches to writing about,
153–154
art and literature, 165
balanced representation of
characters, 165
Campbell's guards and, 159–160
character evaluation in, 81, 158
editor's notes and, 150–151
example outlines for, 18–27
example paragraphs for, 41–42,
44–46
example thesis statements for,
12–13
Faust and, 169, 171
genre classification, 166–167
Gettysburg Address and, 163
historical figures mixed with
fictional, 160
introduction of 1966, 152
mental illness, 157–158
as metafiction, 59, 150, 152, 161–162
moral of, 152–153
philosophical issues of text, 164
points of view in, 167–168
posing as memoir, 72, 87, 149–150
publication of in 1961, 149
the soldier and, 80
style of spy novel, 162
title significance, 169
truth theme of, 151, 154–156

Vonnegut as "editor," 151
war not focus of, 161
Mother Night, sample topics
  absurdism and black humor, 168
  allegiance, 156–157
  art and literature, 165–166
  Campbell's guards, 159–160
  comparison of Campbell and Jones,
    171
  comparison of Campbell here with
    his character in *Slaughterhouse-
    Five*, 171–172
  comparison with Mailer's *Armies of
    the Night*, 172
  comparison with Mailer's *Barbary
    Shore*, 172
  Doctor Abraham Epstein and
    mother, 160–161
  dual nature of man, 165
  epigraph of, 168, 170
  genre classification, 166–167
  hide and seek as symbol, 168–170
  historical figures, 160
  history repeating and forgotten, 163
  Howard W. Campbell Jr. analysis,
    159
  identity, 154–156
  mental illness, 157–158
  morality and ethics, 164–165
  patriotism and espionage, 162=63
  point of view analysis, 167–168
  propaganda, 163
  structure (form), 167
  title analysis, 169
  truth theme of, 151, 154–156

Newton Hoenikker (*Cat's Cradle*), letter
  written by, 174–176
Nystrom Paul, 211

Online Writing Lab (OWL), 55, 57
Orwell, George, 94, 116, 146–147
outlines
  flawed, 16–18
  formal, 31–40

informal, 27–30
purpose of, 15
well-written, 18–27
OWL (Online Writing Lab), 55, 57

paragraphs, body
  coherent paragraph examples,
    42–46
  unified paragraph examples,
    40–42
Parakilas, James, 103
parenthetical citations, 55–56
Paul Proteus (*Player Piano*)
  complexity of character, 109,
    110–111
  lie detector scene, 120–121
  looking over battlefield, 104
  playing piano, 103
  sound of machinery and, 105
philosophy and ideas
  Breakfast of Champions, 237–239
  Cat's Cradle, 188–191
  Mother Night, 1i64–166
  Player Piano, 116–119
  Sirens of the Titan, The, 139–141
  Slaughterhouse-Five, 211–213
  writing about, 8
  writing about Vonnegut, 84–86
Phoebe Hurty (*Breakfast of Champions*),
  226–227, 230
Piano Roles (Parakilas), 103
plagiarism, 59–61
Player Piano
  American history portrayed in, 84
  as American protest literature, 113,
    115
  capitalism and, 113–114
  changed American landscape
    depicted in, 115–116
  characters struggling with
    uselessness, 108–109
  comparison with later works, 100
  consumerism and, 83
  contextual elements in text, 102
  contrasting imagery in, 120

dangers of technological progress in, 106–107

dehumanization of characters in, 76, 104

dystopia and, 116–117

evolution of Vonnegut's style, 101

fictional representations of war, 82

first published novel, 71

ghost motif in, 119

Ghost Shirt Society and, 115

historical references, 114

interaction between human and nonhuman characters, 110–111

interplay between man and machine, 105–106

posing as science fiction, 72, 86

published in 1952, 112

satire and social commentary, 119

as semiautobiographical work, 102

the soldier and, 80

symbolism of title, 102–104

uniforms and costumes, 120

women in novel, 108–109, 111–112

Player Piano, sample topics

capitalism, 113–114

comparison with *Brave New World/ or We*, 122

comparison with later novels, 121–122

contrast in, 120

dehumanizing effects of technological advancement, 107

dissidence and revolution, 115

division by social class, 114–115

dystopia, 117

faith, 117–118

historical references, 114

Industrial Revolution and America's changed landscape, 115–116

Kroner, 111–112

lie detector test, 120–121

pairing of Shah of Bratpuhr and Ewing J. Halyard, 111

Paul Proteus, 110

postwar life compared to treatment of others, 122–123

progress, 108

purpose, 108–109

satire and social commentary, 119

science fiction genre, 118–119

uniforms and costumes, 120

women in novel, 108–109, 111–112

Polenberg, Richard D., 138

postmodernism

Breakfast of Champions, 239–240, 243

Slaughterhouse-Five, 218–219

preparing to write, 9–10

primary sources

documenting, 55–56

using, 50–55

punctuation of quotations, 54

quotations

accuracy of, 52–54

integrating, 50–52

punctuation of, 54

reading to write

Breakfast of Champions, 222–229

Cat's Cradle, 174–180

Mother Night, 149–153

Player Piano, 100–105

Sirens of the Titan, The, 125–128

Slaughterhouse-Five, 198–203

religion and faith, 84–85

"Report on the Barnhouse Effect," first short story, 71

Roe, Nicholas, 240

Romanticism (Roe), 240

Roosevelt., Franklin D. (FDR), 137–138

Salo (Sirens of the Titan), character analysis of, 134

sample essay, 61–68

sample topics. *See title of work followed by* sample topics

Sandburg, Carl, 5–6

science fiction genre, 87–88

252

Bloom's How to Write about Kurt Vonnegut

Scott, Sir Walter, 168, 170
secondary sources, documenting, 56–57
similes, 5–6
Sirens of the Titan, The
    authenticity of, 142–143
    consumerism and, 83
    dehumanization of characters in, 76
    fate and free will as theme, 140
    fictional representations of war, 82
    meaning of life as major theme,
        128–130, 139–140
    messenger motif in, 133, 135
    minor characters and, 132
    opening of, 125–126
    overturned expectations in, 127–
        128, 132, 137, 141–142
    and *Player Piano*, 145–146
    posing as science fiction, 72, 86,
        127, 141, 142
    publication of in 1959, 125
    relationships depicted in, 131
    science fiction and, 88
    science fiction tag inaccurate,
        125–127
    the soldier and, 80
    space travel and, 138–139
    symbolism in, 143–145
    time symbolism in, 131–132
Sirens of the Titan, The, sample topics
    accidental in novel and
        Slaughterhouse-Five, 147
    age of space exploration, 138–139
    authenticity of, 142–143
    Beatrice's painting analysis, 144–
        145
    comparison of Rumford with FDR,
        137–138
    comparison with Orwell, 146–147
    comparison with *Player Piano*, 146
    deserter here compared to one in
        Red Badge of Courage, 147–148
    fate and free will as theme, 140
    fountain as symbol, 144
    journey and transformation,
        133–134

love and friendship, 131
Malachi Constant analysis, 133
meaning of life, 129–130, 139–140
the messenger, 135
novel as satire, 143
novel as science fiction, 142
religion and faith, 141
Salo analysis, 134
setting as symbol, 144
structure of work, 143
time, 131–132
title significance, 135–136
war as treated here, 139
wealth, 130–131
Slaughterhouse-Five
    banning of, 202
    Bloom on, vi–viii
    brash language and imagery of, 202,
        218
    chapter 1 of, 200–201, 207
    Children's Crusade motif, 201,
        216–217
    Christianity and, 85, 212–213
    climax of, 213–214
    conclusion of, 205
    consumerism and, 83
    cultural and political events,
        208–209
    death as understood by aliens in, 85
    death examples in, 204
    disorder of, 214–215
    disputed message of, 211
    example conclusions for, 48–50
    example introductions for, 46–48
    example thesis statements for,
        14–15, 26–27
    fatalism and, 212
    formal outline for, 31–40
    historical events in fiction, 203
    hybrid of history and science
        fiction, 212–213, 214
    imagery of, 215–216
    informal outline for, 27–30
    message of seeing and, 205
    metafiction and, 201–202, 215–216

Miller's *Death of a Salesman* and, 217
nonlinear storytelling in, 84, 208
overview of, 198–199
as postmodern work, 218–219
postwar modern condition, 208
publication of in 1969, 198
relationship with other Vonnegut works, 217
sample essay, 61–68
semiautobiographical nature of, 199
Shakespeare and, 217–218
the soldier and, 80
soldiers in, 207
structure lacking in, 72
as tragicomedy, 213
Vonnegut's best-known work, 202
World War II and, 82–83
Slaughterhouse-Five, or The Children's Crusade: A Duty-Dance with Death.
  See Slaughterhouse-Five
Slaughterhouse-Five, sample topics
  Billy Pilgrim analysis, 206
  Céline and novel, 219
  Children's Crusade motif, 216–217
  death, 204
  Dresden firebombing, 208, 209–210, 217
  effects of war, 204–205
  faith and religion, 212–213
  fatalism, 212
  form of novel, 214–215
  futility, 211
  metafiction usage, 215
  postmodernism and novel, 218–219
  postwar In U.S., 210, 218
  science fiction in novel, 214
  sight references, 205
  the slaughterhouse as symbol, 216
  the soldier, 207
  Valencia and Lily, 207
  Vietnam War, 208, 209
sources
  primary, 50–56
  secondary, 56–59

symbols. *See* language, symbols, and imagery

The Era of Franklin D. Roosevelt, 1933–1945 (Polenberg), 138
themes
  Breakfast of Champions, 229–232
  Cat's Cradle, 181–183
  Mother Night, 153–158
  Player Piano, 105–109
  Sirens of the Titan, The, 128
  Slaughterhouse-Five, 203–205
  writing about, 2
  writing about Vonnegut, 74–77
thesis statements
  location of, 13
  for *Mother Night*, 11–12
topics, sample. *See title of work followed by* sample topics
topics and strategies
  Breakfast of Champions, 229–245
  Cat's Cradle, 174–196
  Mother Night, 153–172
  Player Piano, 105–123
  Sirens of the Titan, The, 128–148
  Slaughterhouse-Five, 203–219
  writing about Vonnegut, 73–94
transitional techniques, 43, 44, 48

Vonnegut, Jane Marie Cox (wife), 71
Vonnegut, Kurt, writing about
  background of, 70–71
  biographical content of works, 72
  Bloom on, vii
  capture by Germans, vi, 70–71, 198
  Cat's Cradle as thesis in anthropology, 191
  character analysis and, 77–78
  cultural content explored, 72, 74–75, 81–82
  dark themes as technique, 72–73
  enlistment in U.S. Army, 198
  as ironist, vii
  mislabeled as science fiction writer, 118–119

novels are genre hybrids, 86, 118
point of view varied, 75
supporting your argument on, 73
Vonnegut, Kurt, writing about, sample
  topics
  absence of heroes or villains, 81
  absurdism and black humor, 86–87,
    88
  black humor and absurd, 86–87, 88
  compare a single element across
    Vonnegut's works, 93
  compare Vonnegut with another
    author, 93–94
  consumerism and postindustrial
    revolution, 83
  contrast, 91–92
  death, 85–86
  dehumanization and effects of
    science and technology, 75–76
  evolution of form, 88–89
  family, 79–80
  fate and free will, 75
  fiction as autobiography, 89

Kilgore Trout, 79
language, 90–91
mental illness, 76–77
metafiction, 89–90
people in groups, 80–81
quest for meaning, 77–78
religion and faith, 84–85
science fiction, 87–88
setting as symbol, 91
the soldier, 80
tragicomic figure, 78–79
United States as portrayed by
  Vonnegut, 83–84
war, 82–83
Vonnegut Effect, The (Klinkowitz), 59

Winston Niles Rumfoord (*Sirens of the
  Titan*)
  character of, 127
  modeled on FDR, 135–136,
    137–138
  wealth and, 130
works cited pages, 56, 58–59